Europe's Position in the New World Order

edited by
Péter Balázs

Europe's Position in the New World Order

edited by
Péter Balázs

Published in 2014 by
CENTER FOR EU ENLARGEMENT STUDIES

Distributed by
CENTRAL EUROPEAN UNIVERSITY PRESS

An imprint of the
Central European University Limited Liability Company
Nádor utca 11, H-1051 Budapest, Hungary
Tel: +36-1-327-3138 or 327-3000
Fax: +36-1-327-3183
E-mail: ceupress@ceu.hu
Website: www.ceupress.com

224 West 57th Street, New York NY 10019, USA
Tel: +1-212-547-6932
Fax: +1-646-557-2416
E-mail: martin.greenwald@opensocietyfoundations.org

ISBN 978-963-8982-20-9

This publication was sponsored by the Hungarian Scientific Research Fund (OTKA) under the project "The changing world order and its implications for the wider Europe" (OTKA 84079).

Library of Congress Cataloging-in-Publication Data

Europe's position in the new world order / edited by Peter Balazs.
pages cm
Includes bibliographical references and index.
ISBN 978-9638982209 (pbk.)
1. European Union countries—Foreign relations—21st century. I. Balázs, Péter, 1941– author, editor of compilation.

JZ1570.A5E865 2013
341.242'2—dc23

2013026158

Printed in Hungary

Table of Content

Introduction

Péter Balázs, PhD.

The European Union (EU) has succeeded to considerably expand its influence during the past twenty years. The three rounds of enlargement and the strengthening of the EU's economic and political presence in its neighborhood are among the most remarkable successes of its post-Cold War history. The European Union is one of the key facilitators of stability in the Western Balkans; it represents an institutional and normative anchor for Eastern Neighborhood countries and acts as a partner for a thriving economic partnership with most of the Mediterranean states. During the past few decades, the Union was able to actively mold its regional environment by offering the benefits of integration and/or economic co-operation, based on a finely tuned selection of instruments. The number of EU member states has doubled in less than 15 years, providing a good deal of credibility for Brussels' *normative power*. (Manners, 2008) The co-operation with the EU and its main benefit – membership – became achievable for an unprecedented number of external actors, and the continued belief in it provided significant leverage for the Union. Moreover, the EU and its member countries became stakeholders in US hegemony. (Toje, 2008)

Despite all controversies, individual European states and the EU acted keenly and in strong co-operation with the United States in the continent's neighborhood. Closer co-operation with the EU and a possible accession to the community had been a common strategic fundament for US and European policies vis-à-vis Turkey, the Western Balkan countries and even for the Eastern partners: Belorussia, Ukraine, Moldova, Azerbaijan, Georgia and Armenia. Besides NATO, the EU itself became the strongest institutional link in the transatlantic community – a well accepted fact both in Brussels and Washington. The Union – and some of its member states – also developed a strong coercive authority due to their dominance in foreign trade, pointing beyond policy tools traditionally associated with soft power. (Nye, 2004) On the basis of these instruments, and its increased global weight, the EU was able to acquire a strong influence and an institutional credibility in its broad neighborhood, spurring a vivid intellectual debate on the EU's international "actorness". (Hill, 1996)

During the past few years, however, the changing international order, the deterioration of European competitiveness and the need for internal compromises have begun to challenge the belief in the Union's future capabilities to actively mold its environment, bringing the problem of the capabilities-expectations gap once again to the fore. (Ginsberg, 1999) First, decreasing US attention towards Europe due to President Obama's "pivot to Asia" and the resulting changing nature of the transatlantic relationship began to put it in question the very fundaments of the EU's role in the international context that had existed since the 1950s. Second, the Union's swiftly decreasing share in the global economy – particularly trade and investments – have undermined its prestige and regional influence. Third, the Union was hit hard by the 2008 global financial crisis, pulling the eurozone to the edge of a meltdown and spurring a range of political and economic questions that stress the boundaries of the European project. This internal turmoil further weakens the EU's magnetism, its institutional-normative pull for the immediate neighborhood.

Furthermore, the EU faces a major challenge in each of the three distinct dimensions of the immediate environment in which it has to act. One, a reinvigorated Russia has demonstrated ambitions to act as an alternative source of benefits for states in the Eastern neighborhood seeking to escape EU conditionality – a development which may prove especially problematic in the case of Ukraine. Two, partner states in various external actions are typically not fully committed to the transformatory vision of the EU and have remained more opportunistic actors than fully aligned supporters of this vision. This is in stark contrast to the experiences of the 1990s and of Central European enlargement, the primary example cited in support of the EU's effective normative power. Three, the EU's public has also looked at some dimensions of external actions with increasing reservations, especially with regards to Turkey. As a result, enlargement – beyond Croatia – is distinctly a hard sell, while other programs lack the clear political will that would propel them forward. Domestic considerations in key member states lead to an increase in symbolic, safe and all too success-dependent interaction at the cost of deep reform.

The EU and its member states will have to adjust to this complex new situation in order to preserve and further strengthen their leadership in the wider Europe. The Union will have to keep its credibility as the main facilitator of integration, stability and welfare, and it will need to launch new sectoral initiatives in order to remain an attractive aim for elites. All these steps need to be taken in a rapidly changing global environment, with a competent European leadership that is able to reverse the declining fortunes of the organization. The current research seeks to contribute to the solution of this complex Gordian knot by analyzing the interaction between the aforementioned two processes: the EU's adaptation to the changing global environment, and the in parallel evolving influence of the Union on the wider European environment. Taking a comprehensive look at the changes in the EU and its environment, the present volume is structured along five clusters of questions. The first group assesses the realignment of US foreign policy – i.e. the pivot to Asia and the decreasing attention toward Europe – and its impact on the Union's external influence. Is the European model of external action capable to address neighboring actors alone? Is a European leadership in wider Europe possible without the hard security guarantees of the United States? The second group shifts attention to the possible consequences of the EU's gradually decreasing share in global economy? Can cultural, institutional and political benefits compensate for a lesser extent of economic co-operation in the regional environment?

1. How could the EU preserve its integrating credibility with more bleak accession perspectives? Can the Union's normative, institutional power survive Europe's decline? Can the Union provide stakeholders' rights for the neighbors in general or in particular policies?
2. How can the EU involve its regional partners in global governance? Can it distribute its benefits, channel their interests and harmonize their policies in the new international order?
3. Are the existing patterns of external actions sufficient to produce synergies and permanently create win-win situations?

The state of the art

The European Communities did not seek to become active global players until the end of the Cold War. Accordingly, the academic debates about the EC's (and later EU's) regional influence and its stance in global affairs were for a long time centred on the realist-functionalist debate. The realist-neorealist discourse was sceptical about the EU's purportedly subjective international stance and interpreted its actions as an "interstate alliance whose primary purpose is to strengthen the position of individual states in an interdependent and highly competitive global economy". (Gilpin, 1996, p.19) The functionalist-intergovermentalist interpretations focused on the integration and its negotiation process as the basic constituency of the Union.

The end of the Cold War initiated the development of a number of new external policies (CFSP, enlargement), it marked a major move in the organisation's convergence "from policy to polity" (Chryssochoou, 2001, p. 6) and led to an emerging debate about the European identity. All this resulted in the inclusion of the Union's external actions into the previously existing theories of integration. Neo-functionalism, with its multi-level interpretations (Lindberg, 1963; Tranholm-Mikkelsen & Jeppe, 1991) and liberal inter-govermentalism (Moravcsik, 1993) provided new theoretical patterns. Yet, the mainstream of the discourse was without doubt constructivism, which went as far as influencing official EU communication. Constructivism provided the dominant and most popular explanation for and interpretation of the Union's regional expansion during the last fifteeen years, facilitating Brussels' influence through its normative and socializing power. (Checkel, 2006)

Recently, the debate concerning the "Post American world" (Zakaria, 2008) also triggered a new debate about Europe's and the EU's global role. It brought new popularity to "civilizationalist" (Danilovskiy, Spengler) as well as realist theories, which claim to provide a clear explanation for Europe's decline, evidently visible in the continent's economic performance. However, constructivist and inter-govermentalist theorists – so successful in explaining the Union's expanding influence since the end of the Cold War – have come to challenge their view in a number of regards. The emergence of the debate on Europe's future and, particularly, on its regional influence is the dominant academic issue in EU studies for the years to come. Our research provides an audit of EU regional and sectoral policies in its regional environment, exploring the major trends and possible EU responses to them. It is the first coherent contribution from Hungarian authors to this emerging international issue, a major milestone both in Hungarian IR and EU studies.

Bibliography

Avery, G. et al. (Eds.) (2007). *The people's project? The new EU Treaty and the prospects for future integration.* Brussels: European Policy Centre.

Bale, Tim (2005) *European politics. A comparative introduction.* Houndmills: Palgrave Macmillan.

Barnes, I., & Barnes P. M. (1995). *The enlarged European Union.* London: Longman.

Batt, J., Lewis, P. G., & White, S. (Eds.) (2007). *Developments in Central and East European politics.* London: Palgrave Macmillan.

Bruter, M. (2005). *The emergence of a mass European identity.* Houndmills: Palgrave Macmillan.

Checkel, J. T. (2006). *Constructivist approaches to European Union.* ARENA. Working Paper Series.

Chryssochoou, D. N. (2001). *Theorizing European integration.* London: SAGE Publications.

Commission of the European Communities (1977). *Report of the Study Group on the Role of Public Finance in European Integration [MacDaughall Report], Vol. II.* Brussels: Commission of the European Communities.

Crowe, B. (2005). *Foreign minister of Europe.* London: Foreign Policy Centre. Retrieved from fpc.org.uk/fsblob/395.pdf.

Csaba, L. (2006). A fölemelkedő Európa. Budapest: Akadémiai Kiadó.

Delcour, L., Tulmets, E. (Eds.) (2008). *Pioneer Europe? – Testing EU foreign policy in the neighbourhood.* Bade-Baden: Nomos.

Diez, T., Wiener, A. (Eds.) (2004). *European integration theory.* Oxford: Oxford University Press.

Dinan, D. (2004). *Europe recast. A history of European Union.* London: Palgrave Macmillan.

Dinan, D. (2005). *Ever closer union: An introduction to European integration.* Houndmills: Palgrave Macmillan.

Eilstrup-Sangiovanni, M. (2006). *Debates on European integration: A reader.* Houndmills: Palgrave Macmillan.

Forsyth, M. (1981). *Union of States: The theory and practice of confederation.* Leicester: Leicester University Press.

Ash, T. G. (1999). History of the present: Essays, sketches and despatches from Europe in the 1990s. London: Alen Lane.

Grevi, G., Helly, D., & Keohane , D. (Eds.) (2009). *European Security and Defence Policy: The first 10 years (1999-2009)*. Paris: Institute for Security Studies.

Heywood, P. M., Jones, E. Rhodes, M., & Sedelmeier, U. (Eds.) (2006). *Developments in European politics*. Houndmills: Palgrave Macmillan.

Hill, C. (1996). *The actors in Europe's foreign policy*. New York: Taylor & Francis.

Hix, Si. (2005). *The political system of the European Union*. Houndmills: Palgrave Macmillan.

Howorth, J. (2007). Security and defence policy in the European Union. Basingstoke: Palgrave Macmillan.

Huntington, S. P. (1996). *The clash of civilizations and the remaking of world order*. New York: Simon & Schuster.

Jeffrey, C. (2001). *The regional dimension of the European Union: Towards a third level in Europe*. London: Frank Cass.

Kagan, R. (2003). *Paradise and power: America and Europe in the new world order*. London: Atlantic Books.

Kelley, J. (2006). New wine in old wineskins: Promoting political reforms through the new European Neighbourhood Policy. *Journal of Common Market Studies, 44(1)*, 29–55.

Kierzkowski, H. (Ed.) (2002). *Europe and globalization*. Basingstoke: Palgrave Macmillan.

Keukeleire, S., & MacNaughtan, J. (2008). *The foreign policy of the European Union*. Basingstoke: Palgrave Macmillan.

Lindberg, L. (1963). *The political dynamics of European economic integration*. Stanfor: Stanford University Press.

Manners, Ian (2008). Normative power Europe: A transdisciplinary approach to European studies. In C. Rumford (Ed.), *Handbook of European studies*. London: Sage.

McCormick, J. (2005). *Understanding the European Union: A concise introduction*. Houndmills: Palgrave Macmillan.

McLaren, L. M. (2005). *Identity, interests and attitudes to European integration*. Houndmills: Palgrave Macmillan.

Meunir, S., & Nicolaidis, K. (2005). The European Union as a Trade Power. In: Hill, C., & Smith, M. (Eds.), *International relations and the European Union. (pp. 39–63)*. Oxford: Oxford University Press.

Miszlivetz, F. (2004). *Az Európai konstrukció*. Doctoral Dissertation. Budapest: Hungarian Academy of Science.

Monnet, J. (1978). A bold, constructive act. In J. Monnet, *Memoirs. (pp. 288–317)*. Garden City: Doubleday & Company.

Moravcsik, A. (1993). Preferences and power in the European Community: A liberal intergovernmentalist approach. *Journal of Common Market Studies, 31(4)*, pp. 473–524.

Moravcsik, A. (1995). Liberal intergovernmentalism and integration: A rejoinder. *Journal of Common Market Studies, 33(4)*, pp. 611–628.

Nelsen, B. F., Stubb, A. (Eds.) (1994). *The European Union: Readings on the theory and practice of European integration*. Houndmills: Palgrave Macmillan.

Nugent, N. (Ed.) (2004). *European enlargement*. Houndmills: Palgrave Macmillan.

Nugent, N. (2006). *The government and politics of the European Union*. Houndmills: Palgrave Macmillan.

Nye, J. S. (2004). *Soft power: The means to success in world politics*. New York: Public Affairs.

O'Brennan, J. (2010). *The EU and the Western Balkans: Stabilization and europeanization through enlargement (Europe and the nation state)*. London: Routledge.

Palánkai T. (1994). *Az európai integráció gazdaságtana*. Budapest: Aula.

Payne, A. (Ed.) (2004). *The new regional politics of development*. Houndmills: Palgrave Macmillan.

Puchala, D. J. (1972). Of blind man, elephants and integration. *Journal of Common Market Studies, 10*, pp. 267–284.

Rosamond, B. (2000). *Theories of European integration*. London: Macmillan Press.

Shearman, P, & Sussex, M. (2004). *Europe's security after 9/11*. Aldershot: Ashgate.

Taylor P. (1993). International organization in the modern world: The regional and the global process. London: Pinter.

Toje, A. (2008). *America, the EU and strategic culture: Renegotiating the transatlantic bargain*. New York:Routledge.

Tranholm-Mikkelsen, J. (1991). Neo-functionalism: Obstinate or obsolete? A reappraisal in the light of the new dynamism of the EC. *Millennium – Journal of International Studies, 20(1)*, pp.1–22.

Urwin, D. W. (1995). *The Community of Europe. A history of European integration since 1945*. London: Longman.

Wallace, H., & Wallace, W. (2000). *Policy-making in the European Union*. Oxford: Oxford University Press.

Zakaria, F. (2008). *The post-American world*. New York: W.W. Norton & Company.

Global trends and the foreign policy of the European Union Challenges and response mechanisms

Péter Balázs, Ph.D.

The position of Europe in the current international setting is as uncertain as it was in 1992, when the European Union was formally established. This has much to do with the actual structure of the Union, which features one of the most complex sets of decision and policy making ever to come into being. This complexity is not restricted to internal issues, but also, significantly, characterizes the external policies of the Union as a whole. The European Union, as an entity, has proven to be a cumbersome actor in the field of diplomacy and international relations, always playing second fiddle even to its actual member states. However, since the enactment of the Lisbon Treaty, a number of significant trends can be identified, which are attempting to lead toward a better integrated foreign policy. The purpose of this chapter is to analyze the place of the European Union in the global setting. This can be best achieved through the use of a case study: the foreign policy of the Union from an institutional perspective. The study will attempt to identify the latest trends in this area, and to underline the enabling features as well as the bulwarks in relation to the EU becoming a more unified actor in the field of international relations.

Theoretical background

The foreign policy of the European Union may be analyzed according to a number of interpretative frameworks. These assign different roles to international actors and describe the dynamic of the relationships that occur among them according to different sets of rules. For the purposes of this study, a short overview of the dominant theories is necessary. This is useful firstly to define the main concepts used, thereby clearly circumscribing the field of study. Secondly, a short literature review is necessary in order to better explicate the theoretical options available and their usefulness for an institutional approach in relation to the study of the European Union in the international framework.

Traditionally, the dominant debate in the field of international relations concerning the dynamic of inter-state relationships was between realists and functionalists. Realism, in the domain of international relations, highlighted the role of states as the main actors on the international stage. According to realists such as Waltz, the international system is defined by a lack of order. States act on this anarchic stage in line with what they perceive as their own national interest. (Slaughter, 2011) This rationalist model allows for little or no long-term association between states, and emphasizes power as the main organizer. Power may manifest itself in manifold ways: economically, militarily and so forth. Power creates coercion and consent – two key concepts of realism. States either possess enough power to enter into inter-state mechanisms via consent, or they are coerced into doing so. Mearsheimer states that the international scene is regulated by four assumptions. Firstly, all states must safeguard their existence vis-à-vis other states via military power. Secondly, states must act as rational actors in order to ensure their survival. Thirdly, all states must possess military capacity, as they are unsure of their neighbor's intentions. Fourthly, as a conclusion, Great Power politics can be equated with the study of international relations. (Slaughter, 2011) Such a theoretical framework may have difficulty explaining many of the phenomena concerning the continued existence of supra-national organizations like the EU, or of military organizations such as NATO.

Functionalism denies the primacy of the state on the stage of international relations, and deems it a mode of organization which belongs to the past. Beginning with David Mitrany, theorists have underlined the shared interests of states, and their need to group into supra-national organizations. Functionalism and neo-functionalism furnished many of the conceptual definitions and base assumptions with which organizations such as the European Union operate. Neo-functionalism attempts to explain the dynamic of recent international developments by utilizing the concept of spillover. This concept assumes that states, recognizing their common interests in various fields such as trade and economy, will coalesce and create mechanisms and institutions which aid the better functioning of these fields. This institution creation leads to spillover into other areas as well. Spillover can therefore be both functional (in related areas, such as economy) and political (the creation of supra-national organizations among countries which previously coalesced in other areas). (Slaughter, 2011) A sub-variant to the functionalist approach is institutionalism. American scholar Robert Keohane contends that a rational state may recognize its own interests, and promote them through cooperation. Moreover, institutions themselves create rules, norms, and decision mechanisms which negate the innate lack of trust between states argued by realists. Institutionalism also asserts that common sets of norms, agreements, and institutions also increase the level of information that states share among themselves. Therefore, the mistrust between states that realists argue for can be circumvented, as states realize that their non-adherence to norms will be known beforehand. In addition, it is argued that institutions are more efficient in regulating inter-state relationships, as they concentrate and bureaucratize each step of the relationship. It would be more costly, and less time-effective for states to regulate each facet of diplomatic relations through the mechanism of ad-hoc agreements, rather than institutions. (Slaughter, 2011) The institutionalist-functionalist approach, therefore, explains most of the success reported by international and supra-national organizations, for example the European Union.

Though the main theoretical tenets have been synthesized above, something should also be said about recent critical approaches to international relations. These underline key elements about the nature of inter-state relationships and the functioning of organizations such as the European Union. The most significant of these belongs to American political scientist Andrew Moravcsik. In what has become known as the theory of liberal intergovernmentalism, Moravcsik hypothesizes that the main actors of international relations are not states, but individuals and interest groups. It is the interests of these groups and social categories that states serve. The global distribution of these groups determines the relationship between states, as well as the configuration of the international order. The ideological, economic or other types of interests these groups might have may also have significance, alongside rational necessities, such as the survival of the state. (Slaughter, 2011)

For the purposes of this study, the theory of institutionalism is the most appropriate. The focus will be on the importance of institutions, and their role in building common interests and strengthening the European Union. This is to be achieved by building common institutions such as a common foreign policy. Foreign policy shall be defined as the totality of instruments available to the Union, which it can utilize to take a common position in international affairs that affect a large part, or totality of its members, or to build its own position as an actor in international affairs. The building of such institutions has been in the pipeline since the early 1950s. This study will adopt a diachronic approach, in order to reveal the genealogies of the problems which affect the building of a common foreign policy. The new developments brought by the Lisbon Treaty, and how it seeks to overcome these issues, shall be the focus for the main body of the study. In this manner, the current state of affairs, as well as the institutional readiness of the Union, shall be presented and analyzed.

The foreign policy of the Union: from the beginnings to the Lisbon Treaty

The first move toward a common foreign policy was made as early as 1950 with the so-called Pleven plan, which was named after the then prime minister of France, Rene Pleven, whose brainchild it was. It called for the creation of a European army, with the participation of all occidental European states, including Germany, and was France's counter-proposal to NATO, which was also forming at the time. In February 1951 representatives of the states met in Paris, the outcome being very different from what Pleven had envisaged. In 1952 the European Defense Community (EDC) was born. (Hill & Smith, 2000) The treaty of the EDC was ratified by Germany and the Benelux Countries by 1954. However, the treaty was never ratified in France, and so the EDC became a stillborn project. The case of the EDC, even at that early stage, highlighted two important trends. The first was the leading role of France in common European foreign policy projects and institution-creating attempts. The second was the desire of the same country to seemingly do two conflicting things at once. France attempted to create a common European foreign policy, in order to shore up the role of Europe on the global stage, while at the same time attempting to "safeguard" against any loss in domestic state authority. (Hill & Smith, 2000) This dilemma is characteristic for the Union to this day, and it can be identified as the main barricade against efficient creation of institutions and response mechanisms. At first glance the dilemma seems difficult to grasp – the representatives of the same states enacting conflicting pieces of legislation and policy. However, once we apply Moravcsik's theory of liberal intergovernmentalism the conundrum can easily be explained. European states are governed by groups which have conflicting interests, and these manifest themselves in the creation of common policies. The creation of a common foreign policy of the Union is therefore tributary to a common set of interests between the leading factions in each national government.

The resounding failure of the European Defense Community led the European states away from seeking direct solutions to the problem of having a clearcut institutional framework for foreign policy. However, the Treaty of Rome ushered in a new set of foreign policy instruments. When they established the European Economic Community (EEC) the signatories of the treaty embedded two important provisions. The first was the creation of a common external trade tariff. Article 110 of the treaty stated that the tariff and subsequent customs union were enacted to contribute "to the harmonious development of world trade, the progressive abolition of restrictions on international trade, and the lowering of customs barriers." It continued: "in respect of all netters of particular interest to the common market … proceed within the framework of international organizations of an economic character only by common action." The EEC members were to adopt a united front in matters of trade and economy. The second important provision of the Treaty of Rome was the possibility of other states joining the EEC. The possibility of enlarging the EEC was addressed in article 237, which stated that any European state may apply to join the community. The Treaty also stated that the EEC had a "legal personality". (Hill & Smith, 2000)

This was the beginning of what has since become known as European "soft power". The Treaty of Rome created a set of tools for the fledgling European community, with which it could both directly and indirectly influence its neighborhood. Common treaties in the fields of trade and economy allowed the members of the EEC to negotiate tariffs globally, and more successfully. This is consistent with the theory of institutionalism, which, as described above, highlights the efficient functioning of institutions and their bridge-building functions. Secondly, the prospect of enlargement created the possibility for the EEC to become a strong normative partner in its direct neighborhood. The legal personality of the EEC was also a significant precedent, and it would reappear, as we shall see, in the Lisbon Treaty.

The next important step toward an integrated foreign policy was made in 1969. French president Georges Pompidou presented his ideas at the EEC summit in The Hague, which became known as his "triptique". The triad of completion, deepening, and enlargement constituted the main tenets for the external action of the European Community in the future. The report of Belgian foreign minister Etienne Davignon, a year later, established the bases for the European Political Cooperation (EPC). The mechanisms of regular high-level meetings between representatives of the member states and of consultations between foreign ministries were set up. The subsequent Copenhagen Report (23rd of July, 1973) codified the provisions of the EPC by enacting meetings between foreign ministers of the member states four times a year, plus whenever it was deemed necessary. (Hill & Smith, 2000) It is important to stress that these institutional developments were created against the backdrop of increasing international pressure: the 1970s and 1980s witnessed a number of significant international confrontations (the Soviet invasion of Afghanistan, the Arab-Israeli wars, the invasion of the Falkland Islands, and so forth).

This led to the creation, after two waves of enlargement, of the Single European Act in 1985. It codified the boundaries of the European Political Cooperation. It also defined the roles of the European Council, the European Commission and the European Parliament within the EPC. The Council was to take the lead, as foreign policy decisions still remained largely the domain of inter-state consultations, with the important role of assistant given to the Commission. The Parliament retained the secondary role of a consultant body. (Hill & Smith, 2000)

The Maastricht Treaty of 1992 brought further developments for the foreign policy of the European Union. It replaced the EPC with the Common Foreign and Security Policy (CFSP), becoming a pillar in the now "three-pillared" European Union. The CFSP was created to "safeguard common values, the fundamental interests and the independence of the European Union; to strengthen its security and its member states in all ways, to preserve peace and strengthen international security; to promote international cooperation; to develop and consolidate democracy and the rule of law, respect for human rights and fundamental freedoms..." (article J.I.2. of the Treaty of the European Union – TEU). These objectives were to be achieved through joint action. The Presidency of the European Union was to represent it in matters of CFSP. The general guidelines of the CFSP were to be defined and implemented by the European Council, on the basis of unanimity. Foreign policy was to be debated by the Council of Ministers. The Commission became affiliated to the CFSP through the joint right of initiative it received. The areas of interest for the foreign and neighborhood policy of the EU were also defined and categorized geographically. (Ginsberg, 2001; Hill & Smith, 2000)

The CFSP after Lisbon

The Lisbon Treaty of 2007 (entering into force in 2009) ushered in a number of changes in the way in which the European Union implements its external policies. Its main contributions were the creation of specialized institutions for regulating and administering the foreign policy of the Union. Thus the offices of the High Representative of the Union for Foreign Affairs and Security Policy and the

President of the European Council were created. The European Union as such was given legal personality, acknowledging its role as a formal actor in international relations. In this way, the "three-pillared" European Union was abolished. (Carbone, 2010; Griller & Ziller, 2008)

One of the main provisions of the Lisbon Treaty was to detach the CFSP from other areas of the external relations of the Union. (Griller & Ziller, 2008) This has led to a better conceptual circumscription of what the CFSP is and what it entails. However, the Treaty still specifically states that it does not affect the power of Member States to conduct their foreign policy (Declaration numbers 13 and 14) and that it does not increase the power of the Commission to initiate decisions nor of the Parliament in this domain (Declaration number 14). Article 3, section 5 of the Lisbon Treaty defines the objectives of the foreign policy of the European Union as following:

> In its relations with the wider world, the Union shall uphold and promote its values and interests. It shall contribute to peace, security, the sustainable development of the Earth, solidarity and mutual respect among peoples, free and fair trade, eradication of poverty and the protection of human rights, in particular the rights of the child, as well as to the strict observance and the development of international law, including respect for the principles of the United Nations Charter

Beyond its lofty goals, the codification of these objectives involve a number of legal consequences that also affect other areas of EU policy. For example, common trade agreements with foreign states should also take into consideration human rights and environmental issues. One of the main criticisms brought to this formulation of the objectives of EU foreign policy is the fact that the issues are not linked to one another. For example, respect for human rights is not linked to the issue of security. This can lead to inconsistencies in the pursuit of the objectives.

Under the Lisbon Treaty, the decision-making process within the confines of the CFSP has become codified. It is still based, at its core, on the agreement between the member states and on unanimity. There was an attempt, during the drafting of the Treaty, to inject a number of situations in which the decisions could be made according to Qualified Majority Voting, but the results were inconsistent. One of the exceptions was, according to the Treaty:

> When adopting a decision defining a Union action or position, on a proposal which the High Representative (…) has presented following a specific request from the European Council, made on its own initiative or that of the High Representative.

Since the High Representative cannot initiate such moves, the starting point for a Qualified Majority Vote is still based on a decision by the European Council taken with unanimity. This means that the member states, through their representatives in the Council, can pre-block any such occurrence.

The increased role of inter-governmental agreement in the system set up by the Lisbon Treaty is also highlighted by the role it ascribes to the Commission. (Carbone, 2010; Griller & Ziller, 2008) Previously possessing the joint right to make initiatives regarding CFSP proposals, the Commission has now been relegated to supporting the initiatives of the High Representative. The European Parliament's consultant role has remained much the same, though the Lisbon Treaty uses stronger wording, emphasizing the right of the elected body to be "informed and consulted". The EP also has the theoretical right to ask questions and make recommendations not only to the Council but also to the High Representative in matters that relate to the CFSP.

The Common Defense and Security Policy (CSDP) has been integrated into the CFSP. The field of activity of the CSDP includes joint disarmament, military advice and assistance tasks, conflict prevention and post-conflict stabilization. The High Representative coordinates such actions in close cooperation with the Political and Security Committee of the Union. The CSDP is strengthened by the formalization and inclusion into the Treaty of the activities of the European Defense Agency. Member States which have higher military capabilities may establish a so-called structured cooperation. The Lisbon Treaty introduces the opportunity for enhanced cooperation within the CSDP, authorized by the Council acting with unanimity. (Griller & Ziller, 2008)

The office of the High Representative and the European External Action Service

The creation of the office of High Representative of the Union for Foreign Affairs and Security Policy can be viewed as an attempt to preserve the main form and function of the Minister of Foreign Affairs of the Union, which was proposed in the draft version of the EU Constitution. (Griller & Ziller, 2008) In this sense, alongside the above-mentioned Council President, it is the most significant institutional step toward a unified external policy and a more integrated Union. However, due to the special nature of the Union, preserved by the Lisbon Treaty, the High Representative is not analogous to a minister of foreign affairs of a national state. The most important role of the High Representative is that of maintaining a balance, in other words to be a bridge-builder. Catherine Ashton, the first High Representative of the Union, has had the difficult task of building convergence on two levels. Firstly, she must alleviate the tensions that might appear between the Council and the Commission. These periodic conflicts represent the frictions between state and central authority. Secondly, the High Representative has to control the diverging trends of the Union's external policies, which relate mostly to economic, financial, and trading issues, and the CFSP, since the two have been formally separated by the provisions of the Lisbon Treaty (see above). These tasks seem difficult to handle, to say the least, as the High Representative is also expected to be seen at a multitude of forums, and be the spokesperson for the European Union.

The multifaceted nature of the office is reflected by its membership both in the Council (as the representative for the CFSP) and in the Commission, as Commissioner for External Relations. The appointment of the High Representative is made according to Qualified Majority Voting by the European Council, with the agreement of the President of the Commission (Article 18 of the Lisbon Treaty). Therefore, both institutions have a say in the activity of the High Representative. The European Parliament has an indirect say in the matter, as it has control over the appointment and dismissal of the Commission (including the High Representative). However, this means that the person retaining the office at that time still retains his Council hat, at least until a new Commission is approved, which might want to appoint a different person for the position of Commissioner for External Relations, in which case an obvious incompatibility would result. (Griller & Ziller, 2008)

The rights and responsibilities of the High Representative are also split between the Council and Commission. She presides over the Foreign Affairs Council, elaborating the Union's external action on the basis of strategic guidelines formulated by the European Council, while ensuring the consistency of the actions (as laid down in the Lisbon Treaty). The High Representative can also take part in the workings of the European Council, where she is a permanent member, but she does not possess the right to vote. She is also a permanent member of the Commission, and fully participates in its decision-making processes. The High Representative not only directly and indirectly influences decision making in the Union, but also participates in the execution of decisions. The Lisbon Treaty says that the High Representative shall put the CFSP into effect, together with the member states of the Union. This can mean preparation of initiatives and materials for the states to decide upon and implement, as well as the overseeing of implementation of ongoing initiatives, and representation of the Union in diverse international forums. In addition, the Representative may also be put in the position of negotiator within the Commission, as she tries to coordinate the divergent policies that affect the external policy of the EU.

The Treaty of Lisbon attempts to alleviate the responsibilities of the office of the High Representative with the creation of the European External Action Service (EEAS), in order to assist and prepare her work. Article 27(3) reads:

> In fulfilling his mandate, the High Representative shall be assisted by a European External Action Service. This service shall work in cooperation with the diplomatic services of the Member States and shall comprise officials from relevant departments of the General Secretariat of the Council and of the Commission, as well as staff seconded from national diplomatic services of Member States.

The EEAS was established by a decision of the Council, on a proposal of the High Representative, who in turn consulted with the European Parliament, after obtaining the Commission's consent. The new EEAS came into being in December 2010. Since then, the institution has experienced several "growing pains". (Griller & Ziller, 2008; Koutrakos, 2011) In theory, one-third of its members should have come from the Commission, one third from the Council secretariat, while one-third were to be from the foreign ministries of member states. In practice, this led to a large amount of cooperation problems, especially since the third sector, coming from national states, has yet to send all of its representatives to the EEAS. (Burke, 2009) The EEAS has also struggled to acquire the kind of experienced staff it needs to serve the enormous demands placed upon the office of the High Representative efficiently. Moreover, budgetary problems can also be identified, as the finances of the EEAS are quite large. This leads to the EEAS being at present a rather flimsy institution, which in turn also weakens the position of Catherine Ashton.

Enlargement and neighborhood policy

The two avenues of "soft" and normative power for the European Union have traditionally been enlargement and neighborhood policies that prepared for future waves of enlargement. Since 2007, the prospects for great enlargement waves have become obsolete. The Union is realistically expected to receive only a few new members in the foreseeable future. The membership of Croatia will occur in July 2013, it being the only certain future member of the European Union at the time of writing. Currently, there are five existing official candidate countries for EU membership: Iceland, Macedonia, Montenegro, Serbia and Turkey. Albania has not had its status as candidate recognized as of yet. Bosnia and Herzegovina is also expected to apply soon to be a candidate for membership, since the country has concluded its association agreement with the Union.

The prospects of EU enlargement are quite slim if we analyze the status of each candidate, even cursorily. Although most of the countries are largely in accordance with the Copenhagen Criteria, they do not satisfy other conditions. Iceland has faced massive economic and financial instability in recent years, and cannot be expected to meet the economic criteria required to join the Union in the foreseeable future. Macedonia and Montenegro are also similarly equipped financially, with incompatible legal and political systems. Montenegro has the added disadvantage of being a new state, in full process of institution creation and defining its regional role. Serbia is facing huge problems in the domestic field, involving an unstable economy, a fraught political system, and corruption issues, just to highlight a few basic matters. The status of the last official candidate on the list, Turkey, is the most complicated. An official candidate since the 1980s, Turkey has been negotiating EU status for over two decades. Its future membership is being held in limbo due to a series of complications it would bring for European stability and identity. Its membership is more or less being officially blocked by France and Germany, as well as a host of other EU members. Thus enlargement cannot be expected, and therefore the Union has to rely on other tools to conduct its foreign policy goals in its immediate neighborhood.

One of the recent tools developed in 2008 by two Eastern members of the European Union, Poland and Sweden, is the Eastern Partnership. The Partnership is meant to be the final piece in the European neighborhood policy triad of the Northern Dimension and Union for the Mediterranean. Its membership consists of Armenia, Azerbaijan, Belarus, Georgia, Moldova, and Ukraine. The Eastern Partnership is viewed as an institutional forum for discussing visa agreements, free trade deals, and strategic partnership agreements with the EU's eastern neighbors. It is not viewed as a step toward eventual membership. The Eastern Partnership is utilized by the Union to promote its norms in the fields mentioned in the Lisbon Treaty, and also as a benign way of extending its influence eastward. It will be administered directly by the Commission.

The evolution of the ENP and ESDP in the East and South

Having presented the structural and institutional innovations brought by the Lisbon Treaty, it is now necessary to critically evaluate the successes and failures of the newly divided European Neighbourhood Policy and the European Security and Defense Policy. This will be achieved via a quick overview of these policies in action over the last decade, with special focus on post-Lisbon developments.

The European Union has a long history of political engagement in the Mediterranean and Middle East. The main vehicle for achieving this was the MEPP (Middle East Peace Process), which was driven by the European Political Cooperation, the precursor of the CFSP. (Whitman & Wolff, 2010) While the main mode of engagement in the area was that of aid programs and economic stimulus and cooperation, the EU also strategically involved itself on a number of other levels, wishing to show its political face to the world. In the Middle East, the EU Border Assistance Mission in Rafah and the ESDP operation at the Egypt-Gaza crossing stand out. While both were temporary interventions, they highlighted the European concept behind strategic interventions in the Muslim World. The main guiding principle followed was that of two-state policy, and assistance in peace-aiding missions. (Whitman & Wolff, 2010)

In 2006, the EU took a considerable stake in relation to intervention in the conflict in Lebanon. While there was a lack of total unity concerning the form of intervention in the war (mainly due to the compliance of the UK with US desires), the European Political and Security Committee debated a military mission under the flag of the EU. The chosen form was an ESDP operation under UN command; this was somewhat achieved through the UNIFIL (United Nations Interim Force in Lebanon) mission which was finally carried out in the country. On the 25 August 2006, UN Secretary General Kofi Annan encouraged Member States to make "substantial contributions" to the force; the mission may be surmised as an EU mission, due to the provenience of the vast majority of troops. This mission also reinforced the political and security approach of the EU in the area: it did not disarm Hezbollah militias on the Israel border, but demilitarized the area. This was done in order to come up with a political solution to the issues of the area which would include all the actors, its main goal being the creation of peace and stability. This move was explicitly stated at the EU Council following the mission, in which Annan called for a consensus with the Lebanese; it was envisioned that the armed militias would be integrated into an institutional framework, such as a future Lebanese army. This reflects the European desire to resolve armed conflicts through the creation of institutions, which in turn would strengthen stability and good governance. (Whitman & Wolff, 2010)

The real catalyst and test for the foreign policy of the European Union in the Mediterranean area was the series of events dubbed the "Arab Spring". The violent upheavals in almost all the countries on the South-Eastern border of the EU have brought a paradigm shift in EU foreign policy in the area, and also informed a number of assumptions about the successes of certain strategic policies in the Mediterranean. The previous assumptions held that the EU should support incremental changes in the legislative and institutional systems of these states, in order to support good governance and, eventually, democracy. (Biscop, 2012) Radical Islam was seen as the holder of popular support. The opinion of policy makers in general was that it had to be kept out of the political game; the secular nature of most of the uprisings, however, disproved the veracity of the assumptions relating to the supposed popular backing for radical Islam.

The initial response of the EU showed the theoretical framework of its external policy, as it offered political support to the presidents of Tunisia and Egypt. (Biscop, 2012) However, the escalation of the conflict and the brutal response, on the one hand, and the realization of the democratic potential, on the other, led the EU to change its approach to finding solutions for the conflicts. The responses given were multifarious in nature, ranging from economic sanctions, humanitarian assistance, and military intervention on the part of a large number of member states (through NATO).

In 2011 the Commission produced two Communications and, through the voice of the High Representative, requested support for their implementation. The communications were essentially a revision of the ENP and the security policy in the Mediterranean area, grouped around a set of four new principles: redefined conditionality, greater differentiation among countries, new tools to support the building of democracy, and a stronger focus on sustainable socio-economic development. This revision of the policy was dubbed "more for more" by political commentators, and views incentives as the main tool of achieving progress in the area. The motto can be surmised as "more money, more market access, more mobility", and appeals to established factors, the political regimes of the area (again the institutional approach). Targeted economic assistance is to be grouped with trade agreements and lifting some of the protectionist bans on market access and mobility that the Southern and Eastern Mediterranean states had to contend with up to now. The SPRING Program (Support for Partnership, Reform and Inclusive Growth) allocated a sum of 350 million euros to the area for 2011 and 2012. Another economic tool was the European Neighbourhood Policy Instrument, which allocated, for example, 160 million euros to Tunisia and 449 million euros to Egypt during the 2011-2013 period. (Biscop, 2012) This reflects the desire to differentiate between the specific needs of each state. This strategic approach was also mirrored in the creation of the EU-Tunisia Task Force in 2011, which grouped together representatives of the Tunisian and European governments, the EU Commission and External Action Service, as well as various financial actors. Another institutional strategy was the creation of the Civil Society Facility, which was endowed with a budget of 22 million euros for the 2011-2013 period. The stronger commitment to democracy and the encouragement of factors that favor the building of democracy in the countries of the area is well reflected by these strategies. The High Representative has also worked closely with certain political organizations in the area, such as the Arab League and the African Union. These meetings, however, still retain only a semi-official status, as the EU has not formally recognized the Arab League as a partner. (Biscop, 2012)

The communications and the strategic moves of the EU in the South-Eastern Mediterranean zone are certainly positive moves on the theoretical level. However, the practice of implementation will be the proof of the pudding. Since the Arab Spring, the EU has maintained good relations with the states of the South-Western Mediterranean, an area in which it has traditionally done well due to French political influence. We have noted some examples of the types of incentives that Tunisia receives above; similar programs have tackled the developments in Morocco as well. In Libya, the EU chose to intervene militarily, assisting the rebel forces in the overthrow of Gaddafi's regime. After the cessation of hostilities, the EU has moved to set up a Delegation in Tripoli. The country was integrated within the ENP and its sub-element, the Union for the Mediterranean, and its assets were unblocked.

Egypt has remained one of the most problematic test cases for EU foreign and neighborhood policy. Hostilities and protest have still not stopped, and the conflict between the secular and religious factions still looms large in Egyptian society. The EU has a number of economic and political interests in pacification of the country, notwithstanding its overall desire to promote democracy and good governance in the area. In this sense, the Union has been very careful about making any decisive moves that might favor a particular party, beyond economic incentives and aid, which were mentioned above. Similarly, EU policy toward Syria was one of official condemnation, coupled with economic sanctions (Biscop, 2012) The rate of success of these measures is debatable, since the regime has not seemed to respond to them. The EU's policy in the area, as we can see from the cases of Egypt and Syria, is still somewhat conceptually split between the old and new approaches, and reflects mixed theoretical assumptions about the area.

In its Eastern neighborhood, the European Union has to face a completely different situation compared with that in the Mediterranean. The Eastern area is one of frozen conflicts, and is marked by the presence of a competitor which possesses real political, cultural, military and economic power of its own: Russia. Due to this reality, the strategy of the EU has been very different, adapted to the needs of a careful policy in the area. (Dabrowski & Maliszewska, 2011; Whitman & Wolff, 2010) Its main principles and objectives are capacity-building and monitoring. The EU has generally avoided making any decisive intervention in the area, and has attempted to evade the role of conflict mediator. This, however, was the exact role it was pushed into in 2008 by the military conflict which broke out between Georgia and its northern neighbor, Russia. The EU came out as a successful broker of the agreement between the two parties, mainly through the successful mediation of the French EU Presidency. The "Six-Point Agreement" was reached on 1 August, and on 1 October an EU Monitoring Mission was set up in Georgia to oversee the process. (Dabrowski & Maliszewska, 2011; Whitman & Wolff, 2010) The conclusion of the 2008 conflict was that the EU can, at times, successfully act as an united actor on the stage of international relations.

Apart from this isolated event, the Neighbourhood Policy of the Union still seems to rely on the traditional concept of conditionality. (Dabrowski & Maliszewska, 2011; Whitman & Wolff, 2010) Since EU membership has been confirmed to be unrealistic for the near future, confirmed since Ukraine's bid after the Orange Revolution, this reliance leads to a weak overall influence of the Union in the area. The Eastern Partnership has not done much yet, in real terms, to dynamize the relationship between the EU and its Eastern neighbors. Some of the novel elements included the raising of financial incentives. The EU has increased its financial assistance to the ENP envelope by 350 million in 2010–13, and redeployed 250 million already allocated, singling out a number of 'flagship initiatives', such as an Integrated Border Management Programme, a facility for small and medium enterprises (SME), a range of different energy-related projects, and cooperation on the prevention of and response to disasters. (Kostanyan, 2012)

In the aftermath of the Arab Spring, there still remains a niche for EU activity in the post-Soviet area, especially since the United States has scaled down its commitment to Eastern Europe and the Caucasus. However, how the EU shall go about this is still unclear. Among the experts, for example, Stefan Meister from DGAP (The German Society for Foreign Policy) (Meister 2011) has argued for a stronger emphasis on German-Polish co-management of the Eastern policy, using existing institutional tools such as the "Weimar triangle". (Makarychev and Deviatkov 2012) However, after conclusion of its term holding the EU presidency, Warsaw declared that expectations of its leading role might be misplaced, especially in the Caucasus where Poland did not want to take on the frozen conflicts, thus the initiative fell back on Germany and France. (Kostanyan, 2012; Makarychev & Deviatkov, 2012) Nicolas Sarkozy's visit to Baku and Yerevan immediately after the Warsaw Eastern Partnership summit in the beginning of October 2011 was a direct consequence of this.

The Eastern Partnership during the Polish EU Presidency produced a final declaration at the Warsaw summit, which acknowledged the European aspirations of the Partnership countries and the principle of conditionality known as "more for more". This reflects a similar approach to that of the Union for the Mediterranean. In real terms, however, it is not. (Kostanyan, 2012; Makarychev & Deviatkov, 2012) Most of the tools of the Eastern Partnership remain conditional and technical: visa liberalization, deep and comprehensive free trade. The EU foreign policy in this area remains normative and conditional, bound to the implementation of the norms of the acquis communautaire in a variety of areas. This remains an overall weakness of the European conceptual approach to the area.

The bilateral relations between the EU and each of the six "Eastern partners" are prevalent in the agenda of the Eastern Partnership. The reasons for this are much deeper than simple failures in EU policies: the differentiation and fragmentation within post-Soviet space are so profound that large foreign policy actors such as NATO or Russia are themselves unable to efficiently tackle them with a global approach. One of the competing initiatives, however, is Russian President Vladimir Putin's project for a "Customs Union" of the former Soviet states. In his vision, Russia should act as a nucleus for post-Soviet reintegration. It is projected that the Kremlin will invest large sums in this project, which is (partly) intended to be a clear challenge to the initiative of the Eastern Partnership. However, as a side-note, it is less than clear if Russia possesses the financial basis or political motivation to undertake such a project, and make it a success. (Kostanyan, 2012; Makarychev & Deviatkov, 2012)

Conclusion

The foreign policy of the European Union is, as can be seen from the institutional developments of the past up to the Lisbon Treaty, still tributary to its unique nature. The constant search for its own identity on the international stage has, however, set certain trends in motion. These trends have also gained clout due to the rising international pressures on the Union, and the limitations on its traditional means of international negotiations (such as the imposition of certain modes of behavior through enlargement). The bridge-building feature of institutions will hopefully further succeed in the mission of creating a more integrated European front on the global stage, as the Union seeks to affirm its role in the face of external challenges.

In practice, we may observe a number of trends emerging within the foreign policy approach of the European Union. These stem from a paradigm shift in the theory of foreign policy, brought on by recent changes in its immediate neighborhood, but also as a result of a deeper understanding of the real necessities of each of the countries in Europe's vicinity. The EU has begun to differentiate between the needs of each of its neighborhood areas, and its specific neighbors, and to create tools which provide incentives for the creation of lasting stability in the region and better integration with the Union itself. These moves may herald the development of a foreign policy more suited to respond to external challenges, and quicker to act in times of international crises.

Bibliography

Biscop, Sven, Balfour, Rosa & Emerson, Michael. (2012). "An Arab springboard for EU foreign policy?" *CEPS Paper* (54). Retrieved from http://www.ceps.be/research-areas/eu-neighbourhood-foreign-and-security-policy.

Burke, By Edward. (2009). "Europe's External Action Service: Ten steps towards a credible EU foreign policy." Centre for European Policy Studies, Policy Brief, 1-8. Retrieved from http://www.cer.org.uk/sites/default/files/publications/attachments/pdf/2012/pb_eeas_4july12-5377.pdf.

Cameron, Fraser. (2007). *An introduction to European foreign policy.* New York: Routledge.

Carbone, Maurizio. (2010). *National politics and European integration. From the constitution to the Lisbon Treaty.* Cheltenham: Edward Elgar Publishing.

Cebeci, M. (2012). "European foreign policy research reconsidered: Constructing an 'Ideal Power Europe' through theory?" *Millennium – Journal of International Studies* 40(3): 563-583. http://mil.sagepub.com/cgi/doi/10.1177/0305829812442235 (February 4, 2013).

Dabrowski, M, and M Maliszewska. (2011). *EU Eastern Neighborhood: Economic potential and future development.* New York: Springer.

Dannreuther, Roland. (2004). European Union foreign and security policy: towards a neighbourhood strategy. London: Routledge

Emerson, Michael. (2012). "History does not move in a straight line." CEPS Comme (83): 1-3. http://www.ceps.be/research-areas/eu-neighbourhood-foreign-and-security-policy.

Ginsberg, Roy. (2001). *The European Union in international politics. Baptism by fire.* Boulder: Rowman and Littledfield.

Griller, Stefan, and Jacques Ziller. (2008). *The Lisbon Treaty. EU constitutionalism without a constitutional treaty?* New York: Springer.

Hill, Christopher. (2013) *Actors in Europe' s foreign policy.* London: Routledge

Hill, Christopher, and Karen E Smith. (2000). *European foreign policy: Key documents.* New York: Routledge.

Kostanyan, Hrant. (2012). "The EEAS and the Eastern Partnership: Let the blame game stop." *CEPS Commentary* (September): 1-3. http://www.ceps.be/research-areas/eu-neighbourhood-foreign-and-security-policy.

Koutrakos, Panos. (2011). *European foreign policy. Legal and political perspectives.* Cheltenham: Edward Elgar Publishing.

Laidi, Zaki. (2008). *EU foreign policy in a globalized world normative power and social preferences.* Houndmills: Routledge.

Lucarelli, Sonia, and Ian Manners. (2006). *Values and principles in European Union foreign policy.* New York: Routledge.

Makarychev, Andrey, and Andrey Deviatkov. (2012). "Eastern Partnership: Still a missing link in EU strategy?" *CEPS Commentary* (January): 1-5.

McElroy, G., and K. Benoit. (2011). "Policy positioning in the European Parliament." *European Union Politics* 13(1): 150-167.

Slaughter, Anne-marie. (2011). *International relations, principal theories.* Oxford: Oxford University Press.

Smith, KE. (2003). *European Union foreign policy in a changing world.* Malden: Polity Press.

Whitman, Richard G., Wolff, Stefan. (2010). *The European neighbourhood policy in perspective: context, implementation and impact.* Houndmills: Palgrave Macmillan.

Discourses on the EU's international role and external policies

András Szalai

The European Union (EU) is still seen as a novel, mysterious actor in world politics – in Jacques Delors' words, a true "unidentified political object". The EU is not a state, it does not possess a traditional military, it relies heavily on civilian instruments and it is explicitly normative in its foreign relations. Such a peculiar construct that seems to defy Westphalian notions of international actorness has naturally drawn the attention of many academics, serving as a battleground for cutting-edge theorizing. Both its creation and its operation are complex and unique. As Andrew Moravcsik aptly writes: "in few areas of interstate politics are ideas so often invoked, identities so clearly at stake, and interests so complex, challenging and uncertain." (Moravcsik, 1999, p. 669)

Foreign policy serves as a separate field of research within European studies. Part of the European Union's uniqueness as a political entity lies in its practice of pooling the sovereignty of its member states. Throughout the decades of the "European project", many competencies that were previously the exclusive prerogatives of sovereign states have already been delegated to the supranational level. Foreign policy, one of the key defining characteristics of a sovereign state, has been lagging behind. Diverging member state interests, overbureaucratization and the lack of a strong military instrument has forced scholars to question whether the EU possesses international actorness at all. A group of scholars – most of them quite sympathetic to the European project – have argued that the EU is indeed a unique actor in international relations and many of its weaknesses are in fact the source of its strength. The resulting major conceptual shifts in the past four decades along concepts like "normative power Europe" have moved the original debate from the question of whether the EU has a foreign policy to questions about the nature of the EU's actorness, and the specificities of its foreign policy action.

But the literature on European foreign policy[1] is still far from monolithic, and the continued popularity of contradictory concepts both in academia and in

---

1   The meaning of "European foreign policy" can be manifold, as the political, cultural and geographical borders of Europe proper are hotly debated. In this paper, unless otherwise stated "Europe" will refer to the European Community/European Union and "European foreign policy" will always refer to its foreign policy.

the political discourse seems to attest to a mysterious and unexplainable political entity. Ideas are in abundant supply, and the concepts used include state-like and non-state metaphors, as well as various versions of "power". Qualifiers used to address the EU include "peace community" (Smith, 2003), "normative area" (Therborn, 2001 in Cerutti), "trading state" (Telò, 2001), "neo-medieval empire" (Zielonka, 2006), "colonial power" (Ravenhill, 1985), "military power" (Bull, 1982), "normative power" (Manners, 2002), "structural power" (Keukeleire, 2003), "strange superpower" (Buchan, 1993), "small power" (Toje, 2010), "quiet superpower" (Moravcsik, 2002), "ethical power" (Aggestam, 2008), "civilian power" (Duchêne, 1972) and even "metrosexual superpower" (Khanna, 2004). However, this cacophony of concepts does not make up a theory in the traditional sense. Moreover, some of these notions are normatively biased, and lack scientific rigor and precision. The fact that concepts often simply mirror the official political rhetoric, and that the EU also often defines itself in these academic constructs is a recurring point of criticism in relation to the literature.

Throughout the development of its Common Foreign and Security Policy, the European Union was often burdened by the gap between its modest capabilities and the immense expectations – both internal and external – in connection with its role as an international actor. But a "capabilities-expectation gap" (Hill, 1993) is also present between the academic concepts devised to describe and explain the EU's behavior, and the empirical scholarship they could produce. Current events, such as the financial crisis and the Arab Spring, along with a general enlargement fatigue will once again test the resolve of the EU. Concepts that are the product of a pre-crisis era will once again be tested as to whether they can account for a changing EU in a changing environment.

The goal of this essay is twofold. First, it seeks to present the main concepts used to assess and model the European Union as an international actor. It draws attention to these various concepts evolved throughout the European project and the ways in which they have been embedded in the then current historical-political context. Authors sympathetic to the EU and the values it stands for have tried time after time to redefine the criteria for actorness, most importantly power. In their quest to turn the weaknesses of Europe into strength they frame the Union as an entity that wields its power in a fundamentally different way from traditional political forms, and – most crucially – this difference can be conceptualized as normative. Consequently, as the analysis will show, these concepts can rather be seen as metaphors that often are burdened by a normative bias and are therefore only vaguely defined, lacking the scientific rigor of descriptive and/or predictive theories.[2]

The apparent vagueness of theories has further fueled the highly abstract theorizing about international identity that has left us in need of testable hypotheses. Testing is not only important for theory assessment, but also creates a necessary link between science and political realities – a problem that leads us to

---

2   Curiously, scholars within the same ontological/epistemological camp often lack a common methodology, rendering comparison of their arguments difficult.

the second goal of this study. Thus it will also argue that mature theories of International Relations (IR), most notably neo-realism, can still offer us a scientific toolkit that will enable research to move from endless conceptual arguments to empirical studies – the best way to test our concepts of European foreign policy is, after all, to look at what the EU actually does in the field. Previous concepts have been highly contextual, and conceptual shifts in the literature have coincided with developments within the EU or the general international environment. Recent events, like the massive enlargement that created the EU-27, the Union's growing presence as a global actor, and the financial crisis that plagues European states will again force a radical reinterpretation of popular "models". The realist interpretation of EU foreign policy can contribute to contemporary weak-constructivist approaches that also emphasize empirical research to create a finely tuned, more readily applicable framework that is able to come up with testable hypotheses. As will consistently be argued, mere theorizing is hopelessly contextual and subjective, thus we need to move onto the analysis of what the EU is actually doing in the field.

Theorizing the European Union's International Identity

International Relations (IR)[3] has been dealing with the question of European foreign policy since the mid-1970s. Initial attention was given to the European Community's strengthening economic and diplomatic means, while questions of a common foreign and security policy, along with the EU's global responsibilities as an international actor only entered the academic and political debate in the 1990s. Two concepts are mainly used to assess the EU's international role: "actorness" (Sjøstedt, 1977; Hill, 1993; Caporaso & Jupille, 1998) and "presence" (Allen & Smith, 1990; Elgström & Smith, 2006). Actorness deals with the characteristics and prerequisites of being an international actor: 1) recognition by outsiders, 2) authority, i.e. the legal competence to act, 3) autonomy (distinctiveness and independence from other international actors) and 4) cohesion (the extent to which it is seen as a unitary actor from outside).[4] (Caporaso & Jupille, 1998) Especially in the last category, the EC initially fell short of actorness, but it gradually established "a clear presence", mostly in the economic sphere, acting as a "shaper" or "filter" as it influenced the perceptions of other policy-makers and filtered out certain options. (Allen & Smith, 1990) Though arguments were made in favor of the actorness of the EC (most notably Duchêne, 1972), presence was generally used more because it was seen as an in-between concept and also as a welcome step away from state centrism that was seen as a conceptual barrier to analyzing non-state actors like the EC/EU.

---

3   In this essay, "International Relations" denotes the academic discipline, while "international relations" refers to its object of analysis.

4   To these initial criteria of "actual actorness" Hill (1996) adds practical capabilities to have effective policies.

Since the EC did not possess military powers, seen as a prerequisite for being a true actor, analysts trying to frame Europe as an actor needed to redefine actorness without referring to military power. Such a conceptual move was justified by a radical reinterpretation of traditional power in favor of civilian rather than military instruments, thereby creating the most important cleavage within the academic community along different interpretations of the relationship between civilian/soft and military/hard power. With the establishment of the European Union in 1993, along with its Common Foreign and Security Policy, the debate moved to the characteristics of the EU as an actor. Scholars of European foreign policy not only tried to simply frame the EC/EU as another state-like actor in international relations, but to establish it as a unique, "new type of entity with actor quality". (Buzan & Little, 2000, p. 359) With the question of actorness/presence more or less settled in favor of actorness, the question of whether the EU is a novel, unique type of actor, and if so, whether its uniqueness produces a unique foreign policy became the core elements of continuity within the literature.

The uniqueness argument dates back to when François Duchêne (1972) envisaged the European Community as a model of peace and reconciliation for other parts of the world. The successes of postwar reconciliation and the relative peacefulness of the old continent during the Cold War understandably filled Europeans with pride and a belief that the European project was a truly unique Kantian paradise, which overwhelmed many analysts. The subsequent continuous quest for the "sui generis argument" is perhaps best exemplified by a comment of Christopher Hill (1990) calling for the rehabilitation of the then heavily criticized civilian power Europe concept, since it "allows that [European foreign relations are] sui generic, and [an] unprecedented development in world history which must not be cramped by forcing it into inappropriate conceptual models derived from the study of states."[5] (Hill, 1990, p. 54)

Uniqueness presupposes difference, and the European Union's difference is often established in terms of roles[6] that reflect "a claim on the international system, recognition by international actors, and a conception of identity." (Aggestam, 2006, p. 11) The EU's role in international relations is established in contrast to other major international actors, most notably the United States. Difference and uniqueness lie both in the EU's characteristics and in its actions, and are often normative: the EU *is* a unique actor that *acts* in a unique way. Thus

---

5   Note that uniqueness is not a positive quality for all authors. Robert Kagan (2003), for example, acknowledges the EU's unique, Kantian qualities – in contrast to the more Hobbesian United States – but argues that these lead to passivity, impotence and naďveté in world politics.

6   Role theory posits that "a national role conception includes the policymakers' own definitions of the general kinds of decisions, commitments, rules, and actions suitable to their state, and of the functions, if any, their state should perform on a continuing basis in the international system or in subordinate regional systems." (Holsti, 1970 quoted in Aggestam, 2006)

the EU differs from other powers in both its means and ends: it has "milieu goals" (aimed at shaping its environment) rather than "possession goals" (aimed at interests). (K. Smith, 2002; M. Smith, 2003) While shaping its environment, the EU furthers normative ambitions (e.g. human rights); therefore it represents "something different from states in the international system in that it has not been an actor that only is guided by its self-interest." (Elgström & M. Smith, 2006, p. 3)

The Union's institutional structure is also seen as a source of its uniqueness,[7] along with the historical context of its post-war creation and its hybrid forms of governance. (Whitman, 1998; Manners, 2002) For some authors, these factors also create a distinct European identity that can form the basis of common policy action, and predisposes the EU to act in a normative way (Manners, 2002). This identity itself is thus unique in that it is exclusively value-based. Sonia Lucarelli (2006, p. 49) supports this thesis by arguing that the EU relies on a peculiar interpretation of a set of values and principles that are shared by a large part of the international community, but represents these differently from powers like the US. If the EU has an identity, she maintains, it is based on these values, and not on a common culture (i.e. political identity).

The European Union is also unique with regards to its non-state structure. Despite its growing influence in the world, and its partaking in international negotiations, peacekeeping missions and organizations like the United Nations, the European Union is not presented as a sovereign, only its member states are. The EU pools sovereignty, it is not a state, and it exists in contrast to Westphalian notions of territoriality and sovereignty. (Manners & Whitman, 2003) As a network of states (Zielonka, 2006), it is arguably well-equipped for multilateral negotiations. This is attested by the fact that the EU is heavily involved in institution building and the establishment of rules and norms of multilateral cooperation. Elgström and Smith (2006) summarize the differences between the EU and other international actors in terms of seven observations: 1) pacifism rather than aggression; 2) principles rather than pragmatism; 3) slow, consensual and structural, rather than rapid, conflictual action; 4) networking rather than hierarchical; 5) open rather than closed; 6) contra-normal, rather than conventional.

As this wide variety of interpretations shows, scholars who acknowledge the uniqueness of the EU still disagree about its source, often mirroring the so-called agency-structure debate in IR. (Wendt, 1987; Carlsnaes, 1992) The EU's foreign policy identity/role can be the result of active agency: the EU has a certain identity and acts in a specific way because this is how Europe is, due to its history and culture. (c.f. Manners, 2002) Others, in contrast, would argue that the role the EU fulfills is rather a response to the shifting constellations of power in the international system and is mainly of material origins – as Robert Kagan

---

7   The EU's institutional structure is often also seen as an obstacle to a consistent and coherent foreign policy, due to diverging member state interests, weak institutions with competing objectives and an unclear division of competence among actors. For the detailed "euro-paralysis" argument see Zielonka (1998).

(2003) argues, Europe is Kantian out of necessity, not out of choice.[8] This latter approach is shared by scholars of various schools of thought, ranging from Hedley Bull (1982) to contemporary realists like Adrian Hyde-Price (2006).

Lastly, these various conceptualizations of the EU as a unique entity hint at an implicitly stated, yet crucial question. Arguing that the EU is a uniquely constructed entity – be it due to structure, history or culture – does not necessarily imply that it also acts in a way fundamentally different from other powerful actors. This point, as will be demonstrated in a later section, forms the primary point of criticism raised by contemporary neo-realists against idealist-normative approaches to European foreign policy. The following sections will survey the first theoretical construct used to frame the European Union as a unique actor: civilian power Europe (CPE).

Civilian Power Europe and its Early Critics

Critics have been foretelling Europe's decline ever since the Treaty of Rome, yet the economic and political project has been steadily developing ever since. By the 1970s, the European Community stood as a major economic player, provoking an increased interest in the academic community as analysts tried to tackle the "superpower in the making" (Galtung, 1973) with the toolkit of IR.

In 1972 François Duchêne claimed that Europe at the age of twenty represented a civilian power "long on economic power and relatively short on armed forces", in an age where the decline of power politics cleared the way for a reinterpretation of international relations. This return to the idealism of the 1920s – what Hedley Bull (1982) called "neo-idealism" – argued that there was no longer a point in thinking in terms of a European superpower, as such a power would necessarily be a nuclear state with strong nationalist tendencies. Europe instead needs to wield power along different lines. The lack of an army would in fact be a benefit, as Europe could improve credibility in parts of the world where military power is shunned. Europe should stay true to its model, Duchêne demanded, and not succumb to power politics. Instead, it should become a cohesive international actor with a purpose: to act as a civilizer in international relations in line with its values, setting an example for other states in avoiding war, violence and intimidation. Europe should remain "civilian power Europe."

The key elements of civilian power are the centrality of non-military (most importantly economic) means[9] to achieve ends, the primacy of diplomatic cooperation and persuasion in solving international problems, a willingness to use legally binding supranational institutions to achieve international progress, and civilian control over foreign and security policy making. Therefore, CPE is not pri-

---

8   Kagan even goes a step further when arguing that if European states were still powerful, they would act *exactly* like the US does.

9   These non-military means correspond to Joseph Nye's (2004, 2008) "soft power".

marily described as an actor that does not have access to military means and consequently relies on civilian tools, it also entails a particular kind of approach to solving international problems: a civilian power uses carrots, rather than sticks. (Maull, 1990, 2005; Larsen, 2002) The combination of the power and the normative dimensions constitutes the core of the CPE concept. (Orbie, 2006, p. 125)

Duchêne's initial formulation of CPE was rather vague and unsystematic (Zielonka, 1998), but precisely its vagueness has allowed for different interpretations throughout the past four decades, explaining its sometimes "puzzling popularity" both in policy-making and academic circles.[10] (Orbie, 2006) These diverse interpretations reflect the discursive struggle about the desirability of the EU's growing military capabilities and related normative goals, while references to Duchêne's "pioneering article" lends a certain legitimacy to academic interpretations of the EU's international identity. Contemporary proponents of civilian power Europe argue that military power and civilian power are not mutually exclusive within a civilian power if, and only if, non-military instruments enjoy primacy. Following this reasoning, contemporary proponents of the concept like Knud Erik Jørgensen (2004) claim that if NATO continues to exist the EU could stay a civilian power.

The recurring tension between military and civilian power, along with Jørgensen's remark about the necessity of NATO for CPE to exist, echoes Hedley Bull's (1982) famous critique of Duchêne's argument. Bull completely dismissed the idea of civilian power and called it a "contradiction in terms". Disappointed by contemporary European politics and the wider Cold War, he urged Europe to become a military power in order to be able to cope with the dynamics of world politics. Bull stressed the conditionality of European prosperity on US presence in Europe. As we discussed in terms of the agency-structure debate in International Relations, the question about civilian power – and also about normative power – is whether it is a consciously designed role, or merely the result of adjustment to the international environment and/or the discursive rationalization of the lack of military might. Both Bull and Duchêne were bound by the historical context of the Cold War. While Duchêne's "neo-idealism" was influenced by the successes of European integration and the relative peacefulness of the postwar continent, Bull saw these successes through the bipolar conflict of the Cold War. He argued that civilian power was highly conditional: Europe merely reaped the peace dividend while posing as a civilian power – both its strength in economic terms and its ability to forsake the military instrument were conditional on US interests.

This position was absolutely unsustainable, Bull argued, especially due to the divergence between US and European interests, and the Soviet threat. European military weakness is, however, not inherent in the status of European states, but is "the consequence of [Europe's] own state of mind. (Bull, 1982, p. 156) He therefore urged that "Britain and her Western European partners (…) take steps towards making themselves more self-sufficient in defense and security." (Bull,

10 See e.g. Moravcsik 2009.

1982, p. 152) Europe's "ineffective" civilian power needs seven adjustments[11] – among them a nuclear capability – that would turn the EC into "military power Europe", the only kind of power that makes sense in Bull's Hobbesian world. Without a military capability, Bull famously argued, "Europe is not an actor in international affairs, and does not seem likely to become one."[12] (Bull, 1982, p. 151)

European integration has always been a dynamic process, requiring scholars to constantly revise the concepts they use to describe and analyze the EC/EU. The crucial developments of the late 1980s and early 1990s, most notably the Single European Act (1987) and the Treaty of the European Union (1993) launching the Common Foreign and Security Policy, were also coupled by a fundamental shift in the global balance of power: the end of the Cold War and the fall of the Soviet Union. These fundamental changes both within the EU and in its environment issued a new wave of theorizing in the 1990s. The establishment of the European Union and the creation of a common foreign policy – a crucial element of sovereignty – undoubtedly imbued the European project with actor qualities, shifting the focus of the scholarly debate from actorness versus presence towards the analysis of the specific characteristics of the EU as an international actor. While critics emphasized various shortcomings of the Union and predicted its eventual demise, supportive scholarship culminated in a new key concept that still enjoys popularity in the literature: normative power Europe (NPE).

Acting by Being – Europe as a Normative Power

IR scholarship relating to the post-Cold War era is truly vast and complex. With the fall of the Soviet Union, the United States stood as the world's only superpower, marking the beginning of the unipolar era. These changes in the power structure coincided with the process of globalization gaining momentum, producing shifts in the international environment favoring both the European Union and the growing scholarship discussing its international actorness. On the one hand, economic interdependence and global free trade that accompany globalization furthered Europe's importance as an economic power; while on the other hand, the growing importance of non-state actors in the globalized, "post-Westphalian" world drew attention to the EU as the successful example of the new kind of international actor.

---

11   These are: 1) nuclear forces (minimum deterrence); 2) increasing the size and improving the quality of conventional forces; 3) increasing the role of West Germany in defense; 4) securing the commitment and loyalty of France; 5) a pro-European shift in British politics; 6) defense worked out with careful attention to Soviet policies and 7) a defense that equally takes into account the United States' reactions. (Bull, 1982)

12   Bull's reasoning still haunts the literature: Allen and Smith, for example, argue that the still popular civilian power concept (see e.g. Moravcsik, 2009) should in fact also be a negative term, i.e. the rationalization of military impotence. (Quoted in Ginsberg, 1999, p. 445)

With the end of bipolar conflict, many envisioned what Francis Fukuyama (1992) called "the end of history" – a peaceful international system where liberal values like human rights would rule supreme, and military power would lose in importance. Under this new configuration of power in the 1990s and a relatively peaceful international environment, analysts again reconsidered the meaning and role of civilian and military power, as well as the normative role of the European Union in world politics. As one of the leading figures, Ian Manners argued that even though Hedley Bull may have been right about the conditionality of civilian power in the Cold War, his argument no longer holds in the post-Cold War environment where military power seems less effective, even undesirable. As he argued, both Duchêne and Bull were writing within a Cold War mindset, relying on a traditional understanding of power. This conception of power is outdated, Manners claimed, and its inadequacy is best epitomized by the end of the Cold War itself: communism fell because of norms, not because of material power. Norms, therefore, matter in terms of power and influence, and they do so especially in the case of Europe – the stabilization of Central and Eastern Europe after 1989, and the voluntary integration of these countries into European structures during the 1990s and 2000s signifies the power of European norms in particular.

Manners makes the argument that Europe's power lies precisely in the realm of norms. Normative power is not a new concept, he admits, as it was already discussed by Carr (1991, p. 108) who distinguished between economic power, military power and power over opinion. Duchêne (1973) wrote about Europe as an *"idée force"*, and Galtung (1973, p. 33) argued that "ideological power is the power of ideas." The problem with previous CPE and military power approaches was that they concentrated too much on the presence or lack of state-like qualities with the EU. While focusing on policies and institutions, they privileged "physical power in the form of actual empirical capabilities", mostly economic. (Manners, 2002, p. 238) Normative power, as developed by Manners, seeks to move away from this state-centrism and includes "cognitive processes, with both substantive and symbolic components" to understand the EU's international identity. (Manners & Whitman, 1998; Manners, 2000, 2002) It aims to extend the capabilities-based debate about civilian and military power with a focus on "normative power of an ideational nature characterized by common principles and a willingness to disregard Westphalian conventions." (Manners, 2002, p. 239) NPE states that in the post-Cold War era, the European Union can no longer gain legitimacy by presenting itself as an economic power: the EU now *is* and *acts as* an embodiment of norms, and as such it possesses a much larger influence in world politics than capabilities-based approaches would maintain. (c.f. Lucarelli, 2006)

The Normative Power Europe argument holds that certain characteristics of the EU's organization predispose it to act in a normative way. (Manners, 2002; Whitman, 1998; Manners & Whitman, 1998) Universal norms and principles are at the center of the EU's relations with member states and other actors in world politics. The Union's foreign relations are thus more informed by a "catalogue of norms" – manifested in the Universal Declaration on Human Rights and the European Convention on Human Rights and Fundamental Freedoms – than is the case with other actors. Establishing the EU's normative difference is essential for the NPE concept, since the United States and even the former Soviet Union can be framed as normative powers, promoting their own set of norms. (Sjursen, 2006, p. 240) US foreign policy especially has always had normative undertones and has often emphasized the importance of human rights, irrespective of the party in power. These similarities raise the question of just how exactly the EU differs from the US, since the former is often described as a normative power *in contrast with the latter*. The problem of difference also raises the question of hypocrisy, i.e. the rationalization of *Realpolitik* through the constant reference to norms – a point of criticism that has often been raised against US foreign policy ever since the Monroe doctrine. Given this presence of normative politics in the foreign policy of other actors, Sjursen (2006, p. 241) stresses that in order to salvage the NPE argument it is not enough simply to argue that the EU promotes not only strategic interests but also norms and values. We also need a conceptual apparatus that can help us decide what the legitimate pursuit of norms entails.

The literature on NPE only partially fulfils this requirement – similarly to those on the EU's international identity, works on NPE lack a common vocabulary and methodology. Manners relates the EU's normative difference from other powers promoting norms to three factors: 1) the historical context of the post-war creation of the European project, 2) the EU's hybrid polity and 3) its political-legal constitution. Due to these three factors, the EU "has a normatively *different* basis for its relations with the world." (Manners, 2002, p. 252, his emphasis) These relations are characterized by five "core norms": peace, liberty, democracy, the rule of law, human rights; plus four, more contested "minor norms": social solidarity, anti-discrimination, sustainable development and good governance. As was discussed previously, Manners also argues that these norms and principles are the basis of a distinct European identity.[13] However, it is one thing to claim that the EU is a normative power by virtue of its history, hybrid polity and constitution, and something completely different to say that it acts in a normative (good) way. Manners (2002) rejects the argument that Europe could not really exert normative influence on other parts of the world without the ability and the willingness to use force. (See, for example, Therborn, 1997, quoted in Manners, 2002, p. 241) He emphasizes that "the central component of normative power Europe is that it exists as being different to pre-existing political forms, and this particular difference pre-

---

13   The existence of a common European identity based on a common history and culture is constantly debated. Hill, for example, would disagree with Manners' argument by maintaining that "the EU rests on a relatively weak sense of shared history and identity because of the diverse historical experiences of its members, the EU's lack of influence over education, and its inability to create and manipulate stated goals which national governments themselves use to strengthen communal identities." (quoted in Ginsberg, 1999, p. 436) Nevertheless, even Hill acknowledges that the EU is increasingly associated with a distinct set of principles.

disposes it to act in a normative way." (Manners, 2002, p. 242) "It is built on the crucial and usually overlooked observation that the most important factor shaping the international role of the EU is *not what it does or what it says, but what it is.*" (Manners, 2002, p. 252, my emphasis) As such, the EU *acts by being*, and thus seeks to change the norms in the international system:

The creative efforts of the European integration process have changed what passes for 'normal' in world politics. Simply by existing as different in a world of states and the relations between them, the European Union changes the normality of 'international relations'. In this respect the EU is a normative power: it changes the norms, standards and prescriptions of world politics away from the bounded expectations of state-centricity. (Manners, 2008, p. 45)

For Manners the EU acts as a normative beacon, a prosperous paradise that compels other nations to assume European norms – norms through which the EU has redefined what counts as "normal" in world politics. Importantly, this power is only sustainable if it is felt legitimate by those who practice and experience it. (Manners, 2000, 2002, 2006, 2008) Normative action precedes the maximization of common European interests, Manners claims, which is attested by empirical examples where the EU found itself at odds with other developed countries in terms of norm promotion.[14] Due to this "role model" type of passive norms diffusion, Manners also tries to avoid the charge of cultural imperialism: other nations become like the EU because they want to, not because they are forced to. Through NPE, Manners refutes Bull's 1982 argument – in his 2002 article he concludes that "rather than being a contradiction in terms, the ability to define what passes for 'normal' in world politics is, ultimately, the greatest power of all." (Manners, 2002, p. 253)

Similarly to CPE, normative power Europe emphasizes the EU's reliance on civilian means in international affairs. Traditional (military) power has been losing in relevance since the end of the Cold War, while normative power is gaining in effectiveness in shaping world affairs. But, as noted previously, for Manners normative power is conditional on forsaking military power – the instrumental use of military force would decrease the EU's credibility as a peaceful force. Turning the lack of military force into strength again raises the question of whether being a normative power is a conscious choice or the result of the post-Cold War distribution of power. While US hegemony is no doubt favorable to a secure non-military EU, supporters of NPE like Thomas Risse (2002) would argue that the EU could in fact match the US in terms of military power – since it already matches it in economic power – but willingly chooses not to do so.

By building on the tenets of CPE, normative power Europe emphasizes such reliance on civilian means – e.g. multilateral diplomacy – but its power lies specifically in magnetism. Acting by being, however, is a static, passive approach. It does not have a true notion of power and agency, and therefore is highly apolitical. As such, some analysts (e.g. Romsics, 2011) reject NPE in favor of theories – most notably constructivism and post-modern approaches to EU for-

---

14   Manners (2002) uses the example of the abolition of the death penalty, distinguishing the EU from other civilian powers like Japan. (c.f. Maull, 1990)

eign policy (e.g. Merlingen, 2007) – that remedy these problems. The passivity of the NPE concept clearly became a hindrance in its application with the gradual development of the ESDP/CSDP and the accompanying political discourse that framed the EU as a "more active", "more capable" player with global responsibilities. However, the concept enjoys a huge popularity to this day both in academic and in policy circles, demonstrating the influence of constructivist theorizing on actual policies and political rhetoric.

Challenges to Normative Power Europe

Proponents of normative power Europe reframed the European Union's weakness in military terms and turned it into a source of strength – the lack of military power is often mentioned as a core feature of normative power. The initial slow pace of the CFSP/ESDP process – especially in the military domain – and the EU's failed stabilization attempts in the Balkans reinforced the conviction of many analysts that Europe's strength does and should lie in its civilian instruments and normative attainments. (Rosencrance, 1998, p. 22) However, developments in the 2000s embodied in the EU's 2003 Security Strategy, *A Secure Europe in a Better World*, mounted an increasing challenge against the basic tenets of NPE. With the military instrument improving, *A Secure Europe in a Better World* redefined the Union's role as a responsible global actor that actively relies on its military instrument – a new means to achieve its normative ends, for example the protection of human rights. For NPE scholars the question became whether the lack of military power is a prerequisite for normative power, or are the two in fact compatible?

A majority view within the CPE/NPE school maintains that military capabilities can to a certain extent be embedded within the civilian/normative power concept, transforming the EU from a civilian power "by default" (i.e. out of necessity) to a civilian power "by design". (Larsen, 2002, p. 292) Nonetheless, some scholars have argued against enhancing the EU's military capabilities since "it sends a signal that military force is still useful and necessary, and that it should be used to further the EU's interests. It would close off the path of fully embracing civilian power." (K. Smith, 2000, p. 28) Karen Smith even goes as far as to argue that the development of military capabilities would lead to a security dilemma with the EU's neighbors, effectively rendering the magnetism effect of NPE mute. Other analysts voiced a more modest warning by pressing for moderation in developing the ESDP. Andrew Moravcsik (2003), for example, pressed for a more "civilian" Europe, arguing that civilian power "could be a credible instrument of modern European statecraft", making a big European military force unnecessary.

The above challenge to the core tenets of CPE/NPE could not simply be dealt with through minor modifications. Ian Manners tried to salvage the concept in his 2006 article, "Normative Power Europe Reconsidered – Beyond the Crossroads", in which, though acknowledging the apparent trade-off between developing a military instrument and remaining a normative power, he argues that "the militarization of the EU need not necessarily lead to the diminution of the EU's normative power, if the process is characterized by *critical reflexion*, rather than the pursuit of 'great power'". (Manners, 2006, p. 182, my emphasis) Manners maintains that we can actually find examples of the EU's "normative" use of the military instrument through the concept of "sustainable peace", wherein the EU stresses the need to address the causes of conflict and violence, not just their symptoms. Preventing conflict thus becomes a priority of normative power, and how the EU did in terms of conflict prevention becomes the yardstick of normative power effectiveness. (Manners, 2006, p. 185)

However, "sustainable peace" is already stretching the boundaries of the NPE concept, and post-9/11 signs from Brussels, such as the wording and content of the EU's Security Strategy, indicate a weakening, or at least a fundamentally transformed normative power Europe.[15] *A Secure Europe in a Better World* acts as a "symbolic signpost" for Manners, as it reflects an institutional prioritization of military instruments, even though most of the ESDP missions are non-military. The rhetoric also took a turn: the document mentions "civilian aspects" of the ESDP, revealing a reversal in emphasis between civilian and military instruments. (Manners 2006, p. 189) If the ESDP/CSDP only favored civilian instruments when intervention is not possible or when new threats are encountered, Manners argues, it would subdue normative power. Conflict management at least partially through military means seems like a reasonable option, but would be detrimental to normative power in the original sense: the lack of military means supposedly increased the credibility of the EU. If the EU acquired a full-fledged military, it would look more like a state and consequently a traditional power, and the problem of double standards and normative imperialism would resurface with a vengeance (c.f. Manners, 2002), since civilian power is only a step away from the mission of "civilizing" world politics. Therefore, Manners (2006, p. 195) concludes, "the military tasks (…) should only be attempted under a UN mandate, in a critical reflexive context, on a clear, normative basis."

Ethical Power Europe

The gradual development European Security and Defense Policy led to a widening gap between political realities and the theories that tried to model them. With its new security strategy, the EU repositioned itself as a global, rather than a regional actor, with a range of military and civilian instruments. This new role is articulated in the discourse of universal ethics that defines the European Union as a "force of good" or "peace builder", thereby legitimizing the Union's role in global politics. (Aggestam, 2008) This self-perception is evident in *A Secure Eu-*

---

15   It could be argued that the very existence of such a document, comparable to the National Security Strategy of the US, is uncharacteristic of a normative power.

rope in a Better World that served to justify the EU's acquisition of military capabilities.[16] A contemporary branch of the literature calls this new role "ethical power Europe" (EPE), which also denotes the theoretical framework developed to address the changing international role of the EU. Ethical power Europe is a fundamental conceptual shift away from normative power Europe. It no longer envisions the European Union simply as representing a positive role model for other states, thereby defining what counts as normal, but rather as an actor actively shaping the world with a variety of instruments so that this "world" better serves the "global good" as defined by the European Union. (Aggestam, 2008) Hence the EU no longer acts by being: instead of discussing what the EU is, EPE looks at what the Union is actually doing as an international actor, i.e. how its actions relate to the norms and principles it embodies and seeks to promote, and how it deals with the ethical dilemmas that come with the inherent friction between interests, norms, means and ends.

This new, active role definition follows the previously discussed fundamental change in the strategic-political environment: the EU's acquisition of military capabilities. *A Secure Europe in a Better World* marks the beginning of this new period: the document explicitly aimed at making the EU more "active",[17] "capable" and "responsible", while envisioning a range of new, ambitious tasks in the field of crisis management, peacekeeping, state-building and failed state reconstruction. EPE is not so much a real theory of EU international identity, as a framework to assess these new developments critically: it asks whether we can analytically, descriptively and normatively conceive of the EU in the terms its official rhetoric outlines. Ethical power Europe is thus also a concept embedded in its historical context, but as such it by default represents a challenge to the applicability of concepts developed during markedly different time periods, notably those of CPE and NPE. Most importantly, and in contrast to both CPE and NPE, ethical power Europe encompasses both civilian and military power, while also shifting our attention to what the EU does in the field. For the sake of its assessment it is important to note that by acknowledging the normative turn in the EU's self-definition and thereby bringing ethics into the analysis, EPE is an inherently normative concept and its "ethical part" is continuously contested.

As previously discussed, CPE and NPE consistently framed the EU not as an actor that does not have access to military means, but one that consciously chooses to rely on civilian instruments (persuasion and positive incentives), rather than on coercion. This argument mirrors the dominant political discourse that constructs the Union as an international actor. On the one hand, the image implies that the status of civilian power is not something that is given and static: whether

---

16   Larsen (2002) also identifies a competing discourse on the EU acquiring military capabilities, according to which the move was a necessary tool for gaining international status and prestige.

17   Under the term "being active", the document openly endorses military intervention as a possible instrument for conflict prevention and resolution. (Solana, 2003, p. 11)

the EU remains a civilian power depends on how its power and identity are conceptualized in the dominant discourse. On the other hand, the CPE/NPE framework also means that the EU's access to particular means cannot simply turn it into a different kind of actor. This latter observation is increasingly important with respect to the EU's developing military capabilities. (Larsen, 2002)

In the contemporary dominant discourse, civilian means continue to be articulated together with military capabilities, which nevertheless are not given a pivotal role. The discourse presents these newly gained means as practical instruments that allow the EU to *assume responsibility*, rather than to further assert its identity as such.[18] (Larsen, 2002, p. 291) This process, which the official jargon calls "making the EU more capable", challenges existing theoretical conceptualizations of the Union's international identity that argue that its international identity as a civilian/normative power is conditional on it not using force as a foreign policy instrument. For these approaches, the current discourse as well as the underlying mixed power structure present an anomaly. Not only has the EU been developing military capabilities, these capabilities were integrated into an ongoing discursive reinterpretation of the EU's international identity that seeks to maintain the EU's image as a power led by normative considerations, a "force for good." Ethical power Europe seeks to remedy this new "capabilities-expectations gap" between academic concepts and political realities.

Lisbeth Aggestam, in her 2008 introduction to the special issue of *International Affairs* devoted to the new framework, claims that EPE is a more adequate concept to describe the EU as an international actor than its predecessors for five reasons. First, EPE seeks to move from structure towards agency, i.e. from the EU's institutional make-up to its behavior. Second, unlike CPE and NPE that emphasize the distinction between military and civilian power, EPE is capable of capturing both the ESDP/CSDP process and the changing role of military force in the post-Cold War world. However, whereas both previous concepts are based on the assumption that the utility of military power is decreasing in the world, ethical power Europe instead focuses on the actual ethical dilemma of choosing either military or civilian instruments in foreign policy, and the ways through which the use of power is justified. Third, EPE conceives of the European Union in a broader, international context, rather than simply focusing on its internal characteristics and assuming that they alone determine the EU's role in international politics. While CPE and NPE both claim that ethics are intrinsic to the EU's identity, EPE looks at how normative globalization enabled the EU to assume a more proactive role in global politics by partially drawing on an international ethics embodied in the UN (c.f. the responsibility to protect). Crucially, instead of arguing that global developments reflect the EU's power to shape what counts as normal in world affairs, EPE reverses the argument and instead suggests that these developments legitimized and enabled the EU to take a more assertive global role as a "self-proclaimed ethical power". (Hyde-Price, 2008, p. 29) It fol-

---

18 The emphasis was put on "effective crisis management capacity". (Larsen, 2002, p. 291)

lows from this latter point, Aggestam argues, that we must question the sui generis assumption made by proponents of both CPE and NPE, and ask whether its unique hybrid polity and its "normative difference" (Manners & Whitman, 2003) also make the EU *act* in a unique way, different from any other foreign policy actors (c.f. realist critiques). Finally, EPE not only brings back the "international" but also the "national" into the analysis by looking into the "black boxes" of the member states, left behind by previous approaches. Most crucially, it brings back (state) interests into the dynamics of European foreign policy, and acknowledges that the EU will always have "mixed motivation" – both material and ethical. (c.f. Youngs, 2004) Not only do mixed motivations present a more refined, more operationalizable approach to European politics, they also seek to bridge the gap between normative and rational-material approaches to European foreign policy.

Needless to say, the concept of ethical power Europe was not received positively by the entire academic community. In his contribution to the debate in *International Affairs*, Ian Manners rejected the argument and maintained that NPE is still the best model to describe the EU's impact in world politics, and we should not conflate it with the notion of an ethical foreign policy. However, he goes on to list three ways in which the EU as a normative power can promote its substantive normative principles:[19] 1) living by example, 2) being reasonable, and 3) doing least harm. These three "procedural normative ethics", according to Manners, help us to make sense of how the EU exercises its normative power. (Manners, 2008, p. 46) For the NPE concept the ethics of normative power is therefore located "in the ability to normalize a more just, cosmopolitan world." (Manners, 2008, p. 47)

Throughout his article Manners relies on official EU rhetoric as proof for a working normative power. As was discussed in the introduction, conflating rhetoric with models of foreign policy is a reoccurring problem of the literature and questions the empirical relevance of the said concept – it could just as well be that normative power Europe became popular with decision-makers in Brussels and reality imitated science, so-to-speak. Ethical power Europe has mounted the so far most coherent internal critique of the popular NPE concept by asking how the EU behaves normatively and how it deals with the ethical questions that the use of military force necessarily raises. Looking at Manners' writing, the response to this kind of criticism is rather vague and cannot fully resolve the contradiction between the integration of the military instrument and its use for normative goals on the one hand, and the non-military fundaments of NPE on the other. Not only is the passive acting-by-being concept sterile and apolitical (c.f. Romsics, 2011), it also renders the theorizing of a globally "active and capable" Union problematic. Curiously, Manners himself admits the shortcoming of his theory – albeit only implicitly – by arguing that "it may be simply too early even to con-

---

19   In this particular iteration these core norms are: sustainable peace, freedom, democracy, human rights, rule of law, equality, social solidarity, sustainable development and good governance.

template the extremely long-term vision of an EU that is a normative power: system change from Westphalian self-regarding to post-Westphalian other-regarding is slow and needs partners. In this respect the long-term diffusion of ideas in a normatively sustainable way works like water on stone, not like napalm in the morning." (Manners, 2008, p. 60)

Ethical power Europe is not a monolithic research project – its critical framework hosts a range of diverse approaches from Tim Dunne's (2008) historical analysis to Adrian Hyde-Price's refined neo-realist critique. What these approaches have in common is their shifting focus towards what the EU is doing as a foreign policy actor. In the following I will demonstrate how, despite their ontological and epistemological differences, ethical power Europe shares some of its tenets with contemporary realist critiques of European foreign policy studies, and how realist ideas can contribute to a more empirical analysis of European foreign policy in a changing global environment.

Realism and Contemporary European Foreign Policy

Realist critiques of both the European Union as a political entity and the scholarship that analyzes it date back to the 1970s. Building on the classic framework put forth by Kenneth Waltz's 1979 *Theory of International Politics*, neo-realist analysts have time and again emphasized the anarchic and self-help nature of the international system – a world where cooperation is rare and only temporary. In such an environment, a non-state entity like the EU that is the epitome of interstate cooperation, does not focus on hard power, and is preoccupied with low politics is at first sight an anomaly, presenting a "hard case" for testing realist models. However, most realist scholars have either neglected the EU as an object of analysis, or predicted its imminent failure by focusing exclusively on its weaknesses. Those who dealt with the EU in more detail have argued that it is not a fundamentally new entity, but rather resembles traditional alliances "whose primary purpose is to strengthen the position of individual states in an interdependent and highly competitive global economy" (Gilpin, 1996, p. 19). Consequently, they argue, the EU's approach to world politics cannot be new, irrespective of the rhetoric that frames and justifies it. Yet realist scholars have been consistently proven wrong about the decline of European cooperation (Mearsheimer, 1990), and the "approaching" rift between the US and the EU (Walt, 1998), leading to a relative marginalization of realism within European studies by the late 1990s.[20]

In the 2000s realism returned with a new, refined intergovernmentalist critique of "liberal idealist" concepts of civilian and normative power, epitomized by the scholarship of Adrian Hyde-Price (2006, 2008). While it does not aim to ex-

---

20   Two core elements of Waltzian neo-realism, state-centrism (i.e. states-as-unitary-actors) and anarchy, are compatible with the study of European integration for liberal intergovernmentalism (see Moravcsik, 1993, 2002, 2003, 2009)

plain the black box of policy making, i.e. the fine aspects of European foreign and security cooperation, realism claims to be able to describe the EU as an international actor and the underlying dynamic of the CFSP/CSDP. Though naturally still state-centric, the critique claims to be able to account for both the emergence and development of the EU's foreign policy. The argument is similar to that of earlier realists: the EU is not a unique actor, but a foreign policy tool used by states that conform to neo-realist assumptions – it is not a harbinger of a Kantian international system, but a "collective instrument for shaping [the EU's] external milieu by a combination of hard and soft power". (Hyde-Price, 2006, p. 217). The normative goals NPE claims define the international identity of the EU are only furthered when first order goals – most importantly national security – are secured. (c.f. Waltz, 1979)

Adrian Hyde-Price argues that liberal-idealist approaches have a number of shortcomings that question their applicability: 1) they are reductionist in the Waltzian sense – i.e. they underscore the importance of structural forces; 2) they almost totally neglect power in its more traditional sense (c.f. Romsics, 2011), and do not acknowledge civilian power's conditionality on US power (c.f. Bull, 1982); and 3) they seem to be explicitly normative in that they regard the European Union as a force for good. Additionally, analysts sympathetic to the European project often use neo-realism as a straw man,[21] while being hostile to criticism that questions the above normative beliefs. These arguments in their core can easily be traced back to neo-realism. According to Waltz, in an anarchic international system, security (survival) is the primary concern of states: "when power maximization strategies are counterproductive, states will focus on security maximization until more favorable opportunities present themselves." States focus on relative gains which in turn limits cooperation; while "absolute gains become more important as competition lessens." (Waltz, 1979, p. 195) Since states are preoccupied with security and power maximization concerns, all other concerns are

---

that invokes the EU as a perfect example of cooperation under anarchy. Liberals claim that states themselves are the source of European integration, where each state looks at the EU through the lens of its own preferences. Their conceptual toolkit includes cooperation, mutual gains, and positive sum games. Similarly to realists, liberals claim that when the EU does something, it acts because it is in the interest of its member states. The very same critical points that are stressed in IR theory with regard to rationalist approaches are stressed by scholars of European foreign policy (e.g. Ginsberg, 1989), namely those that overestimate the role of states as unitary actors, while underestimating the role of national leaders sharing a common history, domestic politics and/or external stimuli. But whereas realism became mostly marginalized within European studies, liberal intergovernmentalism has been enjoying unbroken popularity – albeit less so in foreign policy studies – as the "scientific" approach to European politics. (See Moravcsik & Checkel, 2001)

21   For a critique of the misrepresentation of rational-materialist theories see Moravcsik in Moravcsik and Checkel, 2001.

"second order concerns". As mentioned, Hyde-Price sees the EU as the "institutional repository for the 'second-order' concerns of its member states." (Hyde-Price, 2006, p. 223) Consequently, member states only allow the EU to follow an "ethical foreign policy" when it does not conflict with their national interest.[22] Moreover, powerful European states often engage in traditional concert diplomacy to circumvent the CFSP, as is visible in the case of Iran or Libya. While the normative rhetoric is often there,[23] and the EU may also be present as a separate entity, such cases show the limits of a common European foreign policy, which in turn limits the actorness of the European Union.

Based on these basic tenets of neo-realism, the EU's actions should always be analyzed in terms of its member states – especially the more powerful ones – and their interests. The EU for Hyde-Price is not a sovereign actor – only the member states are – but rather an "intervening variable". According to traditional neo-realist theory, great states can choose among three strategies to deal with structural pressures: balancing, buck-passing and bandwagoning; while small states also have the option to "hide" or "transcend" the international system. (Hyde-Price, 2006, p. 224) EU member states are not different: they can use the EU to balance against other powers, they can pass the buck to the US in the Middle East while the Europeans focus on trade and economic issues, or they can align themselves with the strongest state in the system. Also, collective policy has a certain "politics of scale" by promising larger gains than unilateral state action would. (Ginsberg, 1989) The politics of scale is especially crucial for small member states as it enables member states to have a proportionally larger say in international affairs than their power would in itself suggest.[24]

The new distribution of power in the international system after the end of the Cold War created "a unipolar world, and a multipolar Europe" (Hyde-Price, 2006, p. 217), with new systemic pressures. The new role of "regional stabilizer" the EU could fulfill in this altered configuration of power was again conditional on the integration of a unified Germany, and security guarantees provided by the US and NATO. As such, the EU could create the CSFP, focus on developing limited and specialized military capabilities, and continue its economic project. Powerful member states use the EU "as an instrument for collectively exercising hegemonic power, shaping its 'near abroad' in ways amenable to the long-term strategic and economic interests of its member states," (K. Smith, 2003), as a tool for furthering collective economic interests in the global economy, and as an institutional repository for second order concerns. (Hyde-Price, 2006, 2008) The in-

---

22 Prominent examples of the resulting double standards include contentious relations with communist China or the protectionism of the Common Agricultural Policy (CAP).

23 As a fundamentally behavioralist theory, neo-realism disregards state rhetoric and focuses exclusively on state action that in turn can be explained by structural factors, such as anarchy and the current distribution of power.

24 Ginsberg's argument, of course, mirrors the neo-liberal/liberal intergovernmentalist argument for mutual gains and solving collective action problems.

struments applied are based on both "soft" (persuasion, negotiation and compromise) and "hard" power (coercion through conditionality). This shows that the EU is, in fact, not a normative power, but an instrument of collective hegemony that relies on many forms of power, while the failure in the Balkans shows the limits of soft power, as well as the adverse effects of US buck-passing. The EU is not an ethical power either, since the ESDP/CSDP is not a real "European army", but an instrument for coalitional coercive diplomacy. (Hyde-Price, 2006, p. 230)

Realists like Hyde-Price naturally acknowledge that the EU acts normatively, but warn us about the inherent second order nature of normative considerations, as well as about the fundamental contradiction within the EU's role and identity as an international actor. On the one hand, it is a tool for furthering common or shared interests,[25] while on the other hand it tries to be a "force for good", but only if it accepts a problematic cosmopolitan ethics as the basis of its foreign policy action. Yet the tension between traditional and "post-modern" international roles is already evident in the core legal principles the EU seeks to promote: multilateralism (sovereignty) clashes with cosmopolitanism (human rights). (Sjursen, 2006, p. 249) Trying to be both a vehicle for shared interest promotion and a champion of universal norms, the EU seems either cynical or naïve.[26] (Hyde-Price, 2008, p. 33) A controversial ethical foreign policy, as outlined in the notion of EPE, carries some risks in this regard: 1) the EU could be charged with hypocrisy when referring to universal norms, yet clearly following members' self-interests; 2) by relying too much on non-military means it could become weak and ineffective; and 3) it could get bogged down in moral crusading. Through an ethical foreign policy, the European Union runs the risk of becoming a "tragic actor", either by becoming weak and therefore unable to further shared member state interests (tragic in the neo-realist sense), or it could indulge in moral crusading, weakening the credibility and effectiveness of its normative/civilian power.[27] (Hyde-Price, 2008) To avoid tragedy, the EU needs to balance interests with normative goals – it has to become a "calculator", not a "crusader". It should be guided by a "realist ethics" based on a "morality of individuality" and characterized by prudence, skepticism and reciprocity. (Hyde-Price, 2008, p. 40)

This criticism moves away from a critique of the EU as a normative project and offers a powerful explanation for its foreign policy and its international pseudo-actorness. It does not deny that the EU acts in a normative way, as NPE would

---

25 These include the territorial integrity, the prosperity and economic well-being, as well as the political and strategic stability of its member states.

26 Realists often lean towards the first possibility – for example, the EU only acts as a "civilizing power" in the sense that it was used by its most powerful member states to impose "Western" values on post-communist Central and Eastern Europe.

27 The "force for good" rhetoric has an additional problem: it raises expectations about activism, thereby renewing the "capabilities-expectations gap". (Hill, 1993; Aggestam, 2008)

maintain, but emphasizes the contextuality and conditionality of such action, as well as the inherent cheap talk/double standards problem. Some of the points Hyde-Price raises are, in fact, shared by a number of well-known figures in the literature. For example, Hill et al. (1996) acknowledge that member states use the CFSP to further their own national interests, while Zielonka (2006) claims that the CFSP is more like a platform for debate and compromise, than a real policy.

Another brand of realism, neo-classical realism, has also mounted criticism against popular normative concepts of the EU's international identity. Even though it is not a structural theory like neo-realism, at first sight the European Union also seems to be a blind spot for neo-classical realism, since it is not a proper state. To be able to integrate it into their theoretical framework, neo-classical realists – like their structural realist counterparts – have had to show that even though the EU is a non-state entity with unique sovereignty, it nevertheless acts *as if* it were a state. As indicated previously, for Hyde-Price the EU is merely an intervening variable, a tool to promote collective interests – tracing its actions back to its member states, he showed that the Union is not an independent actor, but is like traditional alliances. For some neo-classical realists, however, the EU can be analyzed as a single actor that acts similarly to other "great powers". This conceptualization, though it bears obvious similarities to great- and super-power arguments raised by students of the European Union, is explicitly non-normative.

The most apparent similarity between traditional great powers (i.e. nation states and empires) and the EU, neo-classicals such as Pascal Venesson claim, is that they can have a "grand strategy",[28] which in the EU's case is outlined in its 2003 Security Strategy. Grand strategy "defines, in broad terms, priorities and criteria for policy choices regarding security so that ends and means can be balanced." (Venesson, 2007, p. 14) It clarifies international problems and possible solutions, defines rules of conduct for decision-makers, includes a justification for the polity's conduct of international affairs, establishes priorities and identifies threats. These grand strategies are important because they are an exercise in preference formation.

As *A Secure Europe in a Better World* demonstrates, the European Union builds on its comparative advantage in certain aspects of power to enhance its status and identity internationally. Interestingly, the document combines a set of constructivist and liberal intergovernmentalist assumptions about international relations (e.g. security communities and democratic peace). This view, Venesson argues, comes from practice and is clearly seen as coherent. Thus, practitioners do not see ontological differences as irreconcilable – practice is detached from academic debate. For some, this observation sounds banal, but it once again draws attention to the dangers of conflating official political rhetoric with actual foreign policy.

Contemporary realism guides our attention to questions neglected by normative theories, partly due to their bias. It emphasizes the structural constraints

---

28   On great powers and grand strategy see Kennedy, 1989.

that shape the EU's actorness and highlights the prevailing importance of the concert diplomacy of member states while imbuing the EU with a power concept – albeit a very traditional one – that facilitates the analysis. These critiques are no longer detached from the explicitly normatively stated foreign policy practices of the European Union; thus they narrow the gap between theory and political realities.[29]

Closing the Gap – Future Challenges for Theory

The European Union has expanded its influence greatly in the past twenty years, turning from a regional into a global actor. Using a set of tools ranging from the promise of accession to economic sticks and carrots, it became the primary stabilizer in its neighborhood. With 27 member states, the EU is the world's greatest economic player that simultaneously acts as a trade partner and also as a normative anchor for its Eastern partners. Cooperation with the Union or even eventual membership has become a desired goal for countries from Ukraine to Turkey. Developing its own military instrument, the EU has become a serious partner of the US through NATO, actively upholding Pax Americana and taking up global responsibilities in the protection of human rights. The European Union of the mid-2000s represented a powerful international actor that relies on a mixture of hard and soft power, while maintaining a distinctly normative orientation in its foreign policies.

However, during the past few years the deterioration of Europe's economic power (both in absolute and negative terms), intra-EU friction, and a changing international environment began to challenge the Union's ability to actively mold global affairs, or even its close neighborhood. Analysts point to the possibility that the EU's growing power might have been grossly overestimated and highly contextual: its environment-shaping policy only seems effective when its power is overwhelming and its norms are shared, as was the case in Central and Eastern Europe. (Zielonka, 2008) The CEE states were consciously striving to become members of the European Union and therefore uncompromisingly submitted themselves to the long and difficult accession process. With Croatia's imminent accession, the EU will have reached its limits within this "narrow Europe", a region where the Union's normative-economic magnetism could be the strongest, where the promise of membership was the most valued commodity a state could have. Within the "wider Europe", the EU's new neighborhood is more conflict-ridden (e.g. Caucasus, North Africa) and the new neighbors will probably be less eager to internalize norms than were Central and East European states.

---

29   What is especially important in Venesson's argument, for example, is that he consciously downplays the importance of military power with regards to the EU. He argues that the EU as a "post-modern polity" invented its own "post-modern realism" to be able to cope with an anarchical world.

The EU's role expectations as an international actor are not only shaped by its constituency and other major powers, but also by its neighbors. Shifting borders mean shifting expectations, and since the new neighbors seem less committed to the Union's transformative project, the EU will have to change its means if it wants to hang on to its past ends. These new pressures for a transformed foreign policy approach are coupled with a growing enlargement fatigue within the EU public. As a result, enlargement, the EU's so far most effective foreign policy tool, is a contentious issue for many national governments. These two factors seem to be pushing the EU towards a more symbolic, highly functional and success-dependent interaction with its wider neighborhood, weakening its image as a normative power. The European Union and its member states will have to deal with this changing situation in order to preserve the EU's importance in the wider European region, and they will have to do so under largely unfavorable global political and economic pressures.

The European Union is in the process of taking and preserving an ever growing role in the world. How the EU uses the means at its disposal will have far reaching effects. With such changing circumstances, theorizing about the European Union as an international actor has to follow suit – a growing gap between theory and reality is untenable. There are still many unanswered questions, some raised by reality, some by the theories we rely on to explain and understand it. As Zielonka (2008) aptly notes, we simply do not know what kind of combination of norms and power – i.e. hard and soft power – best serves the EU's interests. This study has aimed to present the wide array of theoretical concepts currently used to assess the EU as an international actor. The discussed concepts have time and again proven to be highly conceptual as they follow the evolving international identity of the European Union. Current trends require yet another leap in theorizing – an analytical tool that is able to assess and explain current and future EU policies on the one hand, and is also able to guide policymaking proper on the other. After all, one should not forsake the belief that a better understanding of political realities can lead to better policies in the long run.

Some current trends in the literature are already encouraging. Contemporary theories like ethical power Europe and its neo-realist challengers seek to abandon abstract theorizing in favor of a closer scrutiny of actual policy. While EPE draws attention to the inherent ethical dilemmas of following common European interests and promoting universal norms with both civilian and military tools, neo-realism emphasizes the importance of the interests of the EU's most powerful states. The frameworks are thus available, and can readily be applied to empirics. The essays in this volume aim to contribute to this empirical, yet theory-guided assessment of a changing Union in a new, wider Europe.

Bibliography

Aggestam, L. (2006). Role theory and European foreign policy: A framework for analysis. In O. Elgström & M. Smith, *The European Union's roles in international politics: Concepts and analysis (pp. 11-30).* New York: Routledge.

Aggestam, L. (2008). Introduction: ethical power Europe? *International Affairs, 84(1),* 1-10.

Allen, D., & Smith, M. (1990). Western Europe's presence in the contemporary international arena. Review of International Studies, *16(1),* 19-37.

Buchan, D. (1993). *Europe : The strange superpower.* Aldershot, Hants, England: Dartmouth.

Bull, Hedley (1982). Civilian power Europe: A contradiction in terms? *Journal of Common Market Studies, 21(1/2),* 149.

Buzan, B., & Little, R. (2000). *International systems in world history: Remaking the study of international relations.* Oxford: Oxford University Press.

Carlsnaes, W. (1992). The agency-structure problem in foreign policy analysis, *ISQ 36(3),* 245-270.

Carr, E. H. (1991) *The twenty years' crisis, 1919-1939: An introduction to the study of international relations.* London: Macmillan.

Cerutti, F., & Rudolph, E. (Eds.) (2001). *A soul for Europe: On the political and cultural identity of the Europeans.* Leuven: Peeters.

Checkel, J. T., & Moravcsik, A. (2001). A constructivist research program in EU studies? *European Union Politics, 2,* 219-249.

Checkel, J. T., (2005). International institutions and socialization in Europe: Introduction and framework. *International Organization, 59(4),* 801-826.

Checkel, J. T. (2006). Constructivist approaches to the European Union" *ARENA.* Working Paper Series: 06/2006.

Duchêne, F. (1972). Europe's role in world peace. In R. Mayne (Ed.), *Europe Tomorrow: Sixteen Europeans Look Ahead.* London: Fontana.

Duchêne, F. (1973). The European community and the uncertainties of interdependence. In M. Kohnstamm & W. Hager (Eds.), *A Nation Writ Large? Foreign-Policy Problems before the European Community.* London: Macmillan.

Dunne, T. (2008). Good citizen Europe. *International Affairs 84(1),* 13–28.

Elgström, O., & Smith, M. (2006). *The European Union's roles in international politics: Concepts and analysis.* New York: Routledge.

Fukuyama, F. (1992). *The end of history and the last man.* New York: Free Press.

Galtung, J. (1973). *The European Community: A superpower in the making.* London: George Allen & Unwin.

Gilpin, R. (1996). No-one loves a political realist. *Security Studies, 5(3).*

Ginsberg, R. H. (1989). *Foreign policy actions of the European Community: The politics of scale.* Boulder: Lynne Rienner.

Ginsberg, R. H. (1999). Conceptualizing the European Union as an international actor: Narrowing the theoretical capability-expectations gap. Pittsburgh, PA: UNSPECIFIED (Unpublished).

Hill, C. (1990). European foreign policy: Power bloc, civilian model or flop? In R. Rummel (Ed.), *The evolution of an international actor: Western Europe's new assertiveness.* Boulder: Westview Press.

Hill, C. (1993). The capability-expectations gap, or conceptualizing Europe's international role. *Journal of Common Market Studies, 31(3),* 305-328.

Hill, C. (1997). Closing the capability-expectations gap? In Seattle, WA: UNSPECIFIED, (Unpublished).

Hill, C., & Smith, M. (2005). *International relations and the European Union.* Oxford: Oxford University Press.

Hollis, M. and Smith S. (1991). *Explaining and understanding international relations.* Oxford: Clarendon Press.

Hyde-Price, A. (2006). Normative power Europe: a realist critique. *Journal of European Public Policy, 13(2),* 217-234.

Hyde-Price, A. (2008). A 'tragic actor'? A realist perspective on 'ethical power Europe'. *International Affairs, 84(1),* 29–44.

Jørgensen, K. (2004). European foreign policy: conceptualising the domain. In W. Carlsnaes, H. Sjursen & B. White (Eds.), *Contemporary European foreign policy.* London: Sage.

Jupille, J., & Caporaso, J. A. (1998). States, agency, and rules: The European Union in global environmental politics. In C. Rhodes (Ed.), *The European Union in the world community.* Boulder: Lynne Rienner.

Kagan, R. (2003). *Paradise and power, America and Europe in the new world order.* London: Atlantic Books.

Kagan, R. (2008). *The return of history and the end of dreams.* London: Atlantic Books.

Khanna, P. (2004). The metrosexual superpower. *Foreign Policy, July 1, 2004,* 66-68.

Kennedy, P. M. (1989). *The rise and fall of the great powers: Economic change and military conflict from 1500 to 2000.* London : Fontana.

Keukeleire, S. (2003). The European Union as a diplomatic actor: Internal, traditional, and structural diplomacy. *Diplomacy & Statecraft, 14(3),* 31-56.

Keukeleire, S., & MacNaughtan, J. (2008). *The foreign policy of the European Union.* Basingstoke: Palgrave Macmillan.

Larsen, H. (2002). The EU: A global military actor? *Cooperation and conflict, 37(3),* 283-30.

Lucarelli, S. (2006). Interpreted values: A normative reading of EU role conceptions and performance. In O. Elgström & M. Smith, *The Eu-*

ropean Union's roles in international politics: Concepts and analysis (pp. 47-66). New York: Routledge.

Lucarelli, S., & Manners, I. (Eds.) (2006). Values and principles in European Union foreign policy. New York: Routledge.

Manners, I. (2000). The foreign policies of European Union member states. In I. Manners & R. G. Whitman (Eds.), Substance and symbolism: An anatomy of cooperation in the New Europe. Manchester: Manchester University Press.

Manners, I. (2002). Normative power Europe: A contradiction in Terms? Journal of Common Market Studies, 40(2), 235.

Manners, I. (2006a). The constitutive nature of values, images and principles in the European Union. In S. Lucarelli & I. Manners (Eds.), Values and principles in European Union foreign policy. London: Routledge.

Manners, I. (2006b). The European Union as a normative power: a response to Thomas Diez. Millennium, 35(1), 167–80.

Manners, I. (2006c). The symbolic manifestation of the European Union's normative role in world politics. In O. Elgström & M. Smith (Eds.), New Roles for the European Union in International Politics. London: Routledge.

Manners, I. (2006d). European Union 'normative power' and the security challenge, European Security, 15(4,: 405–21.

Manners, I. (2006e). The symbolic manifestations of the EU's normative power in world politics. In O. Elgström & M. Smith (Eds.), The European Union's roles in international politics: Concepts and analysis (pp. 66-85). New York: Routledge.

Manners, Ian (2008). Normative power Europe: A transdisciplinary approach to European studies. In C. Rumford (Ed.), Handbook of European studies. London: Sage.

Manners, I., & Whitman, R. (2003). The 'difference engine': Constructing and representing the international identity of the European Union. Journal of European Public Policy, 10(3), 380.

Maull, H. (1990). Germany and Japan: The new civilian powers. Foreign Affairs. 69(5), 1–106.

Maull, H. (2005). Europe and the new balance of global power. International Affairs, 81(4), 775–799.

McCormick, J. (2006). The European superpower. New York: Palgrave Macmillan.

Mearsheimer, J. (1990). Back to the future: Instability in Europe after the Cold War. International Security, 15(1), 5–56.

Merlingen, M. (2007). Everything is dangerous: A critique of 'normative power Europe'. Security Dialogue, 38(4), 435-453.

Moravcsik, A. (1993). Preferences and power in the European Community: A liberal intergovernmentalist approach. Journal of Common Market Studies, 31(4), 473-524.

Moravcsik, A. (1998). *The choice for Europe : Social purpose and state power from Messina to Maastricht*. Ithaca, Cornell University Press.

Moravcsik, A. (1997). Taking preferences seriously: A liberal theory of international politics. *International Organization, 51(4)*, 513–553.

Moravcsik, A. (2002). The Quiet Superpower. *Newsweek, 17 June 2002.*

Moravcsik, A. (2003). How Europe can win without an Army. *Financial Times, 3 April 2003.*

Moravcsik, A. (2009). Europe defies the skeptics: How crisis will make the EU stronger. *Newsweek, 1 August 2009.*

Nye, J. S. (2004). *Soft power: The means to success in world politics*. New York: Public Affairs.

Nye, J. S. (2008). Public diplomacy and soft power. *The Annals of the American Academy of Political and Social Science, 616(1)*, 94–109.

Orbie, J. (ed.) (2008). *Europe's global role: External policies of the European Union*. Aldershot: Ashgate.

Orbie, J. (2006). Civilian power Europe: Review of the original and current debates on cooperation and conflict. *Journal of the Nordic International Studies Association, 41(1)*, 123–128.

Ravenhill, J. (1985). *Collective clientelism: The Lomé Conventions and North-South relations*. New York: Columbia University Press.

Risse, T. (2002). US power in a liberal security community. In G. J. Ikenberry (Ed.), *America unrivaled: The future of the balance of power*. Ithaca: Cornell University Press.

Romsics G. (2011). The 'actorness debate' revisited: What kind of actor? (The EU as a single foreign policy actor). Paper presented at 'Structures and Futures of Europe', 17th Annual Conference of the Hungarian Political Science Association, Central European University, 20-21 May 2011.

Sjursen, H. (2006). Values or rights? Alternative conceptions of the EU's normative role. In O. Elgström & M. Smith (Eds.), *The European Union's roles in international politics: Concepts and analysis, (pp. 85-101)*. New York: Routledge.

Sjursen, H. (Ed.) (2006). What kind of power? European foreign policy in perspective. *Journal of European Public Policy, 13* (special issue).

Smith, K. E. (2000). The end of civilian power EU: A welcome demise or cause for concern? *The International Spectator, 35*, 11–28.

Smith, K. E. (2003). *European Union foreign policy in a changing world*. Cambridge: Polity Press, 2003.

Smith, K. E. (2004). Still "Civilian power EU"? Retrieved from http://www.arena.uio.no/cidel/WorkshopOsloSecurity/Smith.pdf.

Smith, M. (2003). The framing of European foreign and security policy: Towards a post-modern policy framework? *Journal of European Public Policy, 10(4)*, 556.

Telò, M. (ed.) (2001). *European Union and new regionalism*. Aldershot: Ashgate.

Toje, A. (2005). The 2003 European Union security strategy: A critical appraisal. *European Foreign Affairs Review, 10*, 117–33.

Toje, A. (2007). *America, the EU and strategic culture: Renegotiating the transatlantic bargain.* New York: Amsterdam University Press.

Toje, A. (2010). *The European Union as a small power: After the post-Cold War.* New York: Palgrave Macmillan.

Venesson, P. (2007). Europe's grand strategy: The search for a post-modern realism. In N. Casarini & C. Musu (Eds.), *European foreign policy in an evolving international system: The road towards convergence.* Basingstoke: Palgrave Macmillan.

Walt, S. M. (1998). The ties that fray: Why Europe and America are drifting apart. *The National Interest, 54*, 3–11.

Waltz, K. (1979). *Theory of international politics.* New York: McGraw-Hill.

Waltz, K. (2000). Structural realism after the Cold War. *International Security, 25(1)*, 5–41.

Wendt, A. (1987). The agent-structure problem in international relations theory. *International Organization, 41(3)*, 335-370.

Whitman, R. (1998). *From civilian power to superpower? The international identity of the European Union.* Hampshire: Macmillan Press.

Youngs, R. (2004). Normative dynamics and Strategic Interests in the EU's External Identity. *Journal of Common Market Studies* 42(2): 415–435.

Zielonka, J. (1998). *Explaining euro-paralysis: Why Europe is unable to act in international politics.* New York: St. Martin's Press.

Zielonka, J. (2006). *Europe as empire: The nature of the enlarged European Union.* New York: Palgrave Macmillan.

Zielonka, J. (2008). Europe as a global actor: Empire by example? *International Affairs, 84(3)*, 471-84.

The Weakening Magnet?
Economic Prospects of the EU and their Effects on the Neighborhood

Dániel Bagaméri

This chapter analyzes the economic position of the European Union (EU) in its neighborhood. The role of the EU is often described as a magnet which is capable of attracting the countries in its vicinity. The chapter investigates the legitimacy of this pulling power in light of an important overlapping of two crucial challenges that the EU has been facing: its own decreasing competitiveness and the future of the diverse territory in its neighborhood. The intersection of the two raises issues which are at the center of this chapter. Can the neighborhood policy of an EU with decreasing economic competitiveness be successful? How does the European economic situation affect the prospects of further enlargement? What can Brussels offer to the neighborhood in terms of economics? And, after all, does the EU still have magnetic pull vis-à-vis its neighboring countries? If it does, what mechanisms sustain the magnetic force?

This chapter offers answers to these inquiries in five sections. The first one describes the challenges of decreasing EU competitiveness and its effects vis-à-vis the neighborhood policy. The second part deals with the nature and mechanism of EU magnetic power. Thirdly, enlargement policy is analyzed from the point of view of economics. The fourth section is dedicated to the investigation of the economic content of the European Neighborhood Policy. Finally, those trends are discussed which are frequently mentioned to describe the EU's magnetic power as declining.

Decreasing competitiveness and the neighborhood as challenges

The starting point of this analysis is a series of signs that show decreasing trends in the competitiveness of the EU. Competitiveness can be understood as the ability and performance of an economic entity to sell goods and services in international markets. Therefore, it is an important determinant of prosperity. Competitiveness is based on the productivity with which goods and services are produced, which is a reflection of the capacity of an economy to innovate and upgrade. (Porter, 2008) In other words, a more competitive economy is one that is likely to grow faster over time. Although performance can be measured in diverse ways, this chapter outlines the weaknesses of the EU only through three dimensions: GDP, productivity, and human capital.[1] They are certainly not independent from each other.

GDP figures are significant for the purposes of this study as they are widely used to measure living standards.[2] In terms of GDP growth, the recent performance of the EU[3] has been lagging behind both its own past performance and the main reference economies (*Figure 1*). In the EU there has been a gradual lowering of growth rates decade after decade, falling from an average 3% (during the period 1971-1980) to 1.3% (2001-2010). This trend also means that the gap between the EU and its rivals has been on the rise. Furthermore, it has been underperforming in relation to its own expectations. This is most apparently illustrated by the revised and eventually failed Lisbon Strategy which set the ambitious, though unrealistic, goal of the EU becoming the most dynamic and competitive economic area in the world. The future of the European economy does not seem to be any brighter, as stagnation is likely to be the long-running trend: projections for potential economic growth in the EU show an increase of around 1% per annum from 2020 onwards. (European Commission, 2009a)

Figure 1: GDP growth (%)[4]

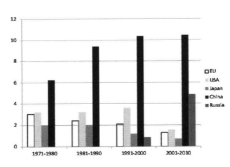

Source: *EUROSTAT, OECD*

---

1   For example, The Global Competitiveness Report 2011-2012 of the World Economic Forum (2011) identifies 12 pillars of competitiveness: institutions, infrastructure, macroeconomic environment, health and primary education, higher education and training, goods market efficiency, labor market efficiency, financial market development, technological readiness, market size, business sophistication, and innovation.

2   Of course, such a measure fails to capture some important qualitative aspects, such as the purity of the environment, the security of employment, and the quality of life.

3   For the sake of simplicity I only use the term EU throughout this chapter, but I always mean the then actual formation and number of Member States of the European integration.

4   Data for Russia are available from 1996 only.

In recent years several studies have shown that one of the principal reasons explaining the slow GDP growth is the insufficient productivity level of the EU. Thus the empirical evidence available (Blanchard, 2004; European Central Bank, 2004; European Commission, 2004a; 2004b; Gordon, 2004; OECD, 2003, 2004; O'Mahony & van Ark, 2003; Prescott, 2004; van Ark, O'Mahony & Ypma, 2007) shows that the EU-15's process of convergence to the higher levels of labor productivity of the US economy stopped in the mid-1990s, producing stagnation in the second half of the decade, and a recession in recent years (*Figure 2*).[5] On the other hand, the United States has experienced accelerating productivity growth since the mid-1990s, which appears to have been a combination of high levels of investment in rapidly progressing information and communications technology (ICT) in the second half of the 1990s, followed by rapid productivity growth in the market services sector of the economy in the first half of the 2000s. (van Ark, O'Mahony & Timmer, 2008) Therefore, as argued later as well, the faster growth of US productivity since the mid-1990s is of a structural and not primarily cyclical nature. (O'Mahony & van Ark, 2003) For Europe to prosper in the future, especially in the face of its rapidly aging population, raising productivity growth rates to or above pre-1994 levels will be crucial.

Figure 2: European Productivity compared to that of the United States (%)

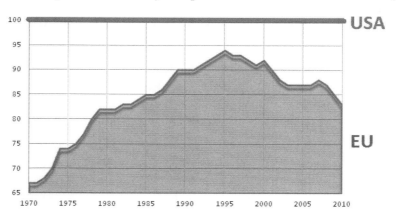

Source: *European Commission, 2002.*

---

5   There is a wide variation across the European Union in productivity performance, both in terms of growth rates as well as levels. A limited number of countries show productivity levels near to that of the US (Germany, Netherlands) or even above it (Belgium, France), whereas others are substantially behind. However, nearly all countries show a recent erosion of their average productivity levels relative to the US. (O'Mahony and van Ark, 2003, p. 7)

Furthermore, in today's modern economies increasing productivity growth greatly depends on the ability to create and absorb knowledge. (Cowan, David & Foray, 2000) A well-trained labor force is the key to productivity. Therefore, Europe needs more highly skilled workers, more investment in research and development, and innovation-friendly market conditions. A network of coherent policies covering improvements in education, science, training, and mobility will therefore be crucial in ensuring that the emerging demand for skills is met on a sustainable basis. (European Commission, 2002) The time when Europe competed mostly with countries that offered low-skilled work at low wages is long gone. Today countries like China and India are starting to deliver high skills at low costs – and at an ever increasing pace. (Schleicher, 2006) This is profoundly changing the rules of the game. It is therefore widely discussed (e.g. van Ark, O'Mahony & Timmer, 2008) that the European productivity slowdown is attributable to the slower emergence of the knowledge economy in Europe.

It should be mentioned that Europe's future human capital standing is also strongly influenced by a number of demographic trends. First, in most countries birth rates are far below replacement levels, resulting in shrinking native populations. Second, political and social barriers in most countries have made managed immigration at levels high enough to close the native demography gap very difficult. Finally, the brain drain, the migration of highly qualified people from Europe, causes losses in productivity and the financial resources of the educational system. It subsequently has a negative impact on the innovative and economic potential. All these unfavorable demographic trends point towards a deteriorating European human capital.

These decreasing tendencies of the EU economy can be attributed to several interconnected factors that are all, in essence, related to its failure to adapt to a rapidly changing environment. The first cause to be noted is the low contribution of employment to growth, which can be explained by the rigidity of the European labor market. (Altomonte & Nava, 2005, p. 165) Second, the EU economy is characterized by an outdated and inflexible industrial structure resulting from a combination of factors: the excessive importance of low and medium-technology industries; the relatively small size of the EU's ICT production sector; and the low rate of diffusion of ICT to other industries in the EU. (Denis et al., 2005) The Sapir Report concludes that the EU economic system is built around the assimilation of existing technologies, mass production generating economies of scale, and an industrial structure dominated by large firms with stable markets and long-term employment patterns. (Sapir, 2007, p. 405) All these have culminated in alarming productivity problems in the EU since this economic establishment no longer delivers in the world of today, characterized by economic globalization and strong external competition. Third, the Single Market Program (SMP) failed to deliver higher growth due to two main reasons: (1) the SMP was never fully implemented since service markets remain highly fragmented, and (2) the SMP excluded the liberalization of labor markets, which largely remains the prerogative of Member States. (Sapir, 2007, p. 406) The fourth set of causes is related to governance problems that render fast and efficient reactions difficult: some of the

EU's methods are obsolete and the system as a whole has become too complex and fragmented. (Sapir, et al. 2003) The fifth factor emphasizes the negative side of enlargements as it is a big challenge to integrate successfully a large number of much poorer countries with weak administrative and regulatory structures, not to mention a relatively short experience of markets and democracy. Sixth, a popular explanation claims that the decreasing pace of economic growth is the outcome of a conscious choice made by Europeans: a preference for leisure over material production. (Sapir et al., 2003, pp. 22-23) All things considered, the underperformance of the EU economy is basically related to insufficient European labor productivity, working hours, and employment rates.

The other challenge of the EU analyzed in this contribution is represented by the relationship with the neighborhood. This is a very diverse territory divided by Brussels into two distinct dimensions. The enlargement segment, on the one hand, comprises the seven countries in the Western Balkans, Turkey, and Iceland, which have been offered the perspective of membership in the EU. The European Neighborhood Policy (ENP), on the other hand, frames the relationship with sixteen of the EU's closest neighbors. The ENP is further categorized as Eastern Partnership (six countries) and Euro-Mediterranean Partnership (ten states). The challenge ahead for the EU is twofold. On the one hand, Brussels needs to give a clear definition in terms of the final objectives of its policies towards the neighborhood. There are political, historical, geographical, and economic interests at stake which make finding the common denominator of the Member States rather difficult. On the other hand, the neighborhood as a whole is characterized by relatively low living standards, security risks, and oppressive political regimes, while Brussels' promise is about stability, prosperity, and, for some countries, membership. Policies towards the region, therefore, entail significant resources on the side of the EU, which poses further questions in light of the aforementioned macroeconomic trends.

The European Union as a magnet: The neighborhood's attraction to the EU

Only a complexity of several factors is able to explain the existence and nature of the magnetic power of the EU vis-à-vis its neighborhood. This section identifies the most significant dimensions of EU magnetism. Although the pulling effect has both ideational and material elements, the analysis rather puts emphasis on the latter as it is more concerned with economics. How does the economic influence of the EU work? What are its peculiarities? The following paragraphs offer an explanation.

The EU has become the most economically attractive region in global politics. The mere facts that the EU is a world leader in terms of volume of GDP, trade, foreign direct investment, and aid indicate that the Union has a great potential to express economic influence in its environment. (Leonard, 2005, p. 5) Furthermore, strong economic ties are also predicted by the gravity model of trade theory, which explains the different intensities of trade integration as an outcome of the size of GDP and geographical proximity of the partners.[6] From this it follows that the Union is the single entity that possesses the largest share in the trade flows of all its neighbors (*Figure 3*). This is indeed true as empirical data reveals, with the exceptions of Belarus and Ukraine (first trading partner being Russia) and Jordan (Saudi Arabia in first position). (European Commission, 2011a)

Figure 3: Share of the EU in the Trade Volume of Neighbors, 2010 (%)

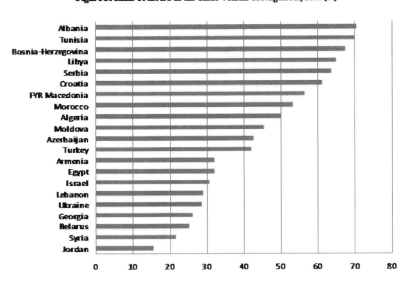

Source: *European Commission 2012.*

The fact that the Single Market is the largest economic area in the world is an essential element of EU power. Such an enormous market with 500 million consumers, EUR 24,400 GDP per capita (Eurostat, 2011a), and a 20% share of world trade (Eurostat, 2011b) attracts non-member countries both for the possibilities it offers and due to the fear of being excluded. The sheer size of its market, therefore, provides the EU with magnetic power. Economic players aim to cultivate good relations with their EU counterparts and to appear with their products in the Single Market as much as possible. This is particularly true of the close neighborhood whose relatively small economies prevent their companies from taking advantage of economies of scale in the domestic field. Expanding to the vast mar-

---

6   The basic theoretical model for trade between two countries (i and j) takes the form of: $F_{ij} = G \ \dfrac{M_i M_j}{D_{ij}}$

Where F is the trade flow, M is the economic mass of each country, D is the distance and G is a constant.

ket of the EU is, therefore, crucial for them, which also contributes to the magnetic pull of the Union.

Furthermore, in trade matters the EU is influential not only because of its aggregated size, but also because it has a unique common policy that operates along federal principles – unlike in other areas. (Tsoukalis, 2005, p. 236) Trade policy is an exclusive power of the EU: only the Union, and not individual Member States, can legislate on commercial matters and conclude international trade agreements. The European Commission acts as the leading voice and has the authority to negotiate with countries outside the bloc on behalf of the Member States. Both in the World Trade Organization and in relations with individual trading partners, EU Member States speak and negotiate collectively and are represented by the European Trade Commissioner. (European Commission, 2012a) This truly common policy of the EU in trade matters makes the appearance of the Union in its external relations as powerful as its economic size suggests. Thus the existence of a single voice and the absence of confusing messages towards its trading partners is also an essential element of EU magnetic attraction.

The living standards and social model EU citizens can enjoy are also among the factors that pull non-member states. The difference between the living conditions of the EU and those of the neighboring countries is all too apparent. In terms of gross domestic product based on purchasing-power-parity per capita the figures of *Table 1* tellingly demonstrate the contrasts.

Table 1: GDP (PPP) per capita in 2011

EU	31,548 USD
Balkan countries + Turkey	11,595 USD
ENP states	9,320 USD

Source: *IMF 2011.*

Furthermore, the Human Development Index, a complex measure of life expectancy, literacy, education, and standards of living, also illustrates why neighboring countries regard the EU as exemplary (*Table 2*). All in all, the EU represents economic prosperity in the surrounding regions.[7]

Table 2: Human Development Index in 2011

EU	0.855
Balkan countries + Turkey	0.747
ENP states	0.768

Source: *UNDP 2011.*

---

7 The public survey carried out by the Opinion Polling and Research project (2011) reveals that the great majority of the population in the neighborhood identifies economic prosperity as the most representative characteristic of the EU.

The fact that the invention of the EU, the euro, has been a success also contributes to magnetism. The euro was established as an accounting currency in 1999 and since then it has been gaining an increasing worldwide role. Today the euro is the second largest reserve currency (Aristovnik & Čeč, 2009) as well as the second most traded currency in the world after the United States dollar. (BIS, 2010) Additionally, the euro has the highest combined value of banknotes and coins in circulation in the world, amounting to nearly EUR 890 billion. The growing importance of the euro is particularly true of the Balkans where an increasing number of countries use the euro as an anchor for their exchange rate policies or as a parallel currency alongside their domestic one,[8] which creates additional links between the neighborhood and the EU.

The ultimate incentive and the final act of pulling neighboring countries towards, and eventually inside, the EU is the possibility of joining the Union. Enlargement has been a win-win situation for both new and old Member States, and the EU as a whole. The most important economic advantages EU accession can offer to non-members are threefold: (1) the inflow of structural funds which might contribute to yearly growth by roughly 1.8 percent (Directorate General for Economic and Financial Affairs, 2001, p. 39); (2) the increased flow of transnational capital into the region;[9] and (3) the various advantages provided by unrestricted access to the single European market. (Mourik, 1997; Robinson, 1963) Positive effects are also present on the side of old members, as several predictions and the experience of the last round of enlargement indicate. (Boeri et al., 2002) However, the advantages are less significant: a 0.7% GDP increase on a cumulative basis in the 2000-2009 decade (Directorate General for Economic and Financial Affairs, 2001, p. 39), due to the relatively smaller size of the economies of acceding countries, whereas costs are even more constrained. The financial contribution by old Member States related to enlargement represents only 0.1% of their GDP. (Bureau of European Policy Advisers and the Directorate-General for Economic and Financial Affairs, 2006, p. 31) Additionally, raising the number of Member States makes the Single Market stronger simply by increasing its size.

One peculiarity of EU magnetic power, which again enhances its effectiveness, is that it can express influence in the political sphere with economic means. It has been noted by several scholars that the EU's most powerful instruments of pressure are in the field of economics. (For instance, Zielonka, 2008, p. 477) The economic capability of the EU involves both 'carrots' and 'sticks', or positive and negative policy tools. The first and perhaps most prominent economic carrot for foreign policy involves the EU's devotion to development aid, particularly among former colonies of EU Member States. The EU also manages to incorporate free trade pacts into many of its most important external relationships. Trade agreements often form the centerpiece of these dialogues, and this incentive encourages non-EU states to accept other political goals important for Europe, par-

---

8   What is more, the euro is the sole currency of Montenegro and Kosovo, and the currency of Bosnia and Herzegovina is directly pegged to the euro.

9   As was demonstrated in the case of Eastern enlargement: .

ticularly democracy, respect for the rule of law, and human rights. In addition, each of these positive measures (financial aid or favorable trade agreements) also involves a negative component: the EU's ability to stop aid or suspend trade negotiations (at a minimum), or impose diplomatic or economic sanctions, including weapons embargoes, on third parties (at a maximum). (Smith, 2005, pp. 165, 168) Consequently, and most importantly in the relations with the neighborhood, through governance by conditionality the EU can achieve political goals by offering gradual market access to its partners.

In view of this, the normative power Europe thesis is often challenged by giving primacy to economic considerations.[10] Proponents of this view argue that the EU's magnet role is conditional upon the material incentives the EU provides, and therefore ideational transfer occurs only because the material opportunity structure of partner states dictates it. (Hyde-Price, 2006) This, in turn, also means that if a strong European economy is not present, the field of maneuvering for EU foreign policy gets constrained. Furthermore, it is crucial to note that economic power has a subtle attribute compared to political one. Economic might draws people in, as argued by some, while political power creates hostility. (Leonard, 2005, p. 28; Rosecrance, 1998) The former encourages other actors to maintain good relations and cooperate with the center, while the latter motivates less influential individual players to form an alliance against it. Therefore, as Rifkin (2004) argues, 'soft power' is able to win greater influence in the long term at considerably less expense.

Magnetic power and enlargement policy

This section investigates how the EU's magnetic power functions by and through enlargement policy. The ultimate rationale of enlargement for the EU can be basically described with four words: peace, democracy, stability, prosperity. The analytical focus of this research is on the economic aspects of enlargement only. To this end conclusions are mainly drawn from the experience of the 2004-2007 accessions, but the recent form of enlargement policy towards the Western Balkans is also considered. Is EU accession beneficial from an economic point of view? How are the economic dimensions of enlargement evaluated?

Enlargement is a very good deal for both the EU incumbents and the new members. A European Commission (2009b) review, five years after the fifth enlargement of the EU in 2004, concluded that: the latest enlargements had brought greater prosperity for all EU citizens and made Europe a stronger player in the world economy; the institutional and legal frameworks and the common policies of the EU played a vital role in ensuring success; entrepreneurs and citizens experienced clear benefits; and the enlarged EU was better prepared to address current and future challenges. Furthermore, public opinion also reflects a positive

---

10 See Andras Szalai's analysis in this volume for an introduction to the normative power Europe literature.

judgment of the latest enlargements. Seventy-six percent of the EU-27 population supports the view that the integration of Central and Eastern Europe (CEE) into the EU has led to growth and modernization in the economies of CEE countries, and 62% agrees with the statement that enlargement has increased prosperity and economic competitiveness for Europe as a whole. (Views on European Union Enlargement, 2009)

Enlargement, in line with the ex-ante estimates (most importantly Baldwin, Francois, & Portes, 1997), has led to increased living standards in the new Member States, while creating export and investment opportunities for the old ones. Income per capita in new Member States rose from 40% of the old Member States' average in 1999 to 52% in 2008, while economic growth averaged 5.5% per year in 2004-2008 compared to 3.5% in 1999-2003. Such progress did not come at the expense of the old countries, which averaged growth of around 2.2% annually in 2004-2008, with a similar figure for 1999-2003. It should be noted, however, that average figures hide significant differences between EU-15 countries because the ones with higher growth rates in their FDI and trade activity with the new Member States have also enjoyed larger increases in their real per capita GDP growth rates. (European Commission, 2009b, p. 18) Enlargement also increased trade opportunities. In 2007, almost 80% of exports from the new Member States went to the rest of the EU. Old Member States also saw their sales to the new members increase to around 7.5% of their total exports in 2007, from 4.75% a decade earlier. All in all, from a macroeconomic point of view enlargement is without doubt a worthwhile investment. On the whole, enlargement is of far greater benefit to the acceding states than to the existing EU Member States.

The positive aggregated outcome of enlargement is manifested through several economic mechanisms. First, one of the crucial requirements of accession is the adoption of all existing legal regulations, the *acquis communautaire*. This is a time-consuming and expensive process for each candidate but it is fostered with EU support, such as the pre-accession instruments.[11] Importantly, the implementation of this secure legal framework attracts investments from old Member States, which have been a key driver of economic transformation in the new ones through boosting growth and employment. (European Commission, 2009b, p. 4) Second, closer commercial ties, and eventually trade integration, foster a more efficient division of labor and strengthen competitiveness in the EU. Third, workers in the new Member States have profited from improved employment opportunities at home and abroad, although labor migration created economic and social problems in some of the new Member States. However, in old Member States concerns raised about massive labor migration prior to enlargement have not materialized. All in all, enlargement means modernization for new members while it provides old ones with market and investment opportunities.

---

11 For example, the Commission expected before the Eastern enlargement that the adoption of the environmental legislation alone would cost between 2 and 3 percent of the annual GDP of acceding states during the transition period of five to seven years. (EUobserver, 2003)

It has also strengthened the economy of the Union as a whole through the advantages of integration in a larger internal market.

Currently the EU is dealing with six candidate countries[12] and three potential candidates.[13] Since 2007 candidate countries and potential candidates have received focused EU funding and support through a single channel – the Instrument for Pre-Accession Assistance (IPA). The total funding for the period 2007-2013 is EUR 11.5 billion. (European Commission, 2012b) For the period 2014-2020 an amount of EUR 14.1 billion is proposed to be allocated "to support candidate countries and potential candidates in their preparations for EU membership and the progressive alignment of their institutions and economies with the standards and policies of the European Union". (European Commission, 2011b, p. 9) Socio-economic indicators show that, with the exception of Iceland, enlargement countries are still well below the EU average and even below the level of the weakest Member States. This relative underdevelopment entails a strong magnetic power on the part of the EU from the perspective of these countries. In addition, the countries in the Western Balkans are still relatively young states formed after the disintegration of the former Yugoslavia. Therefore, in the policy towards the region not only economic considerations should prevail, but political stability, the full establishment of the principles of democracy, and respect for human rights and good governance – all fundamental values of the EU – still need to be strengthened. (European Commission, 2011b, p. 3)

The EU accession process lost momentum before and during the recent economic crisis, and the EU does not seem to be the engine for growth and reforms in the region. The lack of a substantive and comprehensive EU enlargement strategy makes the EU a less appealing actor than its potential would suggest. The ultimate goal of enlargement policy is to fully incorporate its partners into the EU as Member States. The road to achieve this aim, however, seems less well-defined for countries in the Western Balkans. The fact that since Thessaloniki (2003) there has been no new summit indicates the lack of political will in the EU for substantial commitments towards the region. (Miscevic, 2009, p. 22) The EU today faces multiple problems and is troubled with its own difficulties, which makes it noticeable that the EU displays an increasing tendency to neglect the Western Balkan countries. Furthermore, more strictly observing conditions than in previous enlargements gives an impression of double standards for the Western Balkans. There are now signs in public opinion that enlargement fatigue in the EU results in reform fatigue in candidate and potential candidate countries. (Miscevic, 2009, p. 21) Brussels is still lacking a resolution to the dilemma of how to deal with the countries in the Western Balkans and how to keep them inside its sphere of influence without speeding up the accession process to a politically unacceptable level.

12　Croatia, the former Yugoslav Republic of Macedonia, Iceland, Montenegro, Serbia, and Turkey.

13　Albania, Bosnia and Herzegovina, as well as Kosovo under UNSCR 1244/99.

Magnetic power and European Neighborhood Policy

The framework of the EU's magnetic power towards its neighborhood with no enlargement prospects is the European Neighborhood Policy. The purpose of this section is to analyze the content of the ENP from an economic point of view. What is the economic offer of the ENP? How does the magnetic power of the EU appear in and through the ENP?

The ENP strategy is vague and incoherent concerning its *finalité economique*. When it comes to economics the EU offers, in a 2003 Communication, "the progressive participation in a number of EU policies and programs", "increased financial and technical assistance", and "the prospect of a stake in the EU's Internal Market and further integration and liberalization to promote the free movement of persons, goods, services and capital (four freedoms)". (European Commission, 2003, p. 10) The most significant is definitely "the prospect of a stake in the EU's Internal Market", which could lead to a structure similar to that of the European Economic Area (EEA). (European Commission, 2003, p. 15) However, after three years reference to the four freedoms and the EEA disappeared and, instead, the idea of the Neighborhood Economic Community (NEC) was introduced in December 2006. (Gstöhl, 2008) This was conceived as the network of "deep and comprehensive free trade agreements" and legal approximation in related fields (e.g. sanitary and phytosanitary rules, animal welfare, customs and border procedures, competition and public procurement). (European Commission, 2006, p. 4) The European Union, however, still lacks clarity with regard to the substantive and institutional features of an NEC. (Gstöhl, 2008, p. 6) The NEC is, therefore, a less ambitious proposal than the original offer of EEA-like cooperation. This raises several questions about its attractiveness and credibility in non-member states. It is doubtful whether the prospect of the Neighborhood Economic Community is an incentive powerful enough to encourage neighboring countries to carry out significant structural transformation.

It appears clear that incentives are the ENP's weak point. (Milcher & Slay, 2005, p. 4) The Communication of December 2006 on "Strengthening the European Neighborhood Policy" recognized that the policy should "provide more incentives" and that the main problem of the policy is that: "An important part of the incentives of the ENP – for instance in terms of market access and integration and other economic benefits – will only bear fruit later. This creates a real difficulty for partner countries in building the necessary domestic support for reform." (European Commission, 2006, p. 3) The economic benefits of the ENP are, however, potentially considerable. Greater legislative and regulatory convergence with the EU, particularly in those areas important for improved market access, should lead to higher investment and growth, especially if accompanied by greater liberalization of trade in services and agricultural products. (European Commission, 2012c) Furthermore, it is crucial to note that the EU has excluded the mega-incentive of accession as a Member State, and this has decreased the possibilities for exerting stronger leverage over the ENP partners. (Tsoukalis, 2005, p. 240) Considering these points, it seems evident that the EU has yet to find an adequately efficient substitute for enlargement conditionality as a tool for stabilizing its neighborhood.

Not only is the ultimate goal of the ENP obscure, but its public perception in the EU is ambivalent as well. While 61% of the EU population agree that the ENP provides mutual economic benefits, 81% believe it is a great financial burden on the EU. (European Commission, 2006b, p. 48) Furthermore, on the one hand, 75% perceive ENP cooperation an opportunity to enter new markets, while on the other hand, only 65% favor a simultaneous opening of the EU market. (European Commission, 2006b, p. 52) Such dissonant voices also contribute to the limitations of the great potential that the EU economy holds.

The limited efficacy of the ENP can also be explained by the existence of two distinct segments within the same policy. In addition to the common characteristic of strong economic ties with the EU, the ENP comprises very diverse countries. To the East European neighbors, the appeal of the EU's norms of democracy and human rights is especially vivid. (Opinion Polling and Research Project, 2011) However, in the Southern neighborhood the EU is confronted with a drastically different institutional and cultural setting. The Arab states' resistance to EU-promoted ideas and governance methods seem to be greater than for the European neighbors. Consequently, for the Arab Mediterranean neighborhood the economic benefits of regulatory convergence with the EU have to be the prime factor in persuading ruling elites to anchor their economic policies to the EU framework. (Noutcheva & Emerson, 2005, pp. 19-20)

It also renders the working of the magnetic power difficult that neighborhood policy within the EU is subject to a conflict of interests between the Member States. This is further complicated by the fact that the internal conflict has, in fact, two dimensions: one geographic and one political. On the geographic level, the Eastern neighborhood competes with the Mediterranean states for EU funding, with the latter being supported in general by France and Southern EU members. But while there is a clear alliance for a stronger EU focus on Eastern policy, its drivers, notably Germany and the CEE countries, disagree on its political direction, in particular whether membership offers should play a role and to what degree Russia needs to be contained or engaged. (Grotzky, 2008, pp. 9-10)

Weakening magnetic power

The EU has been quite comfortable in the belief that it appears large in relation to neighboring countries because of its sheer economic and political weight. As a result, the EU has been depicted as a pole of 'magnetic attraction' for non-member countries due to its perceived successful politico-economic model. (Rosecrance, 1998; Dannreuther, 2006; Grabbe, 2003) This view seemed to be confirmed both by the Velvet Revolutions of 1989-1991 and the Color Revolutions in Eastern Europe over a decade later. (Rifkin, 2004; Leonard, 2005) There are some indications, however, that the assumptions about the EU's magnetic power need revising. An increasing number of signs suggest that, compared to a decade ago, the EU's attraction is currently in stagnation or decline among the neighboring countries. (Johansson-Nogués, 2011) This section deals with the factors that are often highlighted to support arguments about the weakening magnetic power of the EU. These factors are related to problems of enlargement policy, neighborhood policy, and the internal difficulties of the EU.

First, the lack of visible convergence among the Member States may reduce the expectations of neighboring countries for a fast catching-up process with West European living standards. Neither theory nor the experience of earlier enlargements convincingly supports a hypothesis of automatic convergence. Convergence occurs only in the presence of certain key growth factors and supporting policies. (Sapir et al., 2003, p. 3; Boeri et al., 2002; Baldwin, Francois, & Portes, 1997; Breuss, 2001) Among these the most important ones are the following: (1) market functioning (incentives and competition) and openness; (2) initial income gap; (3) macroeconomic stability and predictability; (4) solid basic policies (e.g. education) and reliable economic institutions; and (5) no 'policy reversals'. (Pelkmans & Casey, 2004, p. 14) Enjoying Western living standards is the prime motive for joining the Union and the lack of closing the gap, therefore, reduces the desirability of accession and the adoption of accompanying measures of reform among non-members.

Second, and in close relation with the previous paragraph, the lack of resources for additional cohesion funds in the case of further enlargement reduces the material benefits of EU membership. This can be explained by the reluctance of most Member States to increase the budget and that of current cohesion territories to give up their massive cash inflows. The perceived outcome for neighboring countries is more constrained financial support to facilitate their convergence with EU standards and, in particular, living conditions.

Third, joining the EU will no longer provide countries with an economic boost of Irish proportions. The reason is simple: unlike Ireland, Spain, and Portugal, the recent applicant countries are given access to EU markets before they formally join the Union; therefore, they can enjoy most of the economic benefits of membership without being a Member State. (Anon, 2001) Thus in the case of Eastern enlargement the process of economic integration with the EU was virtually complete prior to the date of accession. (Bureau of European Policy Advisers and the Directorate-General for Economic and Financial Affairs, 2006, p. 14) Since the benefits of close cooperation with the EU occur during a longer timespan, they are less salient and attached to the EU in the eyes of the wider public. This again can cause frustration with the perceived strength of the EU.

The fourth factor relates to the confused and contradictory messages that are frequently sent by EU actors to the neighborhood. The root cause of this is often the internal contradictions of the EU, which makes it a divided partner when it comes to dialogue. For this very same reason, an unclear strategic vision concerning the enlargement process has had a strong negative impact on the attractiveness of the EU. 'Enlargement fatigue' together with 'enlargement disappointment', notably after the accession of Bulgaria and Romania, is salient both inside and outside the Union. The outcome for the Western Balkans is a long and drawn out accession process where it is difficult to see results. Similarly, the already mentioned confusion around the ultimate goal of the ENP and its weak incentives may decrease the strength of magnetic power in Wider Europe as well.

Fifth, due to the current financial and economic crisis, it started to be questioned even more loudly whether European integration is a success story at all and, therefore, whether it has appeal in the long run. Others disagree and argue that the recent turmoil is not likely to have any direct effect on the overall attractiveness of the EU for neighboring countries. (Batos, 2010, p. 2) However, it is an undeniable fact that the ongoing recession has caused the sharpest contraction in the history of the European Union (European Commission, 2009c, p. 1), and signs relating to the instability of euro economies challenge the so-far increasing trust in the European common currency as well. What was unthinkable for mainstream economists and politicians some years ago is now openly discussed: the possibility of a breakdown of the Eurozone and disarticulation of the EU. As a result, the euro's increase in the share of the worldwide currency reserve basket has slowed considerably since the beginning of the worldwide credit crunch related recession and sovereign debt crisis. (IMF, 2012) The recent depression of EU economies not only made future growth prospects more modest, thereby letting the rivals catch up even faster, but also rendered some internal weaknesses of the integration more visible. The crisis highlighted again the economic interdependence of the EU, while also underscoring the lack of political integration needed to provide a coordinated and effective fiscal and monetary response. In the wake of the global financial crisis and the subsequent debt crisis, the EU has begun to adopt measures for centralizing governance mechanisms and coordinating fiscal and economic policy. If the EU is able to weather the debt crisis, it may very well be able to take the next steps toward becoming a more integrated bloc of nation-states – both politically and economically. If it fails to do so or remains in the recent uncertain condition, this is definitely going to have a negative impact on the attractiveness of the EU and alter some of the patterns and trends which are traditionally attached to the EU economy.

A further major factor that harms the reputation of the EU in the neighborhood is the lack of and/or biased-for-domestic-purposes information about the EU's activity. As was shown in the case of Arab Mediterranean countries, national governments have done little to inform their citizens about the essence of EU policies. (Johansson-Nogués, 2011, p. 12) The true nature of relations between the EU and the state in question is therefore rarely known to the general public in the Arab Mediterranean countries. The wider populace is thus unaware of the extent and/or effects – whether positive or negative – of EU trade and assistance. To make matters worse for the EU, it has often become a scapegoat for local discontent. (Johansson-Nogués, 2011, p. 20) Consequently, in order to secure a stronger influence, the EU could, in particular, find it useful to target the information deficit/slant about itself, its values and its policies which exist in relation to neighboring countries. Therefore, one of the major challenges and opportunities facing the European Union is learning how to portray itself properly to foreign audiences (and to its own citizens as well). (Johansson-Nogués, 2011, p. 23)

As a result of the previously mentioned factors, some signs of decreasing EU magnetic power are very salient. A crucial one is the inconclusive state of the reform processes in many neighboring countries. Indeed, Börzel in her comprehensive survey of the ENP finds more evidence for a *status quo ante* than actual positive reform developments since the 2004 launch of the policy. (Börzel, 2010) What is more, if earlier democratic revolutions in the EU vicinity demanded the Union be the anchor of their political transition processes, such calls were absent in the popular protests sweeping across several Mediterranean countries in early 2011, or in the reform processes beginning in Tunisia and Egypt. (Johansson-Nogués, 2011, p. 2) Thus the EU does not currently appear to be the positive and central referent for determined neighboring countries as is habitually claimed in Brussels circles.[14]

The changes in the public perception of neighboring countries towards the EU also reveal a somewhat alarming trend. In absolute terms both candidate and ENP countries show majority support towards the EU. However, the level of positive attitude is decreasing year by year. (Opinion Polling and Research project, 2011)[15] It is noteworthy that in public opinion the main reasons for the attraction to Brussels are related to trade and economics.[16] What is more, besides the already mentioned ambiguity of EU public opinion towards the ENP cooperation, there is a significant and growing proportion of anti-enlargement sentiment. Only a minority of respondents are in favor of the accession of Ukraine (37%), Montenegro (36%), the former Yugoslav Republic of Macedonia (35%), Bosnia-Herzegovina (35%) and Serbia (34%). Respondents are less enthusiastic about Turkey (30%), Albania (29%) and Kosovo (29%). (European Commission, 2010a, p. 62)

Furthermore, the fact that the EU population also shows declining support for their own country's membership and a deteriorating evaluation of its perceived benefits is also a sign of decreasing magnetic strength and a major challenge for EU legitimacy. The latest Eurobarometer results show that support for EU membership has fallen to 49% (down four points since autumn 2009), which is close to the lowest levels recorded in the last decade. (European Commission, 2010b, p. 11) Additionally, the proportion of respondents who consider that their country has benefited from European membership has fallen by 7 points since the autumn 2009 survey. (European Commission, 2010a, p. 36) The number of re-

---

14   The explanation also lies, in part, in the changing domestic contexts of neighboring partner countries. A close examination of, for instance, Arab Mediterranean countries reveals a series of subtle changes in their domestic political scene in recent years which have come to impinge on elite and popular perception of the Union and have eroded the EU's ability to exert sway and achieve its foreign policy aims.

15   Both the evaluation of relations with the EU in general and the perception of the advantages of EU policies in the home country show a negative trend.

16   See the individual country reports of the Opinion Polling and Research project (2011).

spondents, moreover, who have trust in the EU is rapidly eroding (*Figure 4*), having fallen from 57 percent in 2007, to 34 percent in 2011. Depicting the EU as a scapegoat for many misfortunes, populist parties across Europe are now embracing Euroscepticism to attract new voters beyond the anti-immigration and anti-elite constituencies.

Figure 4: Percentage of respondents who tend to trust the EU

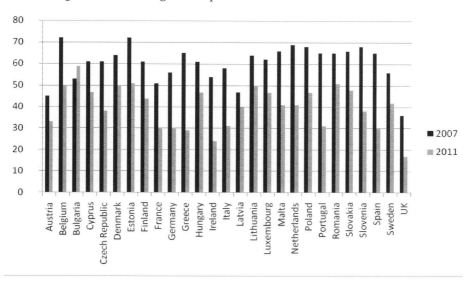

Source: *Eurobarometer, 2012.*

Conclusions

This chapter investigated the intersection of two crucial challenges which the EU needs to address: its decreasing economic competitiveness and its relations with the wider neighborhood. Concerning the economic aspect, it has been concluded that the European model, which worked well for post-war Europe, no longer suits the times. (Blanchard, 2004, p. 3) For much of the post-1945 period Europe practiced catch-up growth based on imitation rather than innovation. For such progress, large firms protected in goods and financial markets could do a good job. But now that European growth must increasingly be based on innovation, now that firms cannot be insulated from foreign competition, the European model has become dysfunctional. It has been indicated that the factors of competitiveness are deeply rooted in the local institutions, people, and culture, which makes improving competitiveness a special challenge because there is no single policy or grand step that can create competitiveness, only many improvements in individual areas that inevitably take time to accomplish. (Porter, 2005) It was suggested that investing in human capital is a vital component in realizing Europe's desire to become a competitive and knowledge-based economy. Additionally and most recently, due to the economic recession and its consequences, the EU is experiencing a major turning point in its history, which makes its future and trend of magnetic power very unpredictable. Although signs of improvement have appeared recently, recovery remains uncertain and fragile since EU countries have not solved a multidimensional equation: how to promote growth in a context of fiscal consolidation. (Eurostat, 2012, p. 5)

The other dimension is the neighborhood which is addressed by two distinct policies in Brussels: enlargement and the ENP. Enlargement, the most effective foreign policy tool of the EU, lost steam a long time ago. Enlargement fatigue in Europe became manifest after the Eastern expansion and it has significantly deepened lately as public perceptions of the EU have become more critical and unemployment figures are rising. What is more, some of the countries with candidate or potential candidate status seem to be having second thoughts about the desirability of membership in a crisis-ridden EU. Especially in Bosnia and Herzegovina, Macedonia, Albania, and Kosovo EU euphoria is gradually being replaced by disillusionment. Where this leaves enlargement after Croatia's accession to the EU in 2013 is unclear. It can be concluded, however, that the EU's influence over (potential) candidate countries is likely to shrink as long as uncertainty about enlargement prevails.

As for the ENP, from the start it has failed to have a meaningful impact on Europe's Southern and Eastern neighborhood. The Arab awakening has been a painful reminder of how marginal the EU's role still is in many neighboring countries. The revolts and revolutions in the Mediterranean region are strategically relevant developments, yet, sanctions aside, these events have unfolded with the EU largely as a bystander. There is no political will in Europe, especially not in times of austerity measures, to either finance large-scale transformation packages or open up European borders for ENP countries. Moreover, even if the EU were in a position to give Mediterranean countries what they wanted, the latter might still turn down European assistance if tied to too many conditions. As long as the EU is mainly trying to extend its own rules to these countries and draw them into a sense of regionalism marked by EU values, it will find it difficult to develop proper partnerships with them. To conclude, the EU has yet to define its own strategy and tools in relation to a territory in its sphere of influence which has no membership prospects, and thus the tested instruments of enlargement policy are ineffective.

Both enlargement and the ENP build upon and reinforce the pulling effect of the EU on the region. This magnetic power involves ideational and material factors, but this chapter's focus was only on the economic side of the attraction. It should be emphasized that this pulling power is not only passive but the EU actively maintains and develops it. The passive dimensions (the sheer size of the Single Market, its legal background, or high living standards) are supplemented with active EU measures (i.e. the politics of conditionality or trade negotiations) which basically offer a share in the common European economic space. Without such an offer made by the EU, the attraction of neighboring countries to the EU would be more limited since rivals (in particular the USA and Russia) are more than eager to strengthen their appearance in the vicinity of the EU. Consequently, Brussels cannot afford a power vacuum in its neighborhood and should keep its magnetic pull working.

It should also be emphasized that the magnetic pull of the EU does not mean the unilateral dependence of neighboring countries but rather interdependence, which in turn means that the EU also needs the neighboring countries as trading and investment partners. Due to its declining competitiveness, the EU is losing momentum in the emerging markets of Asia and in the highly developed North American region, which explains its need to sell its products, in the painful absence of alternatives, in the less dynamic countries of its neighborhood. What is more, EU countries have to rely on their neighbors' energy and agricultural goods as well. All in all, the EU's pulling power really works as a magnet which requires two adequate poles to synergistically interact.

Although there are undeniable tendencies pointing towards a weakening of the EU magnet, they are less related to economics. The problems are more related to politics, internal contradictions, and the lack of a grand European vision and efficient communication. This is very much illustrated by the lack of clarity and substance around the final outcome of the ENP or the road for the countries in the Western Balkans to full EU membership. Reform fatigue is getting stronger in neighboring countries, which needs to be addressed by Brussels. As was argued, the economic benefits of observing the *acquis communautaire* appear slowly and gradually, which makes the full implementation of reforms difficult, and the fact that these potential advantages have been questioned as a result of the crisis causes further uncertainty in neighboring states.

The magnetic power, however, is working because the EU is still the largest single market in the world, the most significant entity in international trade, and a wealthy region. This remains true regardless of the long list of problems. The recommended steps of reforming EU economics are indeed necessary to overcome hardships, but the level of economic development is so much higher in the Union than in the ENP region and the Western Balkans that the magnetic role of the EU remains stable from the perspective of economics. In general, the neighboring countries are on an export-oriented growth track, which attaches their fate to the economic prospects of the EU (as the main trading partner). These countries see their share of exports to the EU growing, which has arisen at least partly from the EU's generous trade preferences for the region (in particular, Western Balkan countries). (Kathuria, 2008, p. 34) The recent economic recession has not reversed the trend of expanding trade relations between the neighborhood and the EU, which is an additional sign confirming that no alternatives to the EU have emerged for these countries. The most recent illustrative example of the strength of EU magnetism was delivered when Croats voted to join the EU with an unexpectedly convincing two-thirds majority saying "yes".

Bibliography

Altomonte, C., & Nava, M. (2005). *Economics and policies of an enlarged Europe*. Northampton, MA: E. Elgar.

Anon. (2001). "The wealth effect." *Economist*. Retrieved from http://www.economist.com/node/622809 (15 February, 2012)

Anon. (2009). Views on European Union enlargement. Retrieved from http://ec.europa.eu/enlargement/pdf/press_corner/publications/eurobarometer_feb2009_summary_20090506_en.pdf

Aristovnik, A., & Čeč, T. (2009). Compositional analysis of foreign currency reserves in the 1999–2007 period. The euro vs. the dollar as leading reserve currency. Retrieved from http://mpra.ub.uni-muenchen.de/14350/1/MPRA_paper_14350.pdf

BIS. (2010). *Triennial Central Bank Survey. Report on Global Foreign Exchange Market Activity in 2010*. Basel. Retrieved from http://www.bis.org/publ/rpfxf10t.pdf

Baldwin, R. E., Francois, J. S., & Portes, R. (1997). The costs and benefits of EU enlargement: The impact on the EU and Central Europe. *Economic Policy 24*, 125-176.

Batos, S. (2010). Countercurrents on the borders? Discovering Europe's limits in the far and near abroad. In *A Weakening European Magnet? – The Attractiveness of the European Union in the New Decade*.

Blanchard, O. (2004). The Economic Future of Europe. *Journal of Economic Perspectives 18 (4)*, 3 - 26.

Boeri, T. et al. (2002). Who's afraid of the big enlargement? London: Centre for Economic Policy Research.

Breuss, F. (2001). Macroeconomic effects of EU enlargement for the old and the new members. *WIFO-Monatsberichte, 74(11)*, 655-666.

Börzel, T. A. (2010). The transformative power of Europe reloaded: The limits of external europeanization. Retrieved from http://www.daad.de/imperia/md/content/de/zentren/boerzel.pdf

Bureau of European Policy Advisers and the Directorate-General for Economic and Financial Affairs. (2006). Enlargement, two years after: An economic evaluation. *European Economy*. Occasional Papers.

Cowan, R., David, P. A., & Foray, D. (2000). The explicit economics of knowledge codification and tacitness. *Industrial and Corporate Change, 9(2)*, 211-53.

Dannreuther, R. (2006). Developing the alternative to enlargement: The European Neighbourhood Policy. *European Foreign Affairs Review, 11(2)*, 183-201.

Denis, C., McMorrow, K, Röger, W., & Veugelers, R. (2005). The Lisbon Strategy and the EU's structural productivity problem. *European Economy. Economic Papers, No. 221*. Brussels.

Directorate General for Economic and Financial Affairs. (2001). The economic impact of enlargement. *Enlargement Papers (4)*.

Eurobarometer. (2012). Retrieved from http://ec.europa.eu/public_opinion/archives/eb/eb76/eb76_en.htm

EUobserver. (2003). Billions of euros needed for candidates to implement EU laws. January 22.

European Central Bank. (2004). Sectoral specialisation in the EU: A macroeconomic perspective, by MPC task force of the ESCB. *Occasional Paper Series, No. 19.*

European Commission. (2002). *Communication from the Commission of 21 May 2002 on productivity: The key to competitiveness of European economies and enterprises.* [COM (2002) 262 final – not published in the Official Journal].

———. (2003). *Wider Europe — Neighbourhood: A new framework for relations with our Eastern and Southern neighbours.*

———. (2004a). *The European Union economy: 2004 Review,* No 6/2004, Directorate-General for Economic and Financial Affairs, Brussels.

———. (2004b). *European competitiveness report.* Brussels, SEC(2004) 1397.

———. (2006a). *Strengthening the European Neighbourhood Policy.*

———. (2006b). *The European Union and its neighbours.*

———. (2009a). Public finances in EMU – 2009. *European Economy (5).*

———. (2009b). Five years of an enlarged EU: Economic achievements and challenges. *European Economy (1).* Retrieved from http://ec.europa.eu/economy_finance/publications/publication14078_en.pdf

———. (2009c). Economic crisis in Europe: Causes, consequences and responses. Retrieved from http://ec.europa.eu/economy_finance/publications/publication15887_en.pdf

———. (2010a). Public opinion in the European Union. Retrieved from http://ec.europa.eu/public_opinion/archives/eb/eb74/eb74_publ_en.pdf

———. (2010b). Public opinion in the European Union. Retrieved from http://ec.europa.eu/public_opinion/archives/eb/eb73/eb73_first_en.pdf. (15 February, 2012)

———. (2011a). Trade – Statistics. http://ec.europa.eu/trade/creating-opportunities/bilateral-relations/statistics/.(15 February, 2012)

———. (2011b). Proposal for a regulation of the European Parliament and of the Council on the Instrument for Pre-accession Assistance (IPA II).

———. (2012a). Trade – Homepage. Retrieved from http://ec.europa.eu/trade

———. (2012b). Enlargement – Financial assistance. Retrieved from http://ec.europa.eu/enlargement/how-does-it-work/financial-assistance/instrument-pre-accession_en.htm

———. (2012c). European Neighbourhood. http://ec.europa.eu/

economy_finance/international/neighbourhood_policy/index_e n.htm

——. (2012d). Trade statistics 2012. Retrieved from http://ec. europa.eu/trade/creating-opportunities/bilateral-relations/countries-and-regions/

Eurostat. (2011). Share of EU in the world trade. Retrieved from http://appsso.eurostat.ec.europa.eu/nui/show.do?dataset=ext_lt _introle&lang=en. (15 February, 2012)

Eurostat. (2012). Eurostatistics data for short-term economic analysis. *Issue number 08/2012*. Retrieved from http://epp.eurostat.ec. europa.eu/cache/ITY_OFFPUB/KS-BJ-12-008/EN/KS-BJ-12-008-EN.PDF

Gordon, R. (2004). Why was Europe left at the station when America's productivity locomotive departed? *NBER Working Paper 10661*.

Grabbe, H. (2003). Europe's power of attraction. *Wall Street Journal, 24 April*.

Grotzky, D. (2008). The European Union and its Eastern neighbour-hood: A strategic failure? In I. Tarrósy & S. Milford (Eds.), *Changing Dynamics of the Danubian Region. New Neighbourhood Policy in the EU. (pp. 9-19)*. Pécs: IDM/IDResearch Ltd/Publikon books.

Gstöhl, S. (2008). A neighbourhood economic community – Finalité Économique for the ENP? *College of Europe EU Diplomacy Paper 3/2008, February 2008*.

Hyde-Price, A. (2006). "Normative" power Europe: A realist critique. *Journal of European Public Policy, 13 (2), 217-234*.

International Monetary Fund [IMF]. (2011). World economic outlook database. Retrieved from http://www.imf.org/external/pubs/ft/weo/2011/02/weodata/index.aspx

IMF. (2012). IMF statistics department COFER database. Retrieved from http://www.imf.org/external/np/sta/cofer/eng/cofer.pdf

Johansson-Nogués, E. (2011). The decline of the EU's "magnetic at-traction"? The European Union in the eyes of neighbouring Arab countries and Russia. Retrieved from http://www2.lse.ac.uk/internationalRelations/centresandunits/EFPU/EFPUpdfs/EFPU-workinpaper2011-1.pdf

Kathuria, S. (2008). *Western Balkan integration and the EU. An agenda for trade and growth*. Washington: The World Bank.

Lankes, H.-P., & Venables, A. (1996). Foreign investment in economic transition: The changing pattern of investments. *Economics of Transition, 4, 331-347*.

Leonard, M. (2005). *Why Europe will run the 21st century*. London: Fourth Estate.

Mattli, W. 1999. *The Logic of Regional Integration: Europe and Beyond*. Cambridge: Cambridge University Press.

Milcher, S. & Slay, B. (2005). The economics of the "European Neighbourhood Policy": An initial assessment. In *Europe After Enlargement*.

Miscevic, T. (2009). Are there any alternatives to the European perspective of the Balkans and the EU Enlargement? In *Stabilisation and Integration Perspectives for the Western Balkans*. Retrieved from http://ec.europa.eu/enlargement/pdf/publication/stabilisation_and_integration_perspectives_for_the_western_balkans_en.pdf

Noutcheva, G., & Emerson, M. (2005). Economic regimes for export: Extending the EU's norms of economic governance into the neighbourhood.

Organisation for Economic Co-operation and Development [OECD]. (2003). *The sources of economic growth in OECD countries*. Paris: OECD.

OECD. (2004). *Understanding economic growth*. Paris: OECD.

O Mahony, M., & Van Ark, B. (Eds.). (2003). *EU productivity and competitiveness: An industry perspective*. Luxembourg: European Commission.

Opinion Polling and Research project. (2011). Retrieved from http://www.enpi-info.eu/

Pelkmans, J., & Casey, J-P. (2004). Can Europe deliver growth? The Sapir Report and beyond. *BEEP Briefing No. 6*. Retrieved from http://www.coleurope.eu/sites/default/files/research-paper/beep6.pdf

Porter, M. E. (2005). What is competitiveness? *Notes on globalization and strategy, 1(1)*. IESE.

Porter, M. E. (2008). *On Competition*. Boston: Harvard Business Press.

Prescott, E. (2004). Why do Americans work so much more than Europeans? *Federal Reserve Bank of Minneapolis Quarterly Review, 28(1)*, 2-13.

Rifkin, J. (2004). *The European dream: How Europe's vision of the future is quietly eclipsing the American dream*. New York: Tarcher.

Robinson, E. A. G. (1963). *Economic consequences of the size of nations*. London: Macmillan.

Rosecrance, R. (1998). The European Union: A new type of international actor. In J. Zielonka (Ed.), *Paradoxes of European foreign policy*. The Hague: Kluwer Law International.

Sapir, A. (2007). European strategies for growth. In M. Artis & F. Nixson (Eds.), *The economics of the European Union: policy and analysis*. Oxford: Oxford University Press.

Sapir, A. et al. (2003). *An agenda for a growing Europe. Making the EU economic system deliver*. Brussels: Independent High-Level Study Group.

Schleicher, A. (2006). The economics of knowledge: Why education is key for Europe's success. *Lisbon Council Policy Brief, 1(1)*.

Smith, M. (2005). Implementation: Making the EU's international relations work. In C. Hill & M. Smith (Eds.), *International relations and the European Union*. Oxford: Oxford University Press.

Tsoukalis, L. (2005). Managing interdependence: The EU in the world economy. In C. Hill & M. Smith (Eds.), *International relations and the European Union*. Oxford: Oxford University Press.

UNDP. (2011). *Human development report 2011*. Retrieved from http://hdr.undp.org/en/media/HDR_2011_EN_Complete.pdf

Van Ark, B., O'Mahony, M., & Ypma, G. (2007). An overview of results from the EU KLEMS growth and productivity accounts for the European Union, EU member states and major other countries in the world. *The EU KLEMS Productivity Report, (1)*, March.

Van Ark, B., O'Mahony, M., & Timmer, M. P. (2008). The productivity gap between Europe and the United States: Trends and causes. *Journal of Economic Perspectives, 22(1)*, 25 – 44.

Van Mourik, A. (1997). The economic theory of customs unions and free trade areas. In M. O. Hösli & A. Saether (Eds.), *Free Trade Agreements and Customs Unions: Experiences, Challenges and Constraints*. Brussels and Maastricht: Tacis European Commission and European Institute of Public Administration.

World Economic Forum. (2011). The global competitiveness report 2011-2012. http://www3.weforum.org/docs/WEF_GCR_Report_2011-12.pdf

Zielonka, J. (2008). Europe as a global actor: empire by example? *International Affairs, 84 (3)*, 471–84.

Post-Lisbon strategies and their implications for a wider Europe

Péter Balázs, Ph.D.

The strategies and policies of the European Union have undergone a great deal of change during the last few years. These mutations are the result of a number of changes and permutations of the world order, in both the political and the financial sense. The European Union, as a supra-national entity, has also seen a shift in its external strategies as well as in its internal structure. The outside challenges now necessitate a novel set of strategic instruments, dealing with economy and trade, infrastructure and foreign policy, since many of the old strategies have become physically impossible to continue or of lesser efficiency. It is the goal of this chapter to outline some of the main strategic moves enacted by the European Union as a body, and also via some of its member states and institutions, acting on its behalf. The chapter also seeks to highlight the manner in which disparate policies create unity or convergence, and address the question of how integrated are the strategies of the post-Lisbon Treaty European Union.

Contributing factors

The main issues and catalysts that urge the development of new strategies come from a variety of sources. First and foremost is the emergence and ratification of the Lisbon Treaty. Born as an attempt to preserve whatever it could from the failed attempt at EU constitutionalism, the Treaty, signed in 2007, came into effect in 2009. (Carbone, 2010; Griller & Ziller, 2008) It brought a whole host of institutional changes to the Union, which have had a great impact on sectoral and global policies. Firstly, the three-pillared EU was scrapped in favor of an institution possessing a legal entity, thus having the theoretical possibility of acting and being represented as a separate unit on the stage of international politics. (Carbone, 2010) This tendency toward institutional integration and unification was strengthened by the creation of two new pivotal offices, the President of the European Council and the High Representative of the Union for Foreign Affairs and Security Policy. The Common Foreign and Security Policy of the Union and the Common Security and Defense Policy became more clearly circumscribed by the text of the Treaty and came under the administration of the High Representative. The details of these policies are still under the firm control of the member states, however, and are subject to inter-governmental negotiations. Nevertheless, the move toward a more coherent and unified front in the field of foreign policy is looming. Similarly, the creation of the office of the President of the Council can also be interpreted as a move toward uniformization, or at least a desire to establish a permanent institution that would aid the facile and swift development of strategies and policies. (Carbone, 2010; Griller & Ziller, 2008)

The Lisbon Treaty also established other changes in the institutions of the European Union. The voting system has been reformed on a number of levels, most significantly in the Council of Ministers, in order to aid decision-making processes. The treaty has expanded the use of qualified majority voting (QMV) in the Council of Ministers by having it replace unanimity as the standard voting procedure in almost every policy area except taxation and foreign policy. Moreover, taking effect in 2014, the definition of a *qualified majority* will change: a qualified majority will be reached when at least 55% of all member states, comprising at least 65% of EU citizens, vote in favor of a proposal. When the Council of Ministers is acting neither on a proposal of the Commission nor on one of the High Representative, QMV will require 72% of the member states, while the population requirement remains the same. However, the "blocking minority" that corresponds to these figures must comprise at least four countries. Hence, the voting powers of the member states are based on their population, and are no longer dependent on a negotiable system of voting points. (Koutrakos, 2011) These moves should create a more streamlined way of creating strategies and policies for the Union, and they signal a move away from the principle of unanimity which characterized EU decision making up to 2009.

Another important contribution of the Lisbon Treaty in the area of creating institutional possibilities which would enable the development of new strategies is the reform of the Union's Neighbourhood Policy. This has been officially split into geographic areas, each given a formal staff in the form of a secretariat, and put under the supervision of the Commission. The Northern Dimension and the Union for the Mediterranean are already part of the regional external policy of the European Union, while the third area is still at the status of a project. The Eastern Partnership, initiated by two interested parties, Sweden and Poland, seeks to provide the Union with a formalized framework to cultivate a good relationship and extend positive influences over its eastern neighbors, especially those of the former Soviet Union. The members include Belarus, Ukraine, Moldova, Azerbaijan, Georgia and Armenia. The Union seeks to cultivate good governance, economic and political reforms, and indeed many of the goals in the preamble of the Lisbon Treaty, through the Eastern Partnership. However, the Partnership is not formally seen as a step toward eventual membership in the Union, since the international status of many of the countries does not allow for that. (Dabrowski & Maliszewska, 2011; Kostanyan, 2012; Makarychev & Deviatkov, 2012)

The weakening economic dominance of the EU is another factor that must be taken into consideration in relation to the development of new strategies. The financial crisis, since its outset in 2008, has hit the Union particularly hard. This is mainly due to the Union's high exposure to the US market, and the interconnectedness of its own banking, monetary and financial networks. A number of financial weaknesses and vulnerabilities of some of the financial and real-estate markets, as well as inadequacies of regulatory systems has left some of the Southern member states in a perilous situation. The imposition of global norms in these areas has become one of the top priorities of the Union, but this would require a step beyond ad-hoc inter-governmental negotiations on issues of economic and financial policy. An acute need is felt for institution building (understood here also as norms and regulations) in these areas. In the backdrop of these developments, other international actors which feature a more solid financial model have affirmed themselves, some in the immediate neighborhood of the EU. Russia is the most significant in this sense, and the efficiency of the above-mentioned Eastern Partnership may be called into question, especially when viewed in the light of two factors. The first is the already described formal admission that the Eastern Partnership would not lead to association agreements with the EU, and end with formal membership. The second is the growing economic, political and diplomatic influence of Russia on these states, which can exert a centrifugal force, driving them back into the Commonwealth of Independent States. Russia can become a serious competitor in the fields of aid and assistance-giving, as more of the EU funds are directed inwards. (Dabrowski & Maliszewska, 2011)

The last significant factor which drives the paradigm shift in EU strategy is the more-or-less formal end of enlargement as a tool of foreign policy. In the spirit of Pompidou's *Triptique*, it is safe to affirm that the EU is undergoing a process of deepening and completion. (Hill & Smith, 2000) The aforementioned institutional changes require enlargement to slow down. In addition, enlargement has run out of steam due to practical considerations. Firstly, from a geographical perspective, the number of European states outside the EU has become quite small. Secondly, they are broken up into at least three categories: a few which will join in the foreseeable future, states which cannot join due to practical considerations, and states which have not applied for membership and are not expected to do so. The first group includes Croatia and Iceland. Croatia's membership in the Union will become official in the summer of 2013 as the country has concluded all required processes and the member states have all ratified its status. Iceland still finds itself at the negotiating table, but negotiations are at an advanced state, and membership is possible in the near future, recent economic issues notwithstanding.

The rest of the states of the Western Balkans find themselves in a secondary status vis-à-vis their relationship with the Union. Most of them are not largely in accordance with the Copenhagen Criteria regarding their judicial and legal systems. Macedonia and Montenegro also have weak economies, with the added disadvantage of the latter being one of Europe's newest states, in full process of institution creation and defining its regional role. Serbia is facing huge problems in the domestic field, ranging from an unstable economy to a fraught political system and corruption matters, just to name a few basic issues. The most important issue barring its promotion to the status of candidate for membership in the European Union is its refusal to recognize Kosovo as an independent state. The status of Turkey is the most contrived. Although it has been an official candidate since 2005 (and has been associated with the EEC since 1987), the country's accession to membership has not made much progress in the last two decades. This is due to certain assumptions related firstly to its size, secondly to its geographic position, and lastly to its non-Christian identity. Turkey's entry into the European Union, as a full member, would mean it would have a big share in decision processes. Due to the reasons listed above, the accession process is non-officially frozen by France, Germany, and a number of other, smaller EU members. Therefore, one can conclude that enlargement is not to be expected in the near future, and that the Union must use other instruments to ensure its foreign policy goals are being met in its neighborhood.

Strategy initiatives since 2010

The most important long-term strategic initiative of the European Union was launched in March 2010 by the European Commission. Entitled the *Europe 2020* strategy, it was announced as a tool of "achieving smart, sustainable and inclusive growth". Growth is expected to be achieved through knowledge and innovation, a greener and more efficient use of resources, and higher employment combined with social and territorial cohesion. (Gros and Roth 2012) The Europe 2020 strategy aims to:

> A. achieve a target for R&D expenditure of 3% of GDP (while also acknowledging the need to develop an indicator that would better reflect innovation intensity);
> B. increase the employment rate of the population aged 20-64 from the current 69% to 75% (through a greater involvement of women, older workers and better integration of migrant workers);
> C. lower the dropout rate to 10% from the current 15% and increase the share of the population aged 30-34 having completed tertiary education from 31% to 40%;
> D. cut the number of Europeans who are at risk of poverty or exclusion by 20 million citizens; and
> E. reduce greenhouse gas emissions by at least 20% compared with 1990 levels or by 30% if the conditions are right, raising the share of renewable energy sources in final energy consumption to 20%, and moving towards a 20% increase in energy efficiency.

In order to achieve these goals, the Commission proposed a series of seven flagship initiatives in the agenda of Europe 2020. The seven flagship initiatives involve: *innovation, youth, the digital agenda, resource efficiency, industrial policy, skills and jobs, and the fight against poverty.* Implementation of these initiatives is a shared priority (according to the categorization made by the Lisbon Treaty), and both the Union and its Member States are required to implement them. The governance methods will be "reinforced" to ensure that commitments are translated into effective action on the ground. The Commission will monitor progress. Reporting and evaluation under both Europe 2020 and the Stability and Growth

Pact (SGP) will be carried out simultaneously (while remaining distinct instruments) to improve coherence. This is expected to allow both strategies to pursue similar reform objectives while remaining separate instruments.

An important characteristic of the relative decline of the EU is correctly identified by the Europe 2020 strategy as the area of innovation and the low expenditure on Research and Development. (Agh & Vertes, 2010; Gros & Roth, 2012; Čolić & Agh, 2012) A decade ago the EU was a relatively close second to the United States (which held the first position globally) in terms of R&D spending. This is no longer the case, as China is now on course to overtake the EU and by 2020, according to present trends, will spend much more in absolute terms.

The share of the EU in global emissions is indeed rapidly declining. However, this is only partially due to the efforts of the EU to reduce its own emissions, given that since 1990 the emissions in emerging markets have increased heavily. In the year 2000, the EU still accounted for 19% of global emissions; today this value is only 12% and by the year 2020 it will have declined to about 10%. By contrast, the share of the emerging Asian nations (non-OECD Asia) will have increased to over 40% of the world's total.

The Europe 2020 strategy makes explicit reference to financial markets. However, this is not followed up with unambiguous goals. The strategy does not contain any concrete measures, in spite of the fact that the financial crisis and the ongoing debt crisis in the euro area demonstrate the necessity for financial stability as a precondition for growth. Furthermore, the results of liberalizing financial markets, which is a part of the Lisbon strategy, have been unsatisfactory. R&D investment has not increased materially as a share of GDP. Instead, the period before 2010 was characterized by a massive misallocation of capital into excessive construction investment in the Baltic States, Spain and Ireland, and excessive consumption in Portugal and Greece. This misallocation of funds affects the efficiency of trans-sectoral policies.

The Europe 2020 innovation benchmark of 3% investment in R&D seems lacking, as Research and Development is too focused on the manufacturing sector. As the main bulk of activities in European economies concern the services sector, with industry retaining the second tier position, the strategy seems maladapted to the real necessities of the EU economy. (Agh & Vertes 2010; Čolić & Agh, 2012) Education has rightly been identified by the text of the strategy as a key element in promoting innovation, increasing employment, and potentially reducing poverty by cutting the rate of school dropouts. The Europe 2020 strategy has weaknesses, which include: an over focus, in the realm of education, on quantitative indicators. (Gros and Roth 2012) This can be related to the abovementioned conceptual issue of linking competitiveness to volume and production. The strategy should take into account qualitative indicators such as the (social) value of the education provided by the universities. This can be achieved practically by paying more attention to university rankings, which would reveal the weaknesses of most European economies in comparison with the US. Thus the definition of innovation, focusing solely on R&D, seems to require improvement. (Gros and Roth 2012)

A skills upgrade in the EU seems key to fostering higher employment rates. Labor market reforms might be successful, as in the case of Germany, but in an aggregated analysis they do not seem to have had a significant impact in terms of increasing employment on average for the EU-27. Second, the (small) employment increase achieved from 2001 to 2010 seems to have been driven to a large extent by a skills upgrade of women in the labor force from below upper-secondary to upper-secondary education. The difference in employment rates for women between those with below upper-secondary and upper-secondary education is particularly large. This suggests that Europe's main employment potential appears to be in the (so far underemployed) female labor force of the two large Mediterranean economies of Spain and Italy. These economies and Europe itself would profit greatly if they were to achieve a substantial skills upgrade of the women in their labor forces. Third, before the big recession the US employment rate was higher than that of the EU because the US had already largely achieved the 2020 targets on education.

Social cohesion had a prominent place in the original Lisbon strategy in 2000, lost some importance in the revised 2005 strategy and in the Europe 2020 strategy, and has been further diminished to an index consisting of three indicators. It is difficult to evaluate if social cohesion can be assessed with such simple variables, and does not require concentrated attention. It would be wise to expand the set of indicators measuring social cohesion. (Gros and Roth 2012) The Europe 2020 strategy should have broadened the set of indicators, for example by including citizens' normative perceptions, and the levels of interpersonal and systemic trust.

At the June 2012 European Council, the President of the Council was invited "to develop, in close collaboration with the President of the Commission, the President of the Eurogroup and the President of the ECB, a specific and time-bound road map for the achievement of a genuine Economic and Monetary Union". (Rompuy, 2012) Building on the Interim Report and the Conclusions of the October 2012 European Council, this report provides the background to the road map presented at the December 2012 European Council. It suggests a time frame and a stage-based process towards the completion of the Economic and Monetary Union (EMU) covering all the essential building blocks identified in the report *Towards a Genuine Economic and Monetary Union* presented at the June European Council. It incorporates valuable input provided by the Commission in its communication *A Blueprint for a deep and genuine EMU – Launching a European Debate* of 28 November 2012. (Rompuy, 2012)

The report was entitled *Towards a Genuine Economic and Monetary Union*. The vision for the future EMU in the report comprises four building blocks:

> § An integrated financial framework to ensure financial stability in particular in the euro area, and minimize the cost of bank failures to European citizens. Such a framework elevates responsibility for supervision to the European level, and provides for common mechanisms to resolve banks and guarantee customer deposits.

§ An integrated budgetary framework to ensure sound fiscal policy making at the national and European levels, encompassing coordination, joint decision making,
greater enforcement and commensurate steps towards common debt issuance. This framework could include also different forms of fiscal solidarity.
§ An integrated economic policy framework which has sufficient mechanisms to ensure that national and European policies are in place that promote sustainable growth, employment and competitiveness, and are compatible with the smooth functioning of EMU.
§ Ensuring the necessary democratic legitimacy and accountability of decision making within the EMU, based on the joint exercise of sovereignty for common policies and solidarity.

These four building blocks offer a coherent and complete architecture that will have to be put in place over the next decade. All four elements are necessary for long-term stability and prosperity in the EMU and will require a lot of further work, including possible changes to the EU treaties at some point in time. (Rompuy, 2012)

The Eurozone heads of state or government decided ion the one hand to establish a *single banking supervisory mechanism* run the by the European Central Bank, and, once this mechanism has been created; and on the other hand to provide the European Stability Mechanism (ESM) with the possibility to inject *funds into banks directly.* (Rompuy, 2012) The recapitalization of Spanish banks is set under these rules, with assistance provided by the European Financial Stability Facility (EFSF), until the ESM comes into effect. The funds will then be transferred to the ESM without gaining seniority status. It was also agreed that EFSF/ESM funds can be used flexibly to buy bonds for member states that comply with common rules, recommendations and timetables. The Eurogroup has been asked to implement these decisions. (Rompuy, 2012)

Under tax policy measures, several member states will launch a request for enhanced cooperation to introduce a financial transaction tax. Member states participating in the Euro Plus Pact will continue their discussions on tax policy issues. In addition to this, leaders took decisions designed to maximize growth, that will apply not only to the eurozone but to all the 27 Member States. An example of this is the 120 billion euros which shall be mobilized in order to increase the European Investment Bank's paid-in capital by 10 billion euros; launch the pilot phase for Project Bonds in transport, energy and broadband infrastructure; and reallocate structural funds in support of SMEs and youth employment, and devote a further 55 billion euros to growth-enhancing measures.

Another strategic move, this time in the field of infrastructure, communications, and transport is the proposed introduction of the new Connecting Europe Facility. With a proposed budget of up to 50 billion between 2014 and 2020, it is "specifically designed to promote growth, jobs and competitiveness through targeted infrastructure investment at European level". (*Connecting Europe Facility,* n.d.) The CEF would be created to support the roll-out of high-performing, sustainable and joined-up trans-European networks in the fields of transport, energy, and broadband and digital services. The European Commission proposed 9.2 billion to stimulate investment in fast and very fast broadband networks and pan-European digital services through the CEF digital. According to the estimates of the Commission, it could stimulate investment worth more than 50 billion, touching 45 million households and over 100 million Europeans, and play a key role in helping Europe reach its fast and ultra-fast Internet targets. Investment in broadband will make Europe more competitive, will help build the Digital Single Market, and will create jobs.

CEF digital is envisaged to support services such as eID, eProcurement, eHealth, Europeana or eJustice where EU-wide interoperability and infrastructures can add value by linking up national systems. The CEF is also designed to help save money for existing institutions: eProcurement could save 100 billion euros a year; cloud computing 250 billion. (*Connecting Europe Facility*, n.d.)

The European Commission first recommended the establishment of the Connecting Europe Facility in June 2011, as part of its EU budget proposal for the next multi-annual financial framework (MFF) 2014-2020. The proposal was submitted to the European Parliament and the Council, and it is expected to be adopted by the two co-legislators before the end of 2013.

The text for the proposal for the Connecting Europe Facility reads:

> Europe needs to grow its way out of the economic crisis. Today, we commit our support to the creation of transport, energy and telecom infrastructure that interconnects Europe and we call for the creation of a Connecting Europe Facility. We need to invest seriously in European networks and this will not be achieved without pan-European investments from the European Union budget. European money needs to be used better. A Connecting Europe Facility will provide real 'added value'... These investments will generate growth and jobs, and will make work and travel easier for millions of European citizens and businesses. It will help to boost Europe's single market and provide security for further investment... (*Connecting Europe Facility*, n.d.)

It can be deduced from the text that the CEF is designed not only to help with the actual improvement of the infrastructure. (*Connecting Europe Facility-Transport* n.d.) This move is linked with the idea of increasing competitiveness, something we have already seen with the Europe 2020 plan. Furthermore, the two are also envisaged to assist with job creation and boosting the economy of the Union. The conceptual linkage into a rough system reveals common trends in EU strategic planning.

In the fall of last year, in a closed meeting, a group of eleven foreign ministers launched an initiative for a more authoritative EU foreign policy, lead by an institutional framework with more power than the current High Representative.

The assemblage, formed from the foreign ministers of Austria, Belgium, Denmark, France, Italy, Germany, Luxembourg, The Netherlands, Poland, Portugal, and Spain, constituted itself as the group for "The Future of Europe". It published its communiqué on the "Future of Europe" on Tuesday 18 September after a meeting held in Warsaw. (*Future of Europe Group Report*, n.d.)

The report concluded that the European Union must enact a "substantial revision" of the European External Action Service (EEAS), putting the High Representative in charge of neighborhood and development policy. The plan also called for a novel defense policy, put under the same authority of the High Representative, with the declared end goal of "creating a European army" for the purposes of common defense. (*Future of Europe Group Report*, n.d.) This is a direct challenge for NATO and other similar organizations, as the ESDP existed until now strictly as a supplement to the activities of NATO, not a replacement for them.

The plan envisages the current High Representative and leader of the External Action Service, Catherine Ashton, to be flanked by neighborhood commissioner Stefan Fuele and development commissioner Andris Piebalgs, whose office controls the EU moneys directed at the Western Balkans, the Middle East, and Africa. The new-model EEAS chief would instead control two "junior" neighborhood and aid commissioners. (*Future of Europe Group Report*, n.d.) The report also calls for more frequent meetings of EU foreign ministers than the current number of four per year, and for decisions in matters of foreign and defense policy to be based increasingly on Qualified Majority Voting, in order to "prevent one single member state from being able to obstruct initiatives." (*Future of Europe Group Report*, n.d.) The report endorsed existing legal proposals to give the European Commission and the European Central Bank more control over national economies (the so-called "two-pack" law on budgetary discipline and a single EU bank supervisor). It also proposed that a single EU President runs the Commission and the EU Council. The appointment to this office should be done through a direct pan-European vote "on the same day in all member states." The report also boldly proposed that EU external borders should be manned by a "European Border Police". (*Future of Europe Group Report*, n.d.)

In conclusion, the "Future of Europe" report envisaged a marked reduction in the authority of nation states, and the creation of unity through institution-building. It proposed that changes to EU treaties should in future be adopted "by a super-qualified majority of the EU member states and their population" instead of by unanimity. (*Future of Europe Group Report*, n.d.)

However, the communiqué has several contradictory phrasings as it noted that "not all participating ministers agree with all proposals". This was probably injected into the text in order to create an escape clause for those who might face a eurosceptic backlash at home. Other problems of the text include its statements that majority-made EU treaty changes "would [only] be binding for those member states that have ratified them" and that "the responsibility of the member states for the composition of their budgets has to be fully respected". (*Future of Europe Group Report*, n.d.)

However, the overall tone of the text is positive, as it also attempts to restore the trust in EU institutions through the concepts of greater democratic "legitimacy" and "visibility." At one point, the text proposes that the European Parliament should be able to initiate legislation instead of just amending or blocking commission proposals. But for the most part the "visibility" boiled down to extra "consultative" powers for MEPs and the creation of a new joint committee for MEPs and national MPs to talk to each other. (*Future of Europe Group Report*, n.d.)

The report also created a new concept, a theoretical possibility for a "pre-in" for EU membership. The "pre-in" refers to an EU country which aims to join the euro one day, and which wants to be able to attend eurozone meetings to find out where the single currency is going. This intermediate stage is envisioned to smooth the process of monetary unification. (*Future of Europe Group Report*, n.d.)

Conclusion

The post-Lisbon European Union has to tackle an inordinate amount of international pressures, coming from a wide variety of areas, including economy, politics, and international affairs. To this end, each its strategic moves are designed to respond to these challenges. Since the issues are often interrelated (competitiveness in the world and the reduction of economic problems), its responses often have a large amount of conceptual cohesiveness. They are also often linked together by similar logic and reasoning mechanisms, displaying the efficiency of inter-institutional and inter-governmental communication that the post-Lisbon EU structure is starting to provide. However, this still does not amount to the kind of coherence needed to become an efficient and coherent actor on the world stage. The European Union seems to possess an inordinate amount of divergent strategic interests, objectives and policies, but has not yet achieved an unified strategy. There are positive signs however, as both the institutional structure of the Lisbon Treaty, and recent developments, such as the "Future of Europe" report show. They indicate certain trends toward further integration and the creation of consistency on the pan-European level.

Bibliography

Agh, Attila, and Andras Vertes. 2010. *From the Lisbon Strategy to the Europe 2020 Strategy: Think European for the Global Action*. Budapest: "Together for Europe" Research Center.

Carbone, Maurizio. 2010. *National politics and European integration. From the constitution to the Lisbon Treaty*. Cheltenham: Edward Elgar Publishing.

Connecting Europe Facility. https://ec.europa.eu/digital-agenda/en/connecting-europe-facility (February 4, 2012).

Connecting Europe Facility-Transport. http://ec.europa.eu/transport/themes/infrastructure/connecting_en.htm (February 4, 2012).

Dabrowski, M, and M Maliszewska. 2011. *EU Eastern neighborhood: Economic potential and future development.* New York: Springer. http://books.google.com/books?hl=en&lr=&id=80jv2dhi7kIC&oi=fnd&pg=PR5&dq=EU+Eastern+Neighborhood.+Economic+Potential+and+Future+Development&ots=uOn95NzJDk&sig=jKUuZoD2_RP00s0Ob-Vc55zxn5U (February 4, 2013).

Dannreuther, Roland. 2004. *European Union foreign and security policy: Towards a neighbourhood strategy.* New York: Routledge.

Future of Europe Group Report. http://www.cer.org.uk/sites/default/files/westerwelle_report_sept12.pdf (February 4, 2012).

Griller, Stefan, and Jacques Ziller. 2008. *The Lisbon Treaty. EU constitutionalism without a constitutional treaty?* New York: Springer.

Gros, Daniel, and Felix Roth. 2012. "The Europe 2020 Strategy." Brussels: Centre for European Policy Studies

Hill, Christopher, and Karen E Smith. 2000. *European foreign policy: Key documents.* New York: Routledge.

Kostanyan, Hrant. 2012. "The EEAS and the Eastern Partnership: Let the blame game stop." *CEPS Commentary* (September): 1–3. http://www.ceps.be/research-areas/eu-neighbourhood-foreign-and-security-policy.

Koutrakos, Panos. 2011. *European foreign policy. Legal and political perspectives.* Cheltenham: Edward Elgar Publishing.

Lucarelli, Sonia, and Ian Manners. 2006. *Values and principles in European Union foreign policy.* New York: Routledge.

Makarychev, Andrey, and Andrey Deviatkov. 2012. "Eastern Partnership: Still a missing link in EU strategy?" *CEPS Commentary* (January): 1-5.

Rompuy, Herman. "TOWARDS A GENUINE ECONOMIC AND MONETARY UNION Report by President of the European Council Herman Van Rompuy." http://ec.europa.eu/economy_finance/focuson/crisis/documents/131201_en.pdf (February 4, 2012).

Čolić, Amela, and Attila Agh. 2012. 18 Srpska pravna misao 57-67 *From Lisbon strategy to Europe 2020.* Zagreb: Institute of International Relations. http://www.spmisao.rs/?page_id=71.

Divided leadership?
The changing transatlantic relationship and its effects on EU external action

András Szalai

In the past two decades the European Union (EU) has succeeded in considerably expanding its influence regionally. Using enlargement as its key policy tool, it managed to stabilize post-communist Eastern Europe and still acts as a solid anchor for the Western Balkans. Apart from its regional successes, in the early 2000s the Union also began to present itself globally as a self-proclaimed great power. Acting as a "normative power" (Manners, 2002), the EU sought to define what counts as normal in global politics, emphasizing norms such as human rights and democracy in its dealings with the world. With the fledgling Common Foreign and Security Policy (CFSP) and the Common Security and Defense Policy (CSDP, the successor of the European Security and Defense Policy – ESDP) the European Union is striving to develop the very capabilities that would imbue it with the characteristics of true actorness in global affairs. (Hill, 1996) Europe as a global power would have not only a clear presence in world politics, but also the matching capabilities to exert influence on other actors. Enthusiastic voices both in Brussels and in the academic world began to see Europe as the world's next superpower (e.g. Moravcsik, 2003), one that would be an equal to the United States in conserving Western dominance in the 21st century, yet would rely on a different set of tools. Consequently, whether the EU would be a partner or a counterweight within the Atlantic Alliance was one of the key questions at the turn of the century.

However, Europe has largely fallen short of these heightened expectations, and during the past few years a changing international system, the Eurozone crisis, the overall deterioration of the competitiveness of Europe's massive economy, as well as the constant pressures for internal governance reform have challenged the belief that the European Union could become a full-fledged global power, and even that it can continue to be a regional stabilizer. These unfavorable changes are coupled with a shift in the nature of the transatlantic relationship. The United States – also struggling with economic hardship – is shifting its focus towards the new centers of the global economy, away from Europe, towards the Asia-Pacific region. Events like America's troubled wars in Iraq and Afghanistan, as well as the ongoing debt crisis have once again given rise to the so-called decline discussion about the end of hegemony, arguing that the US seems to be losing its "unipolar moment" (Krauthammer, 1990) as rising powers such as China or Russia now challenge the superpower even on hard security issues in ways that were unimaginable a decade ago. The US is acutely aware of these global changes and is actively seeking new allies. But within the current state of transatlantic relations, a divided, crisis-ridden Europe is not among the potential candidates. All these factors question the very fundaments of Europe's role in the world order that has been undisputed since the 1950s. With a disinterested Atlantic partner apparently in decline, what role is there for Europe in the world? Can the EU fulfill its role of regional stabilizer at lower levels of American commitment? Is the transatlantic relationship in crisis, or to paraphrase Stephen Walt (1998), are the ties fraying again?

Transatlantic relations – from crisis to crisis

A quick look at the academic literature on the history of the transatlantic alliance could easily give readers the impression that crisis and conflict are business-as-usual in this relationship. Throughout its circa 60 years of existence, the transatlantic alliance has witnessed a series of political crises that periodically propelled analysts and politicians into a frenzy about the end of the Western bloc: Henry Kissinger talked about "a troubled partnership" as early as 1965, during the Vietnam War harsh European criticism of US "imperialism" led to a visible cooling of relations, while the deployment of intermediate range missiles in Europe during the 1980s sparked stark protest against the US, accusing the transatlantic partner of provoking World War III. But the succession of crises did not end with the dissolution of the Soviet bloc. In fact, scholars and policy-makers alike warned that the disappearance of the common threat, the Atlantic Alliance's unity of purpose, would further amplify cultural differences underlying Cold War crises, differences that were deeply rooted in historical experience, geography, language and relative capabilities. (Walt, 1998)[1] The argument went that if NATO did not disband without a *raison d'ętre* by itself, then these differences would surely tear the relationship apart. Without a unifying goal, a stronger, independent Europe would become an actual competitor of the United States. Such fears were not new, as independence from US dominance within the Atlantic alliance has been a recurring point of tension within NATO since its creation in 1949, especially in the case of France. In fact, French president Jacques Chirac's calling for an independent Europe in the late 1990s seemed to reinforce the image of a competitive-assertive Europe in Washington.

Without Soviet forces directly threatening the Eastern borders of Europe and ballistic missiles targeting European capitals, the "transatlantic bargain"

---

1   Walt (1998, p. 6) in particular was right on one point: that a shift in economic attention towards Asia-Pacific will result in some sort of a security shift, too, claiming that "time and resources being finite, [shifting US economic attention towards Asia] heralds an inevitable decline in the level of attention devoted to Europe."

(Toje, 2008) seemed to have lost its purpose. Though NATO successfully reinterpreted its mission globally, the Alliance is far from its former glory. The threat of terrorism could evoke unity for a brief period when NATO's Article V was invoked before the invasion of Afghanistan in 2001, yet heated debates around the invasion of Iraq by the US once again seemed to fit the general trend of "fraying ties". The question whether to support the US operation effectively split the European Union in half, with the UK and the new Eastern member states (Donald Rumsfeld's "New Europe") in favor, France and Germany against. While masses protested against the war in Europe, Americans introduced "freedom fries" and were pouring French wines into the sewers. This transatlantic crisis over the war on terror was seen as representing a whole new quality of tensions, the de facto end of the relationship. (See, for example, Andrews, 2005; Treverton, 2006) The Iraq war was thus nothing more that the last straw in a stretched cooperation between a culturally incompatible United States and Europe, forever paralyzing political cooperation and dialogue across the Atlantic. In his 2003 essay, Robert Kagan famously used the metaphor of Mars and Venus, arguing that the two sides of the Atlantic would never understand each other, since they are from different planets. Deep disagreement about the use of force would spell the end of the relationship under a unilateralist US presidency, while splitting European allies in terms of their support for the global efforts of the US.

Yet the certainty of the oracles foretelling the end of the transatlantic alliance a propos the war in Iraq now resembles the tale of the boy who cried wolf. A lot has changed since 2003. With the ongoing political and financial crisis in Europe, the EU's aspirations for a global role have all but dissipated, pulling the sting of American fears of rising European power. A new, multilateralist US president struck a friendly tone with European allies and, despite a certain disillusionment with his first term, President Obama still enjoys a remarkable level of popularity in Europe that is reminiscent of the Kennedy era. A final Euro-American split along symbolic, cultural lines did not take place.

Nonetheless, even though prophecies about the end of the relationship due to the war in Iraq remained unfulfilled, new challenges have appeared on the horizon that will force both the US and Europe to rethink their relationship. The 2008 global financial crisis propelled the Western world into not only an economic, but also an identity crisis. Analysts today warn us of American decline, and pamphlets about a "post-American world" (Zakaria, 2008) have once again flooded the academic and policy discourse. Apart from deep economic hardship, the emergence of new powers also poses a challenge to the existing world order. "Rising powers" such as China or India are heralds of the relative decline of the US preponderance of power, and the birth of a multipolar world that will not only be shaped by Western states, but also by potential revisionist powers. Both these elements echo E. H. Carr's[2] (1991) prerequisites for a crisis in the international system: the existence of powerful (and potentially resentful) powers on the fringes of the international system, a persistent crisis in the global economy and

---

2   I must thank Asle Toje for bringing this argument to my attention.

a lack of will and/or capacity of the dominant power to maintain the international order. Thus, realist scholars are quick to jump to the conclusion that the 21st century will not be a "new American century" after all. Negativism perhaps reached its bizarre peak recently with a widely publicized book warning American readers about "becoming China's bitch". (Kiernan, 2012)

Battered by two lengthy conflicts and an age of austerity, the US is reinterpreting its global commitments. Having been awarded a second term, President Obama's policies will show continuity. Focusing on domestic economic issues, the President wants to "bring the troops home" from Afghanistan, and cut defense spending. Such a continued domestic focus does not mean isolationism, but rather a form of pragmatism, i.e. bringing commitments more in line with a set of narrowly defined goals. Instead of being the globally active hegemon of the late 1990s and 2000s, the US of the next decade will focus on Asia as a key area of interest, will reduce its military spending – while maintaining a technological edge over its competitors through a flexible force structure – and will work to restore the competitiveness of its economy, a process that is already underlined by a steady growth on the US job market. (c.f. Kupchan, 2012) Meanwhile, a secure second term will enable the US president to focus on his legacy through symbolic actions in the foreign policy arena.

Due to the economic pragmatism of Washington, American attention is necessarily shifting away from Europe. With its economy in trouble, Europe just does not merit the same level of attention as India or China. Simply put, the old continent is no longer the source of the world's problems like it was during the World Wars and the Cold War, and with its global influence still negligible, the European Union does not seem to be part of the solution to these problems either. Hedley Bull's (1982, p. 151) oft-quoted remark about a Europe that is not an international actor and is not likely to become one once again gains relevance as an inward-looking, troubled European Union loses its ability to be a "shaper" of global affairs. Indeed, recent symbolic political hiccups in the transatlantic relationship seem to support the thesis that Barack Obama is a "post-European": the US president missed both the Berlin Wall celebration in November 2009 and the US-EU summit in May 2010. (Meunier 2010) In both trade relations and political relations the US seems to be drifting away from multilateral frameworks to a multitude of bilateral agreements wherein Europe is no longer a partner – for example the so-called G-2 cooperation with the PRC. As a parallel process, the US is "rebalancing" its force structure, which will result in it pulling out troops from Europe – a decision announced in the January 2012 *Defense Strategic Guidance* (Department of Defense [DoD], 2012) – further weakening its presence in Europe and putting the problem of European defense spending once again into the limelight.

After this short review one can already state that the transatlantic relationship may indeed be in danger, but more so due to neglect, not a conflict of norms or interest like many suggested after the war in Iraq. Crucially, prior crises that were attributed to a difference in values, as in the case of the Iraq war, were often the result of the policies of key individuals on either side of the Atlantic. Jacques Chirac argued for an independent European superpower, Gerhard Schroeder won an election with his anti-American populist slogans, and it was George W. Bush who chose to act unilaterally and provoke the resistance of most of the Western world to his messianic foreign policies. Meanwhile, through years of conflicting policies and adverse leadership, both transatlantic publics and elites have remained committed to a continued, close relationship.[3] (German Marshall Fund [GMF], 2011)

The changing foreign policy focus of the US is easy to understand when taking into account current shifts in the global distribution of capabilities, yet it should not come with a deterioration of transatlantic ties. Even though rising powers often seem more important than an aging Europe, economic relations with China, for example, will not necessarily lead to blossoming US-PRC relations. Disagreement between Americans and Europeans on the use of force, the promotion of human rights or even global warming seems paralyzing only from a Western perspective. But the emergence of new actors also brings about the emergence of new views on these and other issues, from trade relations to diplomacy. A multilateral world that is no longer dominated by the West is also necessarily a more diverse one that will require a new culture for conducting global affairs, requiring Americans and Europeans alike to revise their Western cultural biases on what counts as a conflict of values in international affairs. To see this underlying challenge for the US and Europe, we do not even have to venture beyond economic relations, the centerpiece of Western declinism. The G8, a forum grossly overshadowed by Western dominance, gave way to the G20, a more representative group that more meets the requirement of inclusiveness, given the current distribution of power within the world economy. But as Charles Kupchan (2012) rightly notes, ideological diversity within the G20 will pose a problem, one that is at least as difficult as the harmonization of economic interests. Considering this colorful playing field, transatlantic disputes seem like the product of a narcissism of minor differences. (Baldwin, 2009) From an Asian perspective, Europe and North America are essentially indistinguishable culturally. It is indeed easy to overlook the many common values connecting the two sides of the Atlantic (and to emphasize small differences that spur conflict) – that is until confronted with those that do not share these values.

The world is changing, and the transatlantic alliance needs to adjust. The US is leagues ahead in reassessing its policies, but, as this analysis will repeatedly argue, America's newly defined interests still necessitate the maintenance of close transatlantic relations. Americans are weary of the global power struggle, and President Obama seems to hear their pleas. In a sense, this shift seems more

---

3   Both leaders and the public had strongly positive attitudes toward the other side of the Atlantic. The leaders were always more favorable than the public to both the United States and the EU. Ninety-three percent of the EU leaders had positive feelings toward the United States and 91% of the American leaders felt the same toward the EU. Among the general public, 76% of Europeans had a positive attitude toward the United States and 68% of the American public felt likewise toward the EU.

natural than the United States' commitment to the defense of Europe: the US always had a Pacific focus, whereas it only became a true European power under President Roosevelt. Yet what the US could take home from its historical cooperation with Europe is not only about Europeans free-riding on American security guarantees. Atlanticism is more than an ideology for maintaining the Western bloc. (c.f. Calleo, 1970, p. 100) It is institutionalized cooperation, a security community that is underpinned not just by shared interests, but also shared culture. As such, it is also a source of strength. The relationship between the United States and Europe has been turbulent for its entire duration, yet it gave birth to a durable military alliance that has not been approximated anywhere else in the world. Meanwhile, the transatlantic economy became the most integrated and most productive economic area on the globe.

With the transatlantic relationship's centrality to the Western world – and consequently to American hegemony – it is not surprising that a lot of attention has been devoted to its dynamics, and it is common for analyst to look for problems and not successes, thereby continually underemphasizing the stability of the relationship. The Atlantic alliance has endured, and economic relations are as strong as ever. Instead of turning its back to Europe, the US should look for synergies where its allies could be helpful in a new, multipolar world. Europeans are key stakeholders in US hegemony, and they are not without means to assist common goals. While the US is decreasing its commitment in several areas, reliance on partners makes all the more sense. What role Europe can and should play in this world, and along what common interests, is the question of this study.

The current state of the transatlantic relationship

Since its conception, the transatlantic relationship has been one of the core institutions of the Western world. It is a showcase of the United States' "benevolent empire" (Kagan, 1998), the superpower's conscious choice to allow its partners to grow under its hegemony within the Western bloc. This policy is epitomized by the meteoric rise of the Japanese economy in the second half of the 20th century, but it is even more apparent in Europe where the United States supported the integration project right from its humble beginnings, seeing it not as the cradle of a future economic rival, but a source of peace and stability on the old continent. This benevolent post-war policy was highly atypical for victorious great powers, and led Geir Lundestad to describe the American role in Europe as an "empire by invitation" or an "empire by integration". (Lundestad, 1986, 1998) After the destruction of WWII, the old continent was in desperate need of economic assistance under a looming Soviet military threat. This need gave rise to an alliance not of equals but with American dominance: US leadership was readily accepted in Europe for economic benefits (recovery aid and access to US markets), and protection from the Soviet Union through the presence of American troops. Thus the transatlantic relationship was initially based on two pillars: an economic and a military, subsequently institutionalized within the North Atlantic Treaty Organization in 1949.

The Transatlantic Economy

The economic pillar is still one of the most crucial manifestations of US hegemony. By helping its wartime allies and enemies to recover and grow after the war, the United States effectively created economic competitors such as Japan and Germany. Yet these states are still firmly allied to the US, well after the end of the Cold War. Turning potential challengers into stakeholders in its hegemony – its empire by invitation, not by conquest – is by far the greatest accomplishment of the United States. The underlying logic that economic development creates a common good (the process commonly referred to as globalization) guided this policy. Ironically, rising economic power did fuel the decline debate in the case of Japan and Europe alike. During the 1980s both the academic literature and the public discourse were riddled with references to Japan overtaking the sluggish US economy and "colonizing" the States. And as we have seen previously, a strengthening European Union was seen as a potential political-economic counterweight to the US at the end of the last century. Confusion once again arose from blurring the line between a narrowing gap between the US and the rest of the world on the one hand, and absolute decline on the other. In fact, as recent analyses show, the US is far from economic decline, but is instead managing the debt crisis quite effectively. (Krugman, 2012) Even though China, India and the other BRICS are often mentioned as the future focus of US economic activity, a quick look at the transatlantic economy shows that trade relations with China are still far from being comparable with US-EU relations. Johns Hopkins University's annual *Transatlantic Economy* study (School of Advanced International Studies [SAIS], 2011) came up with a number of interesting observations that place "the rise of the Rest" into a new perspective. Despite the recession, the US and the EU have remained each other's most important economic partners. As emerging markets are gaining in strength, the Western lead remains, though transatlantic markets are visibly shifting "from a position of preeminence to one of predominance." (Hamilton & Quinlan, 2011) The US economy seems to be healing, and despite the ongoing debt crisis in Europe, trade, FDI, foreign affiliate income, and mergers and acquisitions could enjoy positive growth in the upcoming years.

In the past 15 years, Europe has been able to maintain its 19% market share in world exports, while both the US and Japan lost in their share to China. Thus, in terms of exports, the European Union and China are the world's leading powers. In terms of foreign investment, Europe is still the primary destination for American firms and vice versa. The study shows that between 2000 and 2010 US firms invested a staggering $1.3 trillion into Europe – over 60% of total US FDI. This share only fell back to roughly 52% in 2010. In turn, US FDI to the BRICS between 2001 and 2009 only took up 3.7% of global American FDI outflows, with China only in 12th place behind European states such as Belgium or Ireland. US investments to India, the other rising economy are even smaller – roughly 60% of FDI directed to Norway.

Europe also continues to be a depository of US assets: on a historical cost basis, the study shows, 2009 US investment positions in Europe were nearly 14 times larger than in the BRICS. The UK alone – with $1.6 trillion in 2008 – has more than Asia, Africa, South American and the Middle East combined. US investment stakes in Belgium at the end of 2009 ($70 billion on a historical cost basis) were comparable with the US investment position in China and India combined ($68 billion). But major US interests in Europe are not restricted to the advanced economies of Western Europe. The United States' collective asset base in the Czech Republic, Hungary and Poland – prominent examples for "New Europe" – are twice the size of corporate assets in India. In turn, the US was the top recipient of EU FDI outflows in 2010. In 2009 EU FDI in the US (1.1 trillion) was almost 13 times higher than that in China and India (85.5 billion). In total, between 2001 and 2009, EU FDI outflows to the BRICS only represented 8.4% of global EU FDI outflows. Surprisingly, this 8.4% was mostly targeted at Brazil and Russia, not China or India. North America is historically a primary destination for European exports: it accounts for roughly 23%, the same share as the Asia Pacific region.

The comparable share of exports to North America and Asia shows that Europe has crucial interests in the same emerging markets that the US is turning towards – the EU is the #1 trading partner for each country among the BRICS. Trade relations are especially close with China, the number one exporter to the EU. So a shifting economic focus towards the Far East is not just a US phenomenon: China's share of EU goods imports between 2000 and 2009 grew to 18.2% from 7.7%; against North America's share that shrank from 23.9% to 15.9%. Thus both the US and the EU have shifted some of their economic focus towards China. But what is of further importance is that the EU seems to be ahead in strengthening its economic relations with China and the BRICS. For example, the EU exports more goods to China than the US, growing with a whopping average of 30% over the past decade (yet the total amount is still less than the EU export to Switzerland).

Thus, in sum we can safely claim that the transatlantic economy is steadily recovering from the crisis and has not suffered significantly, remaining the world's most integrated market. China's doubtlessly increasing economic power is still exaggerated in analyses, partly due to a biased and narrow selection of variables that compare China to its former self. China has high growth rates because it started from a low point, but when compared with the transatlantic economy, or even the US, "China is rising, but it is not catching up." (Beckley, 2011, pp. 44-45) Though a relative shift towards emerging markets is visible both in the US and in the EU, their share compared to transatlantic ties is negligible. Nevertheless, both sides need to recognize their shared interests in dealing with emerging markets, and find avenues for cooperation. Of course, the problem for the EU again is that it has been unable to translate this impressive economic relationship into political benefits: the European Union's member states are hopelessly split on trade issues, as well as political issues such as human rights or Tibet. (See esp. Fox & Godement, 2009) Since the EU is yet again not able to appear with a unified voice, the US is shifting towards a bilateral framework with China (see Wong, 2010) – a dangerous game that will be discussed in a later section of this analysis.

NATO and defense policy

Based on elite and public polls, as well as on economic ties alone, the transatlantic relationship is as healthy as ever. (GMF, 2011) Yet as the evolution of Europe as an international actor shows, economic power is not easily translatable into political power and influence. In fact, one of the biggest fears of European elites is that the US only sees the European Union as an economic power, but cannot take it seriously as a partner in managing global issues, mostly due to the EU's inability to appear unified, and its reluctance to devote resources to defense. To fully assess the state of the relationship, we also need to look at the other pillar, the North Atlantic Treaty Organization.

After World War II, European states accepted American leadership in exchange for economic and military assistance. Due to the state of European postwar economies, this partnership was heavily dominated by the US. However, even within the military alliance, the superpower chose to act uncharacteristically for great powers: it sought to involve its allies in the management of the newly established North Atlantic alliance. Despite American gestures, existing asymmetries lead to continued tension within NATO, with Europeans always asking for a bigger say in the alliance. An additional source of dispute was the credibility of the US nuclear umbrella: would the Americans truly sacrifice New York for Paris? These issues famously lead to French President Charles de Gaulle withdrawing from NATO's integrated military command, and launching the French nuclear program. During the latter half of the Cold War, as the arms race intensified, automated strategies like massive retaliation became untenable. The US had to realize that the only way to appear credible in the eyes of both the Soviets and the European allies was to increase the number of conventional forces in Europe, so that the West was not left with a single, nuclear option. However, Europeans were reluctant to bear the costs of a conventional buildup, raising the problem of burden sharing that is still central to NATO's mission in the 21st century. Europeans have become "security consumers": using American security guarantees, they built down their militaries and reaped the "peace dividend", thereby enabling themselves to enjoy a higher rate of economic growth than would have been possible otherwise. Even though the aggregate military spending of EU states is still second to that of the United States, outmatching that of Russia or China, their armies could not defend Europe from a foreign invasion without US support. (Stockholm International Peace Research Institute [SIPRI], 2011) Even the successful military intervention of 2011 in Libya aimed at implementing UN Security Council Resolution No. 1973 – celebrated as a European victory – could not have been successful without the backing of the United States. In purely military terms, the EU is in essence a free-rider that uses US capabilities through NATO to fill any gaps in its force structure. Apart from the obvious tensions with the US, this heavy reliance on American forces also creates conflict within NATO as membership of the European Union and the Atlantic Alliance does not fully overlap (a total of 21 states are members of both organizations). Turkey, for example, a large contributor to NATO's conventional capabilities that has been at the doorstep of EU membership for decades, is excluded from the consultation process whenever the EU relies on NATO capabilities for its missions. This practice is harming the EU's image in the Muslim country.

American calls for greater burden sharing though frequent, have not been heard. Instead of creating a more capable military, some European states are getting rid of entire branches of their military, with little attention paid to effective interoperability on the European level. (Nemeth, 2012) Europeans can always blame the economic crisis for cutbacks, and in fact they do so repeatedly: according to NATO statistics, by 2011 European defense military spending had fallen by 12% from its already low 2008 level. (Dempsey 2012) But the United States is, of course, facing similar financial constraints. Major cutbacks in defense spending are on the menu in Washington, as demonstrated by the 2011 *Budget Control Act* and the 2012 *Defense Strategic Guidance*. The latter document clearly shows that the new US defense policy will redirect resources from Europe as "US military will continue to contribute to security globally, [the US] will of necessity rebalance toward the Asia-Pacific region." (DoD, 2012) "The withdrawal from Iraq and the drawdown in Afghanistan have created a strategic opportunity to rebalance the US military investment in Europe, moving from a focus on current conflicts toward a focus on future capabilities. In keeping with this evolving strategic landscape, [the US] posture in Europe must also evolve." (DoD, 2012) This "evolution" will bring force reductions in Europe, even though a complete withdrawal seems unlikely, since US troops enjoy the greatest level of interoperability with their European counterparts, as attested by the frequent successful training and military exercises within NATO. Though the air campaign in Libya draws attention to the dependence of European forces on US support, on the other hand it also attests to this excellent interoperability. Looking at official European and American strategic documents, the selection of security threats listed – e.g. hybrid warfare, access to common goods, failed and failing states – requires rapid adaptation, innovation, power projection, and full-spectrum operations and interoperability. (Deni, 2011) The value of such an asset should not be neglected when contemplating US withdrawal from Europe, as it adds a crucial self-interest element to US presence on the continent – if the United States has a vested interest in forward deployment in order to achieve better interoperability, then European free-riding must be dealt with through different means. The importance of Europe for US defense policy will decrease in relative terms, but not in absolute terms. As John Deni (2011) argues, reliance on European allies will be issue-specific and the US will always look for political allies (even military) in Europe, for "coalition warfare is the American way of warfare".[4]

Yet the assumption that the mere existence of NATO will uphold a strong transatlantic relationship seems no longer tenable. As the US loses general interest in Europe, the EU must address American concerns regarding burden sharing. Even though the financial crisis makes the demanded buildup unlikely, this study will argue that the EU has other options. Primarily a civilian power, the European Union has always struggled with a gap between its capabilities and the

---

4   John Deni's remark at the 2011 ECPR conference. Reykjavik, 08.25.2011

role that was expected of it, both by its citizens and the international community. (Hill, 1993) It is a widely shared tenet of neo-realist International Relations scholars that soft power is only as effective as the hard power that backs it up. In light of this rather negative view, the idea of a common European military – the CSDP – seemed a logical step to take. But with this project faltering, and with the US moving its attention elsewhere, what can the EU do to remain on the world stage? This crucial question will be addressed by the next section.

Europe's Role in a Changing Global Environment

The EC/EU has been at the focus of academic research ever since its conception. Enthusiastic voices emphasized its historical uniqueness and potential, claiming that European integration represented something strikingly new in international relations, and was giving birth to a wholly new and unique entity. Critics, on the other hand, drew attention to the contingency of European peace and prosperity on US security guarantees, and noted Europe's lack of real international actorness. (e.g. Bull, 1982) In order to qualify as a true international actor, the EU would need to have not only a common presence in world politics, but also an effective capability to carry out its foreign policy. But the EU also falls short of true actorness in terms of presence: its presence is real enough, but incoherent as third states are still forced to maintain bilateral relations with member states apart from their relations with the Union as an entity. (Hill, 1996, pp. 12-13) The "Europeanist" school, critics argue, downplays the importance of state power and national interests, while emphasizing the importance of supranational European institutions in building a common European identity. These pro-European analyses often mix normative arguments with empirical research, subverting the latter to the former. This tendency is most prevalent in the continued effort to re-define the meaning of power so that the European Union appears as a "post-modern great power", one that no longer relies on military means – means that have become less important since the end of the Cold War – but on "civilian" or "normative" power. (Duchêne, 1972, Manners, 2002) It is still unclear, however, how these concepts relate to international actorness.

The question seemed to have taken another turn in the 1990s, when the European Union first introduced its Common Foreign and Security Policy (CFSP), and later its Common Security and Defense Policy (previously ESDP). Both of these instruments were seen as crucial steps towards true actorness by supporters and critics alike. The EU's 2003 Security Strategy entitled *A Secure Europe in a Better World* redefined the Union's role as a responsible global actor that actively relies on its developing military instrument – a new means to achieve its normative ends, for example the protection of human rights. This global assertiveness dazzled academics and policymakers alike. Javier Solana, then High Representative for the CFSP, famously said that the claim that the European Union is a global player is "not an aspiration but a statement of fact". (Solana, 2005) Notable EU scholar Andrew Moravcsik (2010) has repeatedly argued that the 21st century will be shaped by two major superpowers: the United States and the European Union. By the mid-2000s, EU enlargement in 2004/2007 and the CFSP/CSDP were seen as the road to an independent European Union that is a global competitor of the US. These European global aspirations, as previously mentioned, more often than not provoked hostility in the United States as some Americans understandably asked: "If a unified Europe would define itself largely in opposition to the United States, why should the United States encourage European unity?" (Bereuter & Lis, 2003, p. 48) But the gap between role expectations and European capabilities could not be bridged. The development of the CFSP and CSDP in the end did not enable the EU to become a new pole within the Western bloc, and "opt out" of the United States' empire by invitation. Given the current realignment within American foreign policy, the question posed worldwide, and also within the limited scope of this essay, is: does the US need a still militarily weak Europe in its dealings with the new world order?

The past few years have witnessed a resurgence of realist ideas. With America's global war on terror, its difficulties both in Iraq and Afghanistan, and a global economic crisis looming over the Eurozone, the "Fall of the West" again became topical. Studies about the emergence of new powers and a more confrontative multipolar world, or as Robert Kagan put it, "a return of history", dominate the literature. Using a traditional (realist) capabilities-based understanding of power, the EU does not perform well. As it stands now, the EU still lacks a common "grand strategy" for its foreign policy and is struggling with a major political and economic crisis, as well as with the negative effects of its past two integration rounds. Therefore, Asle Toje (2011), for example, argues that the EU, though still an economic giant, more resembles small powers than super powers like the US. But how can such a "small power" contribute to the management of world politics? Though stories about an American decline are largely overblown, the US is undoubtedly losing its dominance in relative terms. Decision-makers in Washington are aware of the fact that the United States can no longer act alone in the new multipolar world. As President Obama remarked in the foreword of the 2010 *National Security Strategy*:

The burdens of a young century cannot fall on American shoulders alone (…) We are clear-eyed about the challenge of mobilizing collective action, and the shortfalls of our international system. But America has not succeeded by stepping outside the currents of international cooperation. (…) we will be steadfast in strengthening those old alliances that have served us so well, while modernizing them to meet the challenges of a new century. As influence extends to more countries and capitals, we will build new and deeper partnerships in every region, and strengthen international standards and institutions. (Obama, 2010)

But who will be these partners? As we have mentioned, most attempts at involving China in the management of the international system have failed as the emerging Asian giant refused to share the costs on account of it being a developing country. At first sight, Europe again seems like an easy pick. Europe and Americans share a great number of values, and their interests – be it economic or political – often intersect. As Bereuten and Lis (2003, p. 151) note, transatlantic shared interests have been broadening since 9/11: instead of focusing on Euro-Atlantic space, both sides looked beyond their common space and addressed challenges and opportunities in issues like trade liberalization, democracy promotion, conflict management (e.g. the Israeli-Palestinian conflict) and various security issues (terrorism, nuclear proliferation, etc.). Yet European contribution to these issues is often hard to detect. True enough, burden sharing in terms of military costs is still not settled within the Alliance, yet writing off the EU as a "rhetorical superpower" would be a mistake.

The EU is in many ways an "accidental power": its status in the current global order is not the result of some grand design, but an externality of its organic development. (Toje, 2011, p. 10) Due to its specific history, institutions and legal basis, the EU's foreign policy has a distinct sui generic element to it. Not being a state, the EU seems to defy the methods of state-centric theories, and posits a unique set of policy instruments. These instruments are commonly referred to as civilian power, (Duchęne, 1972) and are mostly representative of what Joseph Nye (2004) calls soft power, ranging from cultural and scientific excellence to enlargement, foreign aid and peacekeeping missions. Yet this soft power when compared to manifestations of hard power like aircraft carriers is hard to see – Europe is in many ways a "quiet superpower". (Moravcsik, 2002) Though not as visible as the US and other, more traditional powers, the EU has made a distinct mark in defining what counts as normal in international relations. (Manners, 2002) This mark is mostly traceable in the EU's support for international institutions, multilateral diplomacy, cooperation and persuasion instead of coercion in solving international disputes. As a civilian power, the Union is not primarily described as an actor that does not possess military means and consequently relies on civilian tools (peacekeeping operations themselves require a military instrument), but more importantly, it entails a specific approach to solving international problems: the EU uses carrots, rather than sticks.[5] (Larsen, 2002) This level of soft power is comparable to that of the United States. Yet as realists posit, soft power is often meaningless without some sort of hard power instrument backing it up. Lacking an effective military capability, the EU might often find itself in an unresponsive environment when dealing outside its traditional sphere of influence – arguably normative magnetism is only effective when the targeted state wants to become a member of the Union.

Current US foreign policy trends show a surprising level of pragmatism: the United States seems committed to meeting the challenges of the next decade, and it is also looking for partners on very pragmatic grounds. Old habits are thus reinterpreted: a mere harmony of values and interests between the US and the EU does not simply make Europeans an obvious fallback solution. To put it bluntly, Europeans need to have something to offer the United States that is in the way of sharing the costs of managing global affairs. Since a European military buildup is out of question, such a contribution must be based on European

---

5   Even European "sticks" – e.g. economic sanctions – seem sweet compared to a US drone strike.

soft power. But it is also crucial that Europe wields its power *actively* and in concert with the US. On the one hand, the European model has lost a lot of its magnetism globally, and is being challenged by other models, such as the managed democracy of Russia, or the pseudo-capitalist autocracy of the PRC. The other crucial problem here is the diffuse and incoherent presence of the EU as an actor in relation to global issues. Simply put, the EU finds it hard to appear unified on issues such as human rights in China. Member state interests are, of course, crucial for understanding the European Union. Even authors critical of the EU as an independent entity acknowledge that it serves as an excellent intergovernmental forum for channeling member state interests: the supranational structure of the Union enables member states to have a bigger impact on global issues than their own capabilities would allow. (See, for example, Hyde-Price, 2006; Moravcsik, 1993) Yet consensus is mostly reached on sectoral issues, and a truly common foreign policy is still missing. French activism in Libya, and conflicting Russia policies[6] within the Union are signs of diverging policy interests. Global European presence, due to the EU's limited foreign policy toolkit, is only possible in tandem with the United States. But if the EU wants to appear as a potential partner for the US, effective aggregation and focus of these interests is necessary. Only a Europe with a single foreign policy can occupy a global position that its economic might would allow.

Fortunately, there are some positive developments. The Lisbon Treaty shifted the European balance of power in terms of foreign policy agenda setting: with the creation of the office of the High Representative of the Union for Foreign Affairs and Security Policy, a crucial gateway opened for Europe to be able to appear with a united voice. On the other hand, a two-speed Europe might also contribute to a more unified common foreign policy. With the Eurozone in crisis, euro states are seeking a higher level of integration that necessitates closer cooperation on various policy issues. Though the main goal here is economic stabilization – in some form of fiscal Union – the creation of a more deeply integrated core Europe might also bring closer cooperation on foreign policy issues in the longer term. Naturally, a multi-speed Europe would come with huge political costs as it would create a barrier for the non-Eurozone periphery. However, whatever scenario will unfold in the next few years, a unity of voice will be a prerequisite for an effective European foreign policy, as well as for a continued close transatlantic relationship on global issues. With a divided Europe and a diffuse foreign policy, transatlantic cooperation will lose its global aspect and will become highly issue-specific/sectoral. Such a step back would, however, be harmful not just for European, but also for American interests.

---

6   In this case, the UK can revert back to its special relationship with the US and be confrontative with a more assertive Russia, while Germany might become the key player of a more conciliatory Russia policy within the EU. Such a scenario, of course, would once again damage Europe's ability to appear as a coherent, unified actor on the world stage.

What Use for Europe?

American fears about Europeans continuing to reap the peace dividend while not investing are well founded and understandable. In order to maintain the current quality of transatlantic relations, European guarantees for some sort of a security contribution are essential. But such a contribution does not necessarily have to always take the form of a military buildup. Power, understood as the ability to influence other actors, and the outcome of events, has diverse elements that include soft power, the civilian instruments the EU wields in its foreign policy. If we include soft power in the equation, Europe has a markedly different power structure from that of the United States, but one that represents a formidable asset. The EU should no doubt reinforce its hard power, if only to back up its soft power, but not to counter US power, and not in ways that would duplicate NATO capabilities. Nevertheless, something that realist analysts highly critical of European attitudes within the transatlantic alliance miss due to their emphasis on military power is that though hard power is, of course, important, non-coercive means can often achieve the desired ends. Additionally, hard power itself is more than just military power – economic might can also be wielded in coercive ways, as epitomized by the 1973 oil crisis when militarily weak states of the Organization of Arab Petroleum Exporting Countries lectured the United States.

European power offers a number of avenues through which it could assist US goals. The US has been consciously using international institutions to conserve its hegemony against new challengers. The EU is often overrepresented in these institutions. Take, for example, the G8 where apart from France, Germany, Italy and the United Kingdom, the European Union also has a separate seat. Independent representation is not an accident or a relic of history, but the result of conscious and committed European diplomacy. The EU, deriving its credibility partly from its continued support for multilateralism, has been working hard to increase its visibility in international bodies for decades, mainly in the form of an independent EU representation like the one above, or its enhanced observer status in the United Nations. (Hoffmeister, 2007; Jřrgensen, 2008; Rasch, 2008) Additionally, the European Union is well known to be the world's largest aid donor, using humanitarian and development aid as a foreign policy instrument. (Woolcock, 2011) The EU is also an active peacekeeper, having nearly ten times as many troops involved in peacekeeping institutions than the US, and most of these are under the authority of international institutions, (Moravcsik, 2003) The EU's presence in international bodies, along with its track record of reliance on non-coercive soft power instruments still lends it a level of credibility in the non-Western world. Though not necessarily a model to be followed anymore (c.f. normative power Europe), the European Union still appears as a partner with whom dialogue is possible.

Recent events offer a number of scenarios that show how such cooperation may unfold. Having key interest in the stability of the Middle East, the EU and the US are both strongly committed to solving local conflict. In Libya, a French-initiated humanitarian campaign was able to assist rebel forces in toppling the Gaddafi regime. The joint air strikes demonstrated the high level of interoperability between European and NATO forces, and the fact that the US decided to only support the operation shows that both power sharing and burden sharing are feasible among Atlantic allies without European subjugation to American leadership. For years, both the US and the EU have been working hard to forestall a nuclear Iran. However, reflecting different capabilities and foreign policy cultures, the two approaches differ. While the US does not exclude a military option and appears generally more belligerent, the EU (the EU-3: the UK, France and Germany) relies on a number of economic sanctions that are truly harming the Iranian economy (the latest round was announced in late 2011), while pushing for a negotiated settlement through multilateral frameworks such as the P5+1 (the five permanent members of the UN Security Council plus Germany). These joint efforts in line with joint interests signify how the two allies may find a new framework for cooperation: by playing the game known from Hollywood movies of good cop and bad cop. Whereas the US, a military superpower can take a confrontative stance, the EU can rely on a set of sticks and carrots to force the target country to the negotiating table. Deal with us, and we will deal with the US for you. (Nye, 2006, p. 33) The separation of roles does not have to be so strict, as the EU can also rely on coercive diplomacy in its foreign relations, using its economic power. The strength of cooperation rather comes from its flexibility.

Such a close cooperation – apart from the oft-mentioned unified European voice – needs its institutions. Even though it has been a trusted backbone of the transatlantic relationship, NATO might not be the most appropriate institution for such a task, given its military mission, and also because many issues important for both partners are not NATO issues. A new framework needs to step beyond Cold War mindsets and structures, which also means giving up the safety net that the US provided for Europe through NATO. The United States needs to accept European strategic fatigue as a European buildup is unlikely in an age of extreme austerity. (Brzezinski & Scowcroft, 2008, pp. 204-205) Yet instead of abandoning Europe as an ally, it should strive for a working division of labor in the military realm,[7] while integrating the potential of various other aspects of European power into its foreign policy thinking. Meanwhile, Europeans need to accept this new reality, and seek different channels for transatlantic dialogue. (c.f. Shapiro & Witney, 2009) Transatlantic relations need new institutions, both formal and informal. Such a framework may also be a useful tool for engaging emerging powers like China – an issue that will be discussed in the following section.

Engaging China: from G-2 to G-3

China is an unavoidable force in world politics, a "shaper" of global affairs, and therefore it is a factor to take into account in practically every issue area of importance for both the US and the European Union. The way the EU and the US

---

7   An emphasis on interoperability and a division of labor will secure US presence in Europe, while still offering some level of security to Eastern member states that are most in dread of an American withdrawal.

deal with the Asian giant reflects the problems of the respective foreign policies of the two powers; however, it also shows how these problems can be remedies through closer partnership.

American and foreign authors alike have been warning of China's rising power since the 1990s, arguing that it necessitated global actor engagement. Simply put, every state would soon need to have a sound China policy. Sino-American relations were quite precarious at the turn of the century: while the Clinton administration saw China as a strategic partner, President George W. Bush referred to the PRC as a "strategic rival", and openly confronted the Asian power on the issue of human rights and the grounded spy-plane incident in 2001. Though the common interest in anti-terrorism measures pushed the two states closer after 9/11, the US still continues to see China primarily as a threat. This threat gained a crucial economic component with the global economic crisis, since China is the single largest creditor of the United States. As we have discussed, Western calls for Chinese activism in the fight against recession have gone unheard. Beijing still relies on the old rhetoric: despite the meteoric rise of the economy, the political leadership presents China as a developing power, arguing that once it has achieved a sufficient level of development, it will be able and willing to deal with truly global issues (c.f. Chinese abstinence from the Kyoto Protocol). Yet empirically we see a China that is very much active globally and especially in Africa – take, for example, the Chinese navy's operations off the Somali coast, or the huge number of Chinese workers that needed to be evacuated from Libya. Its hunt for natural resources, and its interest in both the US and European debt will make China's interests clash with those of Europe and the United States. Yet beyond these contentious issues, China is also the biggest trading partner of both Atlantic powers – not counting, of course, each other. This interdependence requires a negotiated approach to the Communist power that is mutually beneficial for the respective economies.

The Obama administration's marked turn towards Asia thus seems an obvious choice, and Europe also needs to have a common China policy if it does not want to be left behind. US policies are still in flux, and largely depend on how China's growing power is interpreted. Whether the US is in decline and whether China is a rising rival seem like academic questions, but in policy terms they have far-reaching consequences: if China is seen as a threat, then the US needs to balance against this threat, but if China's ambitions can be reconciled with American interests and security commitments in the Pacific region, then a less confrontational approach is needed. Foreign policy is all about perceived threats, and China has the capabilities that can make it threatening. To the dismay of many experts, often the US seems to be thinking in worst-case scenarios when it comes to the PRC. Worst-case scenarios can rule out the peaceful, negotiated settlement of conflicts. The current China scare seems more like a fad: it would still take decades for Communist China to overtake the United States. At this early stage of its emergence, US hard balancing in Asia – e.g. building bases in the region – is misplaced as it very well might antagonize the Chinese. Instead, as more moderate voices argue, China should be engaged through diplomatic and economic means that are nevertheless backed by a strong US military presence in the region, one that can credibly deter potential aggression against US allies, most importantly against Taiwan. On the other hand, the Obama administration's diplomatic approach to China so far also seems to posit a number of crucial problems. For one it may be too optimistic. As Secretary of State Hillary Clinton remarked in 2009 after announcing the shift in US foreign policy: "The opportunities for us to work together are unmatched any-where in the world." (Quoted in Economy & Segal, 2009) Dialogue has so far been mostly conducted bilaterally, through the so-called G-2 framework. According to the related rhetoric, the G-2 enables the two powers to work hand in hand on any issue. The approach dates back to 2005, when it was supported by major US estab-lishment figures like Kissinger and Brzezinski. It took the place of the G-3 frame-work that also included the European Union. Yet the EU once again posited its major weakness: lacking a unified voice, it was not taken seriously by the other two members and was dropped in favor of the above bilateral framework. (Wong, 2010) Yet elevating the bilateral relationship of the G-2 raised expectations about the part-nership that cannot be met, and also exacerbate existing differences between Wash-ington and Beijing. As Economy and Segal (2009) argue, the inability of the US to effectively cooperate with China does not stem from a mismanagement of the re-lationship, but from a mismatched set of interests, values and capabilities. It would therefore be a huge mistake from the US side to assume that close bilateral relations could facilitate the harmonization of interests on a wide range of conflictual issues that includes Taiwan, Tibet, human rights and trade relations. Such an assumption is derived from a three-sided false premise that China is a status quo power, name-ly that it can be readily integrated into the existing, US-dominated, world order, that there is a set of core values around which cooperation can be built, and that other actors (great powers and international institutions) will accept China as a shaper of global affairs. (Wong, 2010)

The European Union's approach to China is not without problems either. As the European Council on Foreign Relations' sobering audit on EU-China rela-tions demonstrates, the EU makes a crucial mistake by treating China as a mal-leable polity that can be shaped by European civilian power. (Fox & Godement, 2009) Instead, China appears as a highly pragmatic power that knows how to ex-ploit the EU's weaknesses by splitting European member states along two fault lines: how to manage China economically and how to manage it politically, most notably on human rights issues. As the analysis shows, member states are all over the spectrum on these issues, making a unified policy yet again impossible. Since the EU's economic power is only comparable to that of China when it is pooled, the fact that member states have to deal with China individually – and even in opposition to fellow member states – often means that the outcome of these engagements is not favorable for the European side.

Seeing the problems with both the American and European approaches, the advantages of a joint approach are more tempting. Such a joint approach could lend the flexibility to the partners that they individually lack. Again, the first move lies with the European Union: it needs to develop a common China policy, a policy that is not only a prerequisite for a meaningful transatlantic partnership, but is also key to the effective representation of *common* European economic and political interests. The European Union needs to outgrow its post-Cold War attitudes that allowed it to pass the buck of global management to the hegemon and reap the peace dividend. (See Shapiro & Witney, 2009) Instead, the EU needs to appear more assertive for the United States, it needs to appear as a reliable partner. Such a partner could readily be reintegrated into a G-3 framework.

For a New Transatlantic Bargain

> The 'West' – if it still exists – needs a new narrative for the 21st century, and to underpin this, new institutions and structures of transatlantic dialogue transcending NATO and Cold War patterns are required. To do this constructively and without nostalgia is the main task for the foreign policy makers of the new US administration and the EU. (Guérot, 2009)

Transatlantic relations during the Obama presidency lack the turbulence and conflict both partners were used to for the better part of the 2000s. Even though both sides have repeatedly voiced their commitment to a continuation of the relationship, the United States is shifting its foreign policy focus to Asia and away from Europe – a change that can lead to weakened transatlantic ties, which would mean a fall into second rate power status for the European Union. The real danger for Europe in the short run does not lie in the loss of American hard security guarantees, but in the possibility that the US will exclude Europe from the management of global issues. If the signs truly point to an imminent crisis in the relationship, it will be different from previous ones: it will not be a clash over policies and symbolic issues, but will simply empty out and fade away in total indifference. As we have seen, the exclusion of Europe might seem logical when confronted with the often Babelian decision making of the Union, but in the long run it runs the risk that the US will be left alone with powers that do not share the fundamental values that guide its foreign policy, not to mention its interests. Europe still has weight in global affairs, and this weight is built around its economic and soft power. Due to the broad range of shared interests and values between the two sides of the Atlantic, this odd couple may serve as a crucial negotiator for the West in a multilateral world that is less guided by hard power.

Europe still seeks the US as a partner, but this partnership now has a price. The transatlantic partnership is not an end in itself, and effortless continuation of the post-Cold War setup is now nigh impossible: Europe has been dependent on American support for too long. Without the unity of purpose of the Cold War, and more importantly, in a stagnating economy of scarce resources, unlimited and unreciprocated US guarantees for Europe are a relic of the past. In this relationship, both sides need to change their mindsets, but whereas the US merely needs to be open to the inclusion of Europeans in the management of the international system – especially since emerging powers such as China do not seem to be willing to bear the underlying costs – Europe needs to be more pro-active in building more diversified capabilities and thereby gaining America's trust. On the one hand, with the US withdrawing its forces from the old continent, some level of European buildup will be necessary. But such a buildup can be guided by concerns of interoperability within NATO, rather than in building parallel structures. On the other hand, Europe does not have the necessary funds to match US power, but luckily it does not have to do so. The strength of the transatlantic relationship continues to lie in the compatibility of values, interests and also capabilities. Where Europe lacks the punch (military), the US excels, and where the US invests relatively little (civilian tools such as multilateral diplomacy), the European Union still carries weight. Critics could easily argue that European power is contingent on American hard power, and that it is merely an idealistic illusion, something that only works when circumstances are favorable – mostly in those issues that bear little importance for the global power structure. An effective partnership could remedy the first concern. As for the latter issue, recent events have demonstrated that Europe can still act as a reliable agent of the Western world. In Libya, humanitarian intervention was carried out mostly by European powers, assisted by the United States from the sideline, showing the potential of interoperability of forces within NATO. And in Iran, the US and the EU are putting pressure on the regime to abandon its nuclear program, using different approaches. While the EU relies on economic sanctions and multilateral diplomacy, the US does not exclude a military strike. Whatever the solution to this crisis might turn out to be, it is a clear example of how the European Union can apply both its civilian tools and its hard power (coercive economic diplomacy) in concert with the US. The two powers can continue to play the game of "good cop, bad cop" where a saber-rattling US – with Israel as its proxy – threatens with a military strike, while the EU offers negotiation as a way out for the Islamic republic: talk to *us*, and we will deal with the United States.

A set of common interests, including maintaining free trade, promoting democracy, fighting new security threats and managing rising powers, makes the transatlantic relationship an indispensable tool for both partners. The European Union needs the United States in order to be able to shape global affairs, while the United States needs a strong Europe to share the burdens of managing the international system in conformity with Western values and interests. But it is not about the lack of resources: due to the interconnectedness of the modern international system, the complex set of issues the transatlantic partners are forced to deal with are not exclusively Euroatlantic in their nature – take, for example, the problem of global goods. These issues necessarily involve cooperation with other states. The US will remain the world's strongest superpower for decades to come, but it will not easily have its way anymore. No matter how much the Washington elite shuns multilateral diplomacy for its sluggishness, in many cases the bilateral approach favored by the US in the case of China might not yield the best results, but instead offer the EU a chance to rely on its long tradition of multilateral diplomacy.

In conclusion, the transatlantic relationship needs an institutionalized coordinative framework and a sustainable burden-sharing equilibrium that is acceptable for both parties. Yet such an equilibrium need not be defined in purely military terms: a new world with new challenges requires a diversification of means, one that should include both hard and soft power elements. The European Union does possess the right capabilities to supplement the US toolkit, yet it has been missing the required level of actorness to actually implement them. The Union was more often than not unable to appear with a united voice, forcing the Americans to recite Henry Kissinger's sarcastic remark: if one wants to call Europe, what is the phone number? Instead, the EU needs to develop a unified stance on global issues and appear as an assertive, reliable partner for the United States. A more assertive EU would gain greater influence and be an equal of the US. This is where real partnership starts.

Bibliography

Andrews, D. M. (Ed.) (2005). *The Atlantic alliance under stress: Relations after Iraq.* New York: Cambridge University Press.

Baldwin, P. (2009). *Narcissism of minor differences: How America and Europe are alike – An essay in numbers.* Oxford: Oxford University Press.

Beckley, M. (2011). China's century? Why America's edge will endure. *International Security, 36(3)*, 41–78.

Bereuter, D., & Lis, J. (2003). Broadening the transatlantic relationship. *The Washington Quarterly, 27(1)*, 147–162.

Brzezinski, Z., & Scowcroft, B. (2008). *America and the world – Conversations on the future of American foreign policy.* New York: Basic Books.

Bull, H, (1982). Civilian power Europe: A contradiction in terms? *Journal of Common Market Studies, 21(1/2)*, 149.

Calleo, D. P. (1970). *The Atlantic fantasy: The U.S., NATO, and Europe.* Baltimore: Johns Hopkins Press.

Carr. E. H. (1991). *The twenty years' crisis, 1919-1939: An introduction to the study of international relations.* London: Macmillan.

Cronin, P. et al. (2012). *Cooperation from strength: The United States, China and the South China Sea.* Report CNAS. Retrieved from http://www.cnas.org/southchinasea

Dempsey, J. (2012). "U.S. Sees Europe as Not Pulling Its Weight Militarily" *The New York Times*, Febr. 6, 2012.

Deni, J. (2011) American leadership and NATO: Does forward presence still matter? *European Consortium for Political Research*, 2011 Conference Reykjavik, Iceland. Retrieved from http://www.ecprnet.eu/MyECPR/proposals/reykjavik/uploads/papers/3268.pdf

Department of Defense – DoD (2012). *Defense strategic guidance.* Retrieved from http://www.defense.gov/news/Defense_Strategic_Guidance.pdf

Duchêne, F. (1972). Europe's Role in World Peace. In R. Mayne (Ed.), *Europe tomorrow: Sixteen Europeans look ahead*. London: Fontana.

Economy, E. C., & Segal, A. (2009). The G-2 mirage: Why the United States and China are not ready to upgrade ties. *Foreign Affairs May/June 2009*.

Fox, J., & Godement, F. (2009). *A power audit of EU-China relations*. Report, European Council on Foreign Relations. Retrieved from http://ecfr.eu/page/-/documents/A_Power_Audit_of_EU_China_Relations.pdf

German Marshall Fund of the United States – GMF (2011). *Transatlantic trends: Leaders 2011*. Retrieved from http://www.transatlantic-trends.org

Guérot, U. (2009). Obama and the future of transatlantic relations. European Council on Foreign Relations. Retrieved from http://ecfr.eu/content/entry/commentary_obama_eu_us_ecfr_guerot

Hamilton, D. S., & Quinlan, J. P. (2011). *The transatlantic economy 2011: Annual survey of jobs, trade and investment between the United States and Europe*. Washington DC: Washington D.C.

Hill, C. (1993), The capability-expectations gap, or conceptualizing Europe's international role. *Journal of Common Market Studies 31(3)*, 305-328.

Hill, C. (1996). *The actors in Europe's foreign policy*. New York: Taylor & Francis.

Hoffmeister, F. (2007). Outsider or forerunner? Recent developments under international and European law on the status of the European Union in international organizations and treaty bodies. *Common Market Law Review, 44*, 41-68.

Hyde-Price, A. (2006). Normative power Europe: A realist critique. *Journal of European Public Policy, 13(2)*, 217-234.

Jacques, M. (2009). *When China rules the world: The rise of the middle kingdom and the end of the western world*. New York: Penguin, 2009.

Kagan, R. (1998). The benevolent empire. *Foreign Policy, 111(111)*, 24-35.

Kagan, R. (2003). *Of paradise and power: America and Europe in the new world order*. New York: Knopf.

Kagan, R. (2008). *The return of history and the end of dreams*. New York: Alfred A. Knopf.

Kagan, R. (2012). Not fade away – The myth of American decline. *The New Republic, January 11, 2012*.

Kiernan, P. D. (2012). *Becoming China's bitch: and nine more catastrophes we must avoid right now*. New York: Turner.

Kissinger, H. (1965). *The troubled partnership: A re-appraisal of the Atlantic alliance*. New York: McGraw-Hill.

Krauthammer, C. (1990). The unipolar moment. *Foreign Affairs, 70(1,*: 23–33.

Krugman, P. Is our economy healing? *The New York Times, January 22, 2012* http://www.nytimes.com/2012/01/23/opinion/krugman-is-our-economy-healing.html?_r=2

Kupchan, C. (2012). Sorry Mitt: it won't be an American Century *Foreign Policy Magazine*, on-line edition Retrieved from http://www.foreignpolicy.com/articles/2012/02/06/it_won_t_be_an_american_century

Larsen, H. (2002). The EU: A global military actor? *Cooperation and Conflict, 37*, 283-30.

Layne, C. (2009). The waning of U.S. hegemony—Myth or reality? A review essay. *International Security, 34(1),* 147–172.

Lindberg, T. (Ed.) (2005). *Beyond paradise and power : Europe, America, and the future of a troubled partnership.* New York: Routledge.

Lundestad, G. (1986). Empire by invitation? The United States and Western Europe, 1945–1952. *Journal of Peace Research, 23(3),* 263–77.

Lunderstad, G. (1998). *Empire by integration: The United States and European integration, 1945-1997.* Oxford: Oxford University Press.

Lundestad, G. (2005). *The United States and Western Europe Since 1945: From "empire" by invitation to transatlantic drift.* Oxford: Oxford University Press.

Manners, I. (2002). Normative power Europe: A contradiction in terms? *Journal of Common Market Studies, 40(2),* 235.

Meunier, S. (2010). Do transatlantic relations still matter? Conference forum, *Perspectives on Europe, 40(1).*

Mold, A. (Ed.) (2007). *EU development policy in a changing world: Challenges for the 21st century.* Amsterdam: Amsterdam University Press.

Moravcsik, A. (1993) Preferences and power in the European Community: A liberal intergovernmentalist approach. *Journal of Common Market Studies, 31(4),* 473-524.

Moravcsik, A. (2002). The quiet superpower. *Newsweek, 17 June 2002.*

Moravcsik, A. (2003). How Europe can win without an army. *Financial Times, 3 April 2003.*

Moravcsik, A. (2010). Why is Europe, not China or India, the second superpower of the 21st century? *Radio Interview on WILL/Illinois Public Radio* (27 January 2010).

Nemeth, B. (2012). How to bridge the 'three islands': The future of European military co-operation. *Ideas on Europe: Strategic Snapshot* No. 4.

Nye, Joseph S. (2004). *Soft power: The means to success in world politics.* New York: Public Affairs.

Nye, J. S. (2006). Soft power and European-American affairs. In T. L. Ilgen (Ed.), *Hard power, soft power, and the future of transatlantic relations* (pp. 25-38). Burlington, VT: Ashgate.

Nye, J. S. (2011). *The future of power.* New York: Perseus.

Obama, B. (2010). Foreword: National Security Strategy, May 2010. *The White House.* Retrieved from http://www.whitehouse.gov/sites/default/files/rss_viewer/national_security_strategy.pdf.

Parello-Plesner, J., & Khanna, P. (2012). Stop fretting about Beijing as a global policeman. *European Council on Foreign Relations* Retrieved from

http://ecfr.eu/content/entry/commentary_stop_fretting_about_
beijing_as_a_global_policeman

Rasch, M. B. (2008). *The European Union at the United Nations: The functioning and coherence of EU external representation in a state-centric environment.* Leiden: Martinus Nijhoff Publishers.

Shapiro, J., & Witney, N. (2009). Towards a post-American Europe: A power audit of EU-US relations. *European Council on Foreign Relations.* Retrieved from http://ecfr.3cdn.net/05b80f1a80154dfc64_x1m6b gxc2.pdf

Solana, J. (2005). Speech on 'Shaping an Effective EU Foreign Policy'. *Konrad Adenauer Foundation* (Brussels).

Stockholm International Peace Research Institute (SIPRI) (2010). *Military database: The 15 countries with the highest military expenditure in 2010* Retrieved from http://www.sipri.org/research/armaments/milex/resultoutput/15majorspenders

Toje, A. (2008). *America, the EU and strategic culture: Renegotiating the transatlantic bargain.* New York: Routledge.

Toje, A. (2011). *The European Union as a small power: After the post-Cold War.* New York: Palgrave Macmillan.

Treverton, G. F. (2006). A post-modern transatlantic alliance. In T. L. Ilgen (Ed.), *Hard Power, Soft Power, and the Future of Transatlantic Relations* (pp. 39-59). Burlington, VT : Ashgate.

Walt, S. M. (2012). A new kind of NATO. Blog entry. Retrieved from http://walt.foreignpolicy.com/posts/2012/01/11/a_new_kind_of_nato

Wong, R. Y. (2010). G-3?: Conceptualising a US-EU-China triad in international relations. Conference paper, ECPR 5th Pan-European Conference. Porto, Portugal 23-26 June 2010.

Woolcock, S. (2011). *European Union economic diplomacy: The role of the EU in external economic relations.* Burlington: Ashgate.

Zakaria, F. (2008). *The post-American world.* New York: W.W. Norton & Company.

The EU and Russia – Emerging rival or dynamic partner?

András Deák, Ph.D.

EU-Russia dialogue belongs to the relatively new, but also to the most ambivalent relations of the EU's external policies. The Soviet Union recognized the European Communities as a legal entity only in 1989. During the slightly more than 20 years since then, the relationship has reflected a high level of volatility and divisiveness, both in Russia and especially in and among the European institutions. We have witnessed sympathy and enthusiasm following the political changes, anger and concern during the Chechen wars, hope and skepticism during Putin's first term, and fatigue and perplexity recently. A good deal of the related controversies stem from the inherent conflicts between nation states, in this case a great power such as Russia and the complex nature of the European Union. The latter has hardly anything that can relate to Russia's "Hobbesian" world. The Russian notion of the EU, both in terms of a geopolitical reality and as a modernization model, is weak and often hesitant, even unwilling. Russia would need a strong commitment, an integrationist attitude, in order to enter the labyrinth of European politics, but that has been present only for extremely short periods during the past two decades. At the same time, for the European Union Russia has always represented a great temptation. Russia always seemed to be in its close proximity. Its significance in terms of economy and human ties has always been too strong for the EU to handle the country only as a distant partner, like China or India. The EU always wanted to find an added value for these relations, maybe something less than transformative and integrationist, but definitely something that would represent this increased significance for each other. Russia has been too big to perceive as a distant planet on the European periphery, but too small to regard as a sun of a neighboring system.

Russia and Europe undoubtedly have become much closer during the last 20 years. It is obvious that in all fields of the relations, in economic, human, political and security aspects, ties are stronger and deeper. With reasonable caution this could be qualified as a success story, especially if analyzed in a longer historical context. However, uncertainties around the EU-Russia relationship remain highly tangible. Despite progress in the dialogue, the parties have failed to establish a perspective and a consensus around it. Neither disengagement nor integration are realistic options in such an environment. During the last 20 years a large number of different strategies have been put to the test in the bilateral relations – from soft integrationalism to soft coercion, from containment to pragmatic inclusion – without any particular success. Not unconnected with this, EU-

Russia relations have also remained relatively low-profile, especially if compared with EU relations vis-à-vis other regions. Russia has not built up a true "strategic relationship" with any other major global power, and the one with the EU has also remained largely rhetorical. It was rather the European Union that made some attempts to increase the intensity of the relations in some periods, but these could not bring lasting results. Not surprisingly, some authors even question whether "more" is always "better" in these relations. (Gerrits, 2008, p. 2) At least as long as the possibility of a larger consensus about common strategies is not present, perhaps the existing, pragmatic approach with its day-to-day management of emerging issues may result in more benefits and less political damage for both sides.

Historical overview

During the first half of the 1990s EU-Russia relations emerged in the context of the general post-Socialist transformative logic. Russian democratic and market economy reforms seemed to be on the right path, even if definitely on a more rocky one than those in the Central European region. Russia had been returning to its "European family" after the long decades of Communism. The Partnership and Cooperation Agreement (PCA),[1] signed in 1994, was the first, initial step in putting relations on a more institutionalized foundation. The PCA is a relatively extensive document, with a primary focus on technical and trade issues. It also outlines the institutional setting of the relations and puts them into a very much disputed democratic and human rights conditionality framework. The document set rather humble prospects for progress, like free trade negotiations when Russia joins the WTO. The Russian PCA is very similar to the other Partnership and Cooperation Agreements signed with almost all post-Soviet states over the years. But it is also a very good reflection of the existing realities, opening up the way for an integrationist trajectory. It was a cautious, but necessary step, suggesting a realistic positive scenario for strengthening relations.

Uncertainties arose as early as the mid-1990s, in parallel with the turn in Moscow's policies, a more authoritarian style in its domestic behavior, and harsher foreign policy rhetoric. The first Chechen war (1994-96) caused a long impasse in the ratification process of the PCA and old skepticism regarding Moscow's underlying intentions were revived in the EU. The EP and some national parliaments showed increased unwillingness to approve the document, while the Commission and the Council tried to maintain some sort of cautious engagement. The EU relations reflected a high level of sensitivity regarding Russian domestic policy issues, which concerns are traditionally much less accentuated in bilateral relations. European decision-makers also had to realize that they overlooked a good deal of Russian ignorance vis-à-vis the EU in general. Moscow primarily focused on economic matters, and since the trade-related parts of the PCA came into force

---

1   http://trade.ec.europa.eu/doclib/docs/2003/november/tradoc_114138.pdf

in 1995 due to an interim agreement, it has lost much of its interest. These problems coupled with other, more important issues on the periphery of the EU, such as the Balkan wars and approaching enlargement, put these relations on the back burner. In the second half of the 1990s both parties were pretty much preoccupied with their internal and other, foreign policy issues.

The "golden age" of EU-Russian relations came during Putin's first presidency. The new Russian leader had a profound experience of Russian weakness, economic backwardness and foreign policy isolation. He inherited a humiliated and weak country lacking any certainty that the situation would be much better in the years to come. Russia was highly dependent on the West in terms of financial credits and capital. The small, but influential circle of oligarchs openly lobbied for improving the Western nexus, primarily led by their own private interests and implicitly hoping for additional guarantees of preserving their status and personal wealth. In addition, Putin had a solid German background due to his former work. US policies vis-à-vis Russia did not offer anything reliable during the period of the new Bush administration. Europe was the most accessible partner, a Western anchor for a weak Russia, which could potentially offer everything that was thought necessary by the Kremlin for the modernization of the country. As Dmitry Trenin pointed out in 2001: "It [the EU – A.D.] is the only political-economic 'large space' into which Russia can integrate once her 'large space' – Eurasia – has ceased to exist." (Trenin, 2001, p. 298) Capital, know-how, trade, more leverage in the international arena, all seemed to be at hand in Europe. The EU also had a relatively calm period, it had enough time and resources to respond the Russian engagement.

As Andre Gerrits (2008, p. 1) puts it, "long-term interests are easier to formulate than the policies to realize them". While Russia openly engaged with many European leaders during these years, like Tony Blair or Gerhardt Schröder, and there was a clear notion of an increased set of potential common interests, it was pretty difficult to put these efforts into a comprehensive framework at the practical level. Russia never, not even in these relatively pro-European years, expressed a wish to join the European Union in the long term. What is more, it openly refused to accept any model that would suggest some kind of hierarchy between the sides, and insisted on bilateral and equal negotiations regarding the respective *acquis communitaire*. This became clear when Moscow refused to take part in the Eastern Partnership initiative and Brussels accepted its reservations. The four "Common Spaces" were established to manage the patchwork of the relations and elaborate mutually beneficial compromises.

This was not easy. Russia was not a WTO member, which put a barrier to further trade liberalization. Furthermore, Russia did not have a broad set of foreign investments which could stimulate lobbying and further incentives to approximation. Russia, like other post-Soviet states, remained a predominantly domestic ownership regime, and issues related to external trade were negotiated between a national bourgeoisie and the government. This context traditionally has its constraints in relation to economic opening. Russian skepticism regarding EU jurisdiction in prominent issues like energy, technical standards and foreign policies was high and well understandable. Some of these policies were in the nascent phase, others were pretty far from Russian realities. At the same time European institutions, primarily the European Parliament, and public opinion had an understandable sensitivity to human rights and democratic freedoms in Russia. Even if the deficits of the first Putin years, such as the second Chechen war or the new regulation of the media, could have been interpreted in a normal consolidation narrative, these issues obviously put a stress on the relations. The fact alone that the EU tried to establish a credible conditionality in the relations presupposed the existence of a hierarchy between the sides. Not surprisingly, some years later the concept of "sovereign democracy" was to respond to all these criticisms and close a fruitless debate on conditionality issues. Moscow qualified itself as a "democratic state in its own way" and did not allow others to question this statement. It was a semi-official formulation of the wish to end all US and EU criticism in these fields, and to exclude conditionalities from the relations. A large number of different solutions have been elaborated (Bordachev & Romanova, 2003; Barysch, 2004), a high number of different consultative bodies have been established to provide selective, sectoral integration, and some highly visible summits were held on the EU-Russia level. (St. Petersburg, 2003) However, it is right to say that EU-Russia relations significantly lagged behind the intensity achieved on the general European-Russian level.

It was again Russian domestic politics and US-Russia relations that put an end to this engagement. The 2003-2004 electoral cycle in Russia, the arrest of Mikhail Khodorkovsky, and the color revolutions across the post-Soviet periphery sparked a new wave of mutual disengagement. The EU-Russia dialogue was practically frozen, very well symbolized by the failure to renew the PCA in 2008. The European Union desperately tried to mediate in conflicts like the 2008 August war between Georgia and Russia, or the 2009 January gas dispute between Ukraine and Russia, without any particular success. Despite the US-Russia reset under the Obama administration, there has been no significant recovery in EU-Russia relations. The dialogue has been in an impasse for years and no serious efforts have been made to revitalize it.

This clumsy institutional progress is in sharp contrast with developments on the everyday level. Mutual trade has been growing rapidly during the last 20 years. Russia became the biggest external energy supplier of the EU in the fields of natural gas, oil and coal. Human relations are obviously stronger than ever. Russia has reluctantly accepted the EU's presence in post-Soviet conflict zones such as Transnistria, Georgia and Karabakh, and takes the EU's mercantilist challenge seriously in Ukraine or Moldova. The relations have become more multifaceted and diversified, and even without political interference they lie on much more solid fundaments than two decades ago. Bilateral relations could quickly develop without political and institutional back-up. Excluding conflicts over energy issues, progress was achieved without significant tensions: there have been no serious fears about Russian immigration into the EU, and no concerns about large deficits in mutual trade. But fears are justified – will this weak and fragile relationship be able to manage emerging conflicts in the future?

The four freedoms and Russia

Even though Russia is often qualified as a "security giant, economic dwarf", in particular vis-à-vis the European Union, this statement needs to be critically assessed. Russian GDP is indeed more than 10 times smaller than EU output,[2] but it is still by far the biggest economy in the proximity of the old continent. Russia represents a potentially bigger market than the new members (EU-10) combined, and its output exceeds that of Turkey twofold. In terms of aggregate growth potential it belongs to the BRIC group, significantly and positively extrapolating past growth trajectories. Its sheer size is very well reflected in trade relations with the EU. In 2011 Russia was the third biggest trading partner of the Union after the US and China, accounting for 9.5% of its total external trade turnover.[3] Despite the high share of energy in EU imports, Russia still constituted the fourth biggest export market (7.1% of total exports) for EU goods.

EU-Russian external trade is big in size, but peripheral in structure. Russian exports almost exclusively consists of fuels and raw materials, while EU exports are predominantly high added value machinery and equipment (Figure 1). This phenomenon decreases the short-term gains from a potential trade liberalization process on the Russian side: it will not gain too much in terms of export markets and would decrease the budget's customs revenues. Thus the main rationale behind trade liberalization is the Russian raison d'être, long-term competitive benefits and the drive for technical modernization, arguments which often fail to gain critical support from governments. Trade opening considerations can be offset by the temptation for some protectionism, based on the relatively large market size in some segments. Russian consumption has been booming during the last 12 years, and given its sheer market size Moscow has a strong leverage on trade issues vis-à-vis major companies. A typical example involves new car sales where Russia has a still growing market, which was equal to France in 2011.[4] Protectionist measures in these segments have proved to be relatively successful, forcing almost all major car makers to establish some assembly factories in Russia. Large segments in the agricultural industry can also be seen as an example, where foreign investment entered the country in order to supply the domestic market and by-pass the barriers existing in foreign trade. Not surprisingly, Moscow pursued a gradual and cautious liberalization policy with strong sectoral protectionist measures prior to WTO accession in order to optimize its trade relations. In this light it is still an open question whether Russia would be very much interested in free trade or even opening up large segments of its service sectors.

---

2   1,487.29 vs. 16,300.51 billion current USD; 2.4% vs. 25.8% of world total in 2010 according to IMF World Economy Outlook, 2012.

3   Eurostat, 2012.

4   ACEA, http://www.acea.be/news/news_detail/new_vehicle_registrations_by_country/ and http://aebrus.ru/application/views/aebrus/files/press_releases_files/aeb_newcarslcvs_jan_eng_12_01_2012_09_43_04_file_releases_2012_01_12_13_18_33.pdf

However, the major differences vis-à-vis CEE states and other European peripheries are the structural ones in FDI. Russia does not have a broad fundament of export-oriented foreign direct investments, similar to those in the new members and Western Balkan countries. Net FDI stock as a share of GDP was 5.1% in Rssia, while it was 51% in the Czech Republic and 28.7% in Poland as of October 2012.[5] Most of these investments came into the energy sector, but also to agriculture, machinery construction, banking and insurance. The main attraction, apart from resources, is the steadily growing domestic market. While in the CEE states investors came to get the gains from cheap local inputs, like a professional workforce, and increase their competitive standing in external markets, this is not exactly the case in Russia. Not underestimating the significance of these trends, these investors are not sufficient to provide a solid basis for micro-level integration and to give the necessary bottom-up drive for EU-Russia trade liberalization.

Figure 1: EU-Russia foreign trade composition, 2011

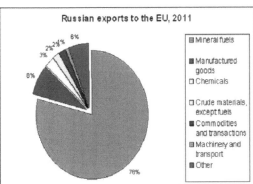

Source: *EC.*

5   OECD, http://www.oecd.org/daf/internationalinvestment/FDI%20in%20figures.pdf

These statistics are important as they demonstrate the difficulties involved in the EU-Russia relations. The bilateral relations cannot be differentiated from the general trade policy trends. The turnover cannot be separated from the mainstream policies on each side. This is particularly true for Russia, where the EU has an almost 50% share in total turnover. Thus polemics about Russian economic modernization or future EU trade policies and their implications for trade and investment policies, as well as normative aspects, directly affect EU-Russia economic relations, in particular negotiations on the Common Economic Space (CES). The drivers in the bilateral relations are basically identical with those in general policy trends. In this respect mutual skepticism is well justified. Russian authors tend to think that only the traditional aspects of trade liberalization, the free movement of goods, services, capital and people, and the approximation of some technical specifications would be beneficial for the country. Normative aspects, environmental and social rules may be counterproductive, given the gap between the developed, mature, highly regulated European economies and the oil-dependent, shaky economy of Russia. (Mau & Novikov, 2002; Sutela, 2005)

Selective approximation is not a popular idea on the European side either. If it is not a selective integration, like the EEA, but some sort of set of special, equal bilateral arrangements with Russia, it would further complicate the already complex external economic system of the EU. Moreover, most of the barriers facing European exporters are non-tariffal, non-normative in character, such as non-transparent customs or visa administration, bureaucracy or corruption. These institutional problems can only be efficiently addressed by universal or at least sectoral free movement regimes, if not by the host country's own decisions. Thus it is not only its integrationist logic, but purely economic rationale that pushes Brussels towards more ambitious targets or restrains it from any further offer.

The parallel integration process in the post-Soviet space further complicates EU-Russia relations. (Ludvig, 2008) Russia has been making serious efforts to establish a Customs Union with some of its neighbors (Belarus, Kazakhstan and potentially Ukraine). The EU looks at these efforts with understandable skepticism and with ignorance. However, the Russian commitment seems to be credible and very well questions not only the relevant target models in EU-Russian relations, but also those in the other bilateral relations. This is particularly important in the case of Ukraine. While the EU has elaborated the concept of DCFTA regimes for the Eastern partners, with a focus on Ukraine, Kiev's entry to the Russian Customs Union would practically exclude this outcome. Not surprisingly the Customs Union is predominantly perceived as being in competition with the EU-related projects, pointing to a situation whereby the EU will have to negotiate on trade and potentially even on harmonization issues with a Customs Union in which Moscow has a dominant role.

Thus even in the economic relations, which will constitute the backbone of the dialogue, it is difficult to outline a final target, the finalité of the cooperation. Despite the economic-oriented mindset of Moscow and the EU's indisputably strong legitimacy in this field, the cooperation lacks a vision or even a short-term perspective. It is not clear to what extent the CES will be based on harmonization of the EU acquis or negotiations and bilateral agreements; whether the result should be similar to "EFTA" and if so, which fields can be included (e.g. energy) or it will be some sort of new model, more similar to that between the US and the EU. If Russian efforts to create a strong Customs Union in post-Soviet space are successful, the question regarding the negotiating subjects can also be raised.

Nevertheless, in the current situation the relations do not really need a final perspective. The WTO accession talks with the EU were open-ended and conducted in a highly pragmatic manner. These clearly showed that the major difficulties were represented mainly by non-trade issues. Disputes arose around services like banking, insurance and air traffic, and in the segment of agricultural subventions. The conventional set for an industrial free trade regime involves a range of accessible solutions and the sides can still move on when the WTO rules are implemented in the bilateral relations. Free trade is strongly supported by some Russian export industries such as the metallurgical and chemical industries, thus the barriers mainly lay in the significance of budgetary income from customs duties and the growing protectionist attitude of Moscow. However, industrial free trade does not constitute a developed form of integration. Unlike the early years of the European Communities, competitive gains and economic approximation rest much more on normative engagement than before. Thus it is difficult to speak about real integration without progress in relation to the other freedoms, namely in relation to the movement of capital, services and people.

The situation is strikingly differentiated in the case of free movement of people. As is demonstrated in Figure 2, delegations in Russia are extremely "busy" in a global comparison, taking the first nine rankings on the list of issued visas. These numbers are even more astonishing if we take into account that some of the more permissive states issue primarily multi-entry visas, like Austria in Moscow or Finland in St. Petersburg (respectively 98.8% and 96%). (Popescu, 2011) These statistics partly underpin Russian criticism that the current visa regime is not in line with the turnover, causes disproportional damage to relations and the further use of these softly prohibitive practices is discriminatory. As different practices on the EU's side show, the national capitals also have varying attitudes: some Southern countries like Italy, Spain or Greece and some neighbors like Finland are actively lobbying for easing the regime. Surprisingly Germany, a long-standing partner, has the most reservations about Russian visa-free travel. As Salminen and Moshes asserted, there seems to be no correlation between the visa relations and political relations. (Salminen & Moshes, 2009, p. 7)

Figure 2: TOP15 EU national foreign delegations by numbers of visa issued

Biggest EU Consulates (by number of visas)	Total Visas Issued
1. Finnish Consulate in St. Petersburg	738,525
2. Spanish Consulate in Moscow	438,182
3. Italian Consulate in Moscow	434,182
4. Greek Consulate in Moscow	327,848
5. French Consulate in Moscow	251,713
6. German Consulate in Moscow	224,920
7. Czech Consulate in Moscow	205,932
8. Finish Consulate in Moscow	125,439
9. Austrian Consulate in Moscow	111,951
10. German Consulate in Kiev	97,171
11. French Consulate in Istanbul	95,650
12. Italian Consulate in Beijing	84,882
13. German Consulate in Beijing	78,573
14. French Consulate in Algiers	74,017
15. French Consulate in Shanghai	73,112

Source: *Popescu 2011.*

Nevertheless, arguments in favor of caution are also justified. Russia is one of the biggest exporters of asylum-seekers together with Afghanistan and Serbia. (Popescu, 2011) Visa-free travel is also a political issue and in a post-Soviet comparison Russia still belongs to the least cooperative countries. It also has conflict zones, like the North Caucasus, which can produce a large number of refugees if the local situation changes. Not surprisingly, visa-free travel has remained a long-term goal since 2003 in EU-Russia relations. Unlike Russian assurances that the whole system can be eliminated as soon as the EU decides to do so, the realistic approach can only be selective, focusing on particular groups. The practice of long-term (five years) multi-entry visas for reliable individuals is the most popular among experts. (Salminen & Moshes, 2009; Batory Foundation, 2009) Still, this is a unique issue with the potential of short-term progress.

Unbundled future? – cooperation in the field of energy

Undoubtedly energy is the most intensive and at the same time the most controversial field of cooperation. Russia has more than a 25% share of supplies of oil and gas in EU markets, and is by far the biggest exporter of these goods to the Community. It has a quasi-monopoly on the Eastern flank of the Union, but even the big economies like Germany, Italy and France are heavily dependent on

Russian energy. In contrast with what many believe, the cooperation has a rather short history. Large-scale oil and gas links emerged only in the late 1970s and early 1980s, even in the Socialist bloc countries, but have been permanently increasing since then, in terms of both volume and significance. For Russia the old continent is the only and exclusive trading partner, its Far Eastern diversification efforts are pretty new developments in this respect.

The EU-Russia energy link is far broader than other similar relations of the partners, and covers not only oil and gas. Russia became one of the major coal exporters to the old continent during the 2000s and the relations also have a nuclear fuel and technology aspect, particularly in the case of post-Socialist members. Even minor-scale electricity exports are present in the case of the Baltic states and Finland. If we look at the map of pan-European infrastructure and energy transfers and ignore political borders, Russia and the EU are in the same entity stretching from the Atlantic to beyond the Urals. Neither the Middle East or the West African suppliers, nor the US has such a strong coupling with Europe.

These relations are to a great extent depoliticized and have an established pattern, very much similar to those of global standards of the particular fuels. Despite the sheer size of the relations and their importance for both sides, it is difficult to find anything particularly specific or qualitatively different from existing global standards. The sides did not provide an added value for the relations, except in terms of size. Russia is no more unique for the EU than Libya, Algeria or Qatar. There is a slow vertical integration process at the corporate level, but its level is far from those in Norway or the Netherlands, and its achievements are definitely not irreversible. In the case of oil and oil products, Russian exporters joined the liquid world market emerging after the oil crises of the early 1970s. The patterns of oil trade have not changed very much since then, resulting in a relative peaceful continuation of oil trade between the sides up to the present day. Apart from some environmental and traffic regulations, generating a number of small-scale policy conflicts between the sides, EU-Russia relations remain rather smooth. The EC does not have a particular regulatory set in this field and Russia does not have a privileged position on the oil market. The same is particularly true for the coal market and with some reservations for the market of nuclear fuels. Not surprisingly, when EU-Russian energy relations are discussed most authors mean exclusively or primarily gas relations. Natural gas represents only one-fifth of the mutual trade in terms of value, but it definitely has a special role due to its fuel specifics.

Energy cooperation also had different narratives and contexts during these years. During the Cold War era West German gas imports became a divisive issue in the transatlantic relations between Bonn and Washington. The US criticized these projects as they provided additional hard currency income for Moscow and posed an energy supply risk for the Alliance. By contrast, at the time of perestroika during the late 1980s, when EC-Russia relations had only started to emerge, close relations seemed to provide synergic effects on the bilateral level. According to the Lubbers plan, heavily lobbied by the EC, cooperation would have been enhanced by European investments into the Soviet, later Russian energy sector, providing more volume for exports to Europe. This would have provided improved economic conditions for the ailing Eastern economy. At the practical level it meant the Energy Charter Treaty, outlining a common, liberalized system for energy trade, transit and investments. Not surprisingly, this transformative effort has gradually lost its attractiveness for most of the involved producers (among others Norway) and for Russia. (Konoplyanik, 2010) It would have constrained sovereignty over national resources and the whole cooperation was heavily consumer-oriented. Russia had been moving away from these Western models as early as the mid-1990s and by the mid-2000s, simultaneously with the growing significance of the sector in the Russian economy, the Kremlin gradually prevented foreign access to the industry.

Nevertheless, even without a transformative potential, energy relations remained multi-faceted and can be considered from many different aspects. Even if the EU-Russia energy link represents one of the strongest bilateral relations globally in its category, these relations are set in the permanently changing global energy patterns. Global sectoral trends, independently from their nature, influence the long-term perspectives of these relations. Furthermore, EU-Russia energy trade understandably has a strong mercantilist aspect. Much of the Russian export revenues come from European consumers. Consequently, market outlooks and growth potentials have a direct impact on sectoral expectations and development strategies, and indirectly on the state and level of Russian welfare. Since oil and gas constitute roughly two-thirds of total Russian exports and half of the budgetary revenues, it would be difficult not to look at this issue as being of increased significance for Moscow. Some of these mercantilist aspects and market growth expectations stem from non-articulated, non-policy factors, such as economic growth in the European economies. Energy demand is determined primarily by economic output, accordingly future growth potential is determined by anticipated economic growth. Many other factors are not directly Russia-related, but policy-oriented, like climate policy or some aspects of the single energy market policies. In these cases the EU pursues unilateral policies and ignores the implications for Russian producers. Furthermore, since the accession of the new members and particularly since the 2009 gas crisis, security of supply has become an important issue in EU policies. This has a strong regional but also an almost exclusive Russian focus, involving an increased political and ideological element.

It is difficult to find a leitmotiv for EU-Russian energy relations in such a complex environment. Security of supply arguments among the new members are often referred to as being among those that influence the relationship. But from a mercantilist point of view this involves only a handful of noisy governments, sometimes with the least dependence on Russian supplies among the EU-8, and with limited potential to change anything significantly on the EU level. On the other hand, climate targets like 20-20-20, environmental legislation about oil products or capacity allocations and legislative packages in relation to the gas markets have a huge input in EU-Russian relations. It is unlikely that the EC would open up these issues for negotiations with external suppliers. These are core common policies, exclusively internal matters of the EU. Thus skepticism, regarding the scope and the nature of the common external energy policy is very well justified, due to the complexity of the issue.

If we look at the history of EU-Russia energy relations through the prism of these three dimensions, namely global energy trends, sector-related policies and security considerations, their combination appeared to be relatively balanced. Until the 2008 financial crisis the notion of future energy scarcity was relatively strong among European decision-makers. The expectation of a future rise in gas imports was particularly strong. According to a DG Tren Study of 2007, the total of European gas imports (EU, Switzerland and the Western Balkans) was set to rise from 304 bcm in 2005 to 639 bcm in 2020. Russia was thought to be essential in covering a good deal of this increase by supplying 196 bcm in 2020 instead of 139 bcm in 2005. (EC, 2007, p. 8) These projections were in line with past EC statements and strategies, and already calculated with the effects of European climate targets and policies. The message was highly encouraging for large-scale Russian investments into gas exports aimed at Europe. Security considerations also had a low profile. In 2006, 77% of the EU-8's total gas imports was from Russia and the issue was considered in a strong foreign and security policy context, while on the EU-25 level the same ratio was only 31% and in Western Europe a further increase in Russian deliveries was thought to be neutral and unavoidable. (Gerrits 2008, p. 46)

This encouraging attitude has changed considerably in less than five years. Due to the US shale gas revolution, the European economic crisis and the relatively high level of past investments into renewables, a relative abundance of natural gas has been perceived by European decision-makers at least for this decade. Thus the notion of scarcity no longer prevented more ambitious and sometimes more confrontative behavior towards external suppliers. Both security of supply considerations and market reform imperatives have moved higher on the EU internal energy agenda. These factors, combined with the situation in the buyers' market, have put more pressure on the existing relationship and contractual relations. Today it is the European Union that has posed a challenge to the existing gas relationship and it would like to achieve a thorough supervision of its main pillars.

The existing long-term financial schemes and contractual regimes with their oil-indexation pricing were a reasonable and the only accessible scheme of gas business during the 1980s and much of the 1990s. Gas markets were primarily fragmented along the borders and dominated by national champions. The liberalization of the industry has only started in the US and British markets. Nevertheless, these schemes were very comfortable for exporters, first of all Russia. The latter had to make huge investments in its homeland, both into production and transport, in order to be able to deliver its output to European consumers. Russian gas fields are located in Western Siberia, in climatic conditions that are pretty harsh, and the gas has to be transported through half of Eurasia, an almost 5000 km long route in order to bring it to the European borders. Russia is the most remote supplier of gas for the old continent, its fields are further than those in Nigeria, Algeria, Norway, Azerbaijan or even some Middle East reserves. For a capital-scarce economy like that of Russia it was relatively difficult to raise the necessary funds. Risks, both in terms of demand security and pricing, were shifted mainly to the consumers.

The situation started to change only at the end of the 1990s. Two factors had a pivotal role in this process: the emergence of new gas technologies like LNG and sub-sea pipelines transforming the patterns of global gas trade, and the leadership of the EC in single market creation with a heavily liberalization-focused mindset. Both factors put pressure on the existing framework of bilateral gas relations. After two packages in gas and electricity regulation, welcomed very skeptically by European corporate actors and national governments, the EC made a strong move to push forward with its own vision for gas business. The third energy package envisages a strongly unbundled set of actors on a single market, where both capacity and trading allocations are made in a rather short-term, high liquidity form. The EC has made additional efforts both in the field of regulation and competition policy in order to enforce these developments. Even if these reforms did not have an anti-Russian character, they posed a challenge to the existing bilateral schemes and questioned their very fundaments.

Understandably, any internal reform can provide only limited say for external actors. As the process deepens, when complex domestic policies must be discussed, the external stakeholders are rarely invited to the negotiation table. Not surprisingly, the EC has had an exclusively inward-looking stance recently and this situation will hardly change until the single European gas market is created around 2015. Consequently, the problems in EU-Russia gas relations point beyond sporadic conflicts, stemming from the usual functioning of the dialogue. They have a clearly systemic character, the clash of two different models: on the Russian side the old, existing patterns, based on the concept of vertical integration and long-term risk management, while on the EC's side a reformed, liberalized European market with hub-pricing, short-term allocations and high liquidity. Both approaches have their own ideologies and philosophy. The conflict between the two models practically handicaps the management of the gas relationship. The DG Competition has already started investigations into Gazprom's European market policy, and oil indexation has been publicly denounced in relation to the Russian company (despite all other suppliers, including Europeans, having oil-indexed contracts). The newly built gas infrastructure, particularly the South Stream pipeline, will face strong criticism and heightened scrutiny during its potential permitting procedure in Brussels.

Thus the relations on the EU-Russia level have the bleakest prospects relative to all the other dimensions of bilateral trade. Contractual responsibility with the big European corporate actors, and responsibility for supply security with the national capitals have gained a relatively clear set of rules during the last 30 years. Conflicts have been manageable with the existing set of institutions and conditions. European gas market reform will overwrite existing rules and reallocate both commercial and supply security responsibilities without a clear and comprehensive target model of the new patterns. Russia's neglect and skeptical attitude derives from these factors, rather than the fear of European unity.

Gazprom is pretty much satisfied with the existing market situation, and the content of the EC policy offers hardly any benefits for it. For Moscow the EC is primarily a trouble-maker on the gas market.

There is no doubt that Europe and Russia have reached an unprecedented level of cooperation in the field of energy. Mutual trade relations and investments have reached a level where it is extremely difficult to move further without qualitative reforms, trust-building, and the shaping of more consistent policies. Interdependence is useful only as long as it provides a better environment for managing external uncertainties than would be the case independently. Today EU-Russia relations have reached a level where these qualitative improvements cannot be achieved either with or without the European Commission. The EC is too influential on the gas market to be ignored, while at the same time its agenda has nothing to offer for Gazprom. Its unilateral policies and market influences may pose an increased commercial, supply or demand risk for the existing patterns and involved parties. EU regulation has been permanently perceived by energy companies as the biggest source of uncertainty on the European market. Gazprom has too much to loose and yet the gains of cooperative behavior are uncertain. Even so, what is certain is that Russia and the EU will remain the most important trading partners for each other in the decades to come. But some sort of diversification, and decreasing the relative dependence on each other seems to be unavoidable. The question is, whether this process can be managed swiftly and smoothly, or relations will suffer long-term damage.

Security and foreign policy cooperation

The security and foreign policy dialogue is the one where Russia may have a substantial input into the relations. Strong EU-Russia cooperation in connection with any regional or global issue would raise the EU's standing significantly in global politics, while Russia could soften its Western image as an isolated and unbending power. But the fruits of cooperation hang rather high. Despite the considerable potential, the historical record of the relations is moderate and controversial. Some controversy originates from the nature of EU foreign policy, a sui generis amorphous and sometimes inconsistent entity, incapable of any cooperation. This was witnessed with the US invasion of Iraq in 2003, when European powers were deeply divided and Russian opposition was far less hostile than that of Germany or France. EU Foreign policy decision making has proved to be lengthy and time-consuming with uncertain outcomes in the past. It is still unlikely that Moscow would provide a place for the EU in its potential grand-European politics.

It is also difficult to interpret EU-Russian foreign policy cooperation outside the transatlantic and US-Russia relations. The former often is mentioned as a facilitator for US-Russian engagement in particular issues and periods (as in the case of Iran or the early 2000s), or as an attempt to soften transatlantic cooperation and outline alternative decision-making forums. Nevertheless, the sides could not formulate their own sets of issues, which could be discussed in an intimate and exclusive way. The common neighborhood (Transcaucasus, Ukraine, Moldova, Belarus) may raise some issue-specific problems in this respect in the future. At the same time, the record of common positions is also very short.

A typical example of this is the Common Space of External Security. The respective roadmap[6] provides a wide range of different fields for cooperation: strengthening the role of the UN and relevant regional organizations, securing international stability globally and in the adjacent regions, promoting the resolution of the frozen conflicts in Europe. Moreover, five priority areas have been defined: strengthened dialogue and co-operation on the international scene; the fight against terrorism; non-proliferation of weapons of mass destruction and their means of delivery, strengthening of export control regimes and disarmament; co-operation in crisis management; co-operation in the field of civil protection. From these five topics only the first priority can be qualified as a genuine EU-Russia one, since all the other four had already been priorities in the NATO-Russia Council (NRC) since the Rome Declaration of 2002. Accordingly, most of these consultations have parallels at the NATO level and bear no significant added-value. Furthermore, divisions are often greater between the EU and Russia than in the respective US-Russian relations. For example, in relation to the fight against terrorism and the Chechen war, European criticism was much more vocal than that of Washington.

The European Neighborhood Policy and particularly the Eastern Partnership were originally met skeptically and adversely in Russia. This was understandable, since the region had been several times declared in official documents as a zone of Russia's primary interests. Furthermore, all this happened in an extremely sensitive period, during the time of the color revolutions (2003-2005). The ideological patterns and narratives of the era automatically put the European efforts into the spotlight and largely presented them as being in harmony with US policies. All this happened despite the humble content of the European offer. ENP partner countries have not received an invitation to the EU, association was ruled out from the beginning, and the resources provided to these countries have not grown significantly. To a large extent the ENP was a rebranding of existing policies and reallocations of intra-EU responsibilities, not a brand new policy vis-à-vis these countries. However, it still opened a policy window for some dedicated new members to extend their influence and ambitions. Thus the Eastern Partnership policy with its Polish dedication was often perceived as identical with the ENP in Russia, one inserted into the tense relational context between the new members and Russia.

The low points of this period were the Russian-Georgian war in August 2008 and the Russian-Ukrainian gas dispute in January 2009. Both conflicts were the culminations of past processes, avoidable but understandable consequences of the emergence of the new elites in Tbilisi and Kiev. Moscow demonstrated its power and readiness to defend its interests in the region, while both Washington and Brussels had no significant input into these conflicts. What is more, neither

---

6   http://eeas.europa.eu/russia/docs/roadmap_economic_en.pdf

the US nor the EU responded to the Russian challenge by increasing their commitment to Ukraine and Georgia, demonstrating the limits of their policies. All in all, since these developments and because of the changing environment of the ENP most of the tensions around the common neighborhood have settled. Moscow does not perceive these policies as having strategic leverage, even if it still tries to minimize the most negative implications of normative rapprochement and elaborate competitive models of post-Soviet integration. But the EU does not represent an immanent danger, its resources and commitment are obviously insufficient to incentivize local elites. This also opens up some room for cooperation in relation to certain specific issues, such as frozen conflicts or soft security concerns.

Conclusion

If we look at EU-Russia relations, it is important to make a distinction between interdependence and integration. There is a high level of interdependence between Europe and Russia. For Moscow the old continent in many regards is almost as important as it was for the CEE states right after the transition. At the same time, the origins and patterns of this interdependence are very much different. In the case of Russia it was a combination of historical legacy, the Soviet collapse and a good deal of inertia that led to the situation. Thirty years ago relations between the Soviet Union and Europe did not resemble to the current state of bilateral ties. The Russian elite has not been against this trend, but has never accepted it as something desirable. Unlike the CEE states, Russia does not want to adjust its policies to these realities. The same is valid for the European Union. During the last 20 years there have been no critical efforts to engage Russia in a more sophisticated manner. Its size and influence have been permanently respected, but only some short-lived initiatives tried to use the relatively high level of interdependence as a fundament for improvement of the relations, as a resource. They were rather a reference to the potential, and in some cases to the European leverage on Russia.

Interdependence can be discomforting, especially if the respective ambitions to make qualitative changes or manage the relationship are lacking. Skepticism is well justified concerning whether the partners can, or even want to further develop their relations in the existing patterns, given the current level of trust and inconsistent models. Thus EU-Russia relations do not need high-level initiatives, short-term goals or visions, but a rather technocratic, medium-level approach. In this respect it is often not the EU-Russia level where such developments occur, rather national, corporate or even civil levels. Maybe the better use of existing resources and small improvements in the relations will generate a higher level of trust in the longer term, as well as some bottom-up forces.

Bibliography

Barysch, K. (2004). *The EU and Russia: Strategic partners or squabbling neighbours?* CER, Retrieved from http://www.cer.org.uk/sites/default/files/publications/attachments/pdf/2011/p564_russia_strat_squabb-940.pdf 23.11.2012.

Bordachev, T. & Romanova T. (2003). Model na vyrost. *Rossiya v global-noy politike, No 2.* Retrieved from http://www.globalaffairs.ru/number/n_868 22.11.2012.

Emerson, M. (2001). *The Elephant and the Bear – The European Union and Their Near Abroads.* CEPS. Brussels.

European Commission (EC), Directorate-General for Research Sustainable Energy Systems: "Energy corridors – European Union and Neighbouring countries" Retrieved from: http://ec.europa.eu/research/energy/pdf/energy_corridors_en.pdf 14.12.2012.

Gerrits, A. (ed.) (2008). *The European Union and Russia: Perception and Interest in the Shaping of Relations.* Retrieved from http://www.clingendael.nl/publications/2008/20081101_paper_gerrits_eu_russia.pdf 22.11.2012.

Konoplyanik, A. (2010). *Rossiya i Energeticheskaya Khartiya.* Gubkin University. Moscow.

Leonard, M., & Popescu, N. (2007). *A Power Audit of EU-Russia Relations,* European Council on Foreign Relations. Retrieved from http://www.kms2.isn.ethz.ch 25.12.2012.

Ludvig, Zs. (2008). *Oroszország és a kibővült Európai Unió gazdasági kapcsolatai.* Akadémiai Kiadó. Budapest.

Mau, V., & Novikov, V. (2002). Otnosheniya Rossii i ES: Prostranstvo Vybora ili Vybor Prostranstva? *Voprosy ekonomiki, 2002(6), 133-143.*

Monaghan, A., & Montanaro-Jankovski, L. (2006). *EU-Russia energy relations: the need for active engagement.* EPC Issue Paper No.45. Retrieved from: http://kms2.isn.ethz.ch/serviceengine/Files/RESSpecNet/17040/ipublicationdocument_singledocument/E0E2E749-43C5-4255-9D2A-900475CD53C7/en/EPC_Issue_Paper_45.pdf 01.01.2013.

Moshes, A. (ed.) (2003). *Rethinking of Respective Strategies of Russia and European Union.* FIIA. Retrieved from: http://kms1.isn.ethz.ch/serviceengine/Files/ISN/10733/ipublicationdocument_singledocument/1E98A871-D44F-40D6-8465-9653F0F26EF7/en/doc_10764_290_en.pdf#page=63 01.01.2013.

NATO-Russia Council (2002). Rome declaration. Retrieved from http://www.nato-russia-council.info/media/69549/2002.05.28_nrc_rome_declaration.pdf

Popescu, N. (2011). On EU-Russia visa free travel, Retrieved from http://blogs.euobserver.com/popescu/2011/09/15/on-eu-russia-visa-free-travel-part-1/ 18.12.2012.

Salminen, M., & Moshes A. (2009). Practise what you preach – The prospects for visa freedom in Russia-EU relations, FIIA Report, Retrieved from http://www.ru.boell.org/downloads/Visa_report_EU-Russia_EN.pdf, 18.12.2012.

Stefan Batory Foundation (2009). *What to do with visas for the Eastern Europeans? Recommendations from the perspective of Visegrad countries*, Retrieved from http://www.batory.org.pl/doc/Recommendations_v4.pdf, 18.12.2012.

Sutela, P. (2005). EU, Russia and the common economic space, *Bofit online, number 3,* Retrieved from http://www.suomenpankki.fi/bofit/tutkimus/tutkimusjulkaisut/online/Documents/bon0305.pdf 23.11.2012.

Trenin, D. (2001). *The End of EURASIA: Russia on the Border Between Geopolitics and Globalization.* Carnegie Moscow Center. Moscow.

Challenging the EU's finalité –
the EU and the Western Balkans

Anna Orosz

Since the end of the Yugoslav war, the Western Balkans region has come to represent the biggest challenge facing the EU foreign and development policy, and has put the EU enlargement process into a new context. As a consequence of the war, the countries in the region face multifaceted political and economic challenges on their way to becoming fully functional democracies and market economies. The basic assumption of this analysis is that the Western Balkan countries are unable to enhance their own development and reach the abovementioned targets the out external assistance. Since the end of the 1990s the European Union has taken the leading role in the promotion of stabilization and democratization of the region. Its efforts peaked in the explicit acknowledgment of the future of the region within the EU at the European Council meeting held in Thessaloniki in 2003.

Despite the commitment expressed by the European leaders, the road toward EU accession is far from being easy for the Western Balkan countries. As pointed out by several scholars (Altmann, F-L., 2005; Calic, M-J., 2004; Bechev, D., 2012), enlargement fatigue in EU member states was already a concern from the very beginning (as a consequence of the two accession rounds in 2004 and 2007) and the slow pace of reforms in the Western Balkans has decreased member states' commitment toward the region. Beyond the uncertain commitment of member states, the lack of a clear strategic approach raised concerns about the implementation of the enlargement process. Though a regional approach has been an essential element of the enlargement process, the EU has not managed to build a real regional strategy in its enlargement policy. As stated by the European Commission's consecutive communications on enlargement strategies, the EU has continued to evaluate candidate and potential candidate countries on the bases of their merits, but so far this strategy has led to the fragmented and mainly reactive enlargement policy and has not been complemented by a coherent regional perspective. Recently Croatia and Montenegro seem to have gained a credible membership perspective, while the other countries could face a never ending candidate status because of unresolved bilateral and domestic disputes. The time factor seriously impacts the credibility of EU membership perspective, and therefore the EU should ensure an attractive vision in order to make potential candidate and candidate countries remain pledged to the accession process.

The economic and financial crisis has significantly undermined the EU's economic stability and competitiveness, as well as the vision of the future EU.

The crisis challenges the integration in various ways, among which three will be highlighted in this chapter. First, the study points out the inability of the EU to tackle the crisis and how the great burden on member states to allow their economy to recover decreases interest in enlargement. Second, metaphorically, it characterizes the enlargement process as shooting at a moving target, but because of the crisis the movement of the target is even less predictable. The unclear and recently very negative vision of the EU might question the incentives to join the Union in general. Third, the study will argue that since the beginning of the 2000s the Western Balkan countries have already reached a high level of integration. Consequently, negative impacts of the crisis have spread around the region causing serious problems for the potential candidate and candidate countries. If the EU is not able to overcome the economic downturn, it could jeopardize former achievements and encourage the Western Balkan countries to look for alternative policy paths.

Under such unfavorable circumstances the question has to be raised: what are the decisive factors which facilitate the continuation of the accession process? This chapter will examine the issue from two perspectives: from the side of the EU and the Western Balkan countries. In the case of the EU, the analysis underlines two main aspects: the costs of a loss of prestige and the recognition of the weakness of its foreign policy tool; and path dependence due to the already reached high level of integration. The analysis will also highlight the complexity of factors influencing the Western Balkans governments' commitment to the enlargement process by analyzing the perspective of membership in terms of credibility, the existence or absence of another actor taking the role of the EU, and the costs and benefits of a reorientation of economic and political networks. In conclusion, the chapter will examine the EU's recent position in the region in relation to these aspects, focusing on tendencies during the crisis period.

Recent state of the enlargement process and the impact of the crisis on the Western Balkans

Since the beginning of the 2000s, the Western Balkan countries have experienced a significant integration process with the EU. As a result, not only did the EU become the most important partner of the Western Balkan countries, but the region reached such a high level of integration that made it dependent on the EU's economic performance. As Dimitar Bechev (2012, p. 1) points out, the Western Balkans became a "periphery of the periphery" of the EU.

As the table below shows, the EU's share in international trade with the region is more than 60%, and the majority of export products of these countries are sold in the EU.

Table 1: Share of EU in import and export of Western Balkan countries

	Share of EU in imports (2010)	Share of EU in exports (2010)
Albania	68.60%	75.40%
Bosnia and Herzegovina	64.80%	72.60%
Croatia	60.70%	61.70%
Kosovo	n.a.	n.a.
Macedonia, FYR	53.40%	61.40%
Montenegro	69.20%	89.40%
Serbia	65.30%	60.20%

Source: *Eurostat*

The financial and bank systems of these countries are based on institutional relations with EU economies. While some countries have already introduced the euro as a country-wide used currency (e.g. Montenegro, Kosovo), others have pegged their currencies either formally or informally to the euro (Bosnia and Herzegovina, Macedonia, Croatia). But even if the currencies are not pegged to the euro, the high dependence on EU markets in exports and in the financial sector makes them vulnerable to negative tendencies in the EU. Banks and companies from Greece, Italy, Austria and Germany have managed to gain significant market share in the region.

According to Eurostat data, as a consequence of the crisis, real GDP growth in the EU fell from 3.2% in 2007 to –4.3% in 2009. Since then the situation has improved somewhat and the GDP growth rate was 2.1% in 2010 and 1.5% in 2011, but unfortunately no real breakthrough has been achieved so far. (Eurostat, 2012d) The economic performances of Southern member states (Greece, Spain, Italy and Portugal) have been particularly weak, which made an EU-level intervention necessary. The unemployment rate has exceeded 10% in the EU-27, while in Spain and Greece it has even surpassed 25%. (Eurostat, 2012c)

As Greece and other weakening member states belong to the most important economic partners of the Western Balkan countries, the negative spillover effects reached the Balkans very quickly. After years of credit boom and high liquidity which boosted economic development, the quantity of loans available and remittances decreased significantly, and consumption seriously plummeted. Production has also been negatively affected by contracting demand in EU markets.

According to a recent Eurostat analysis (2012e), the crisis initially affected countries whose economic performance relied significantly on exports and external financing. In 2009, GDP fell by 6.0% in Croatia and 3.5% in Serbia, while Montenegro's GDP shrank by 5.7%. In Bosnia and Herzegovina GDP contracted by 2.9%. Albania and the former Yugoslav Republic of Macedonia were the least affected by the crisis because they are less dependent on exports. GDP in the former Yugoslav Republic of Macedonia decreased only slightly in 2009 (by 0.9%), whereas Albania managed to achieve a growth rate of 3.3% in the same year. (Eurostat, 2012e, p. 60)

However, in the latter cases the fiscal and monetary policies employed to cushion the impact of the crisis seem to be unsustainable. Macedonia mainly benefited from huge public spending and public investments, while Albania used monetary policy to support economic growth. Accordingly, the Economist Intelligence Unit (hereafter: EIU) estimates a plummet in real growth to 0.7% in Albania (EIU, 2012a, p. 12) as well as a contraction of Macedonia's GDP growth to 1.2% in 2012 as a consequence of the unresolved euro zone crisis. (EIU, 2012d, p. 6) These negative impacts also led to an increase of the already high unemployment rate in the Western Balkan countries (though not to the same extent as in the West European states). This raises many concerns about the possible ways of recovery, which is unlikely to happen until the EU manages to facilitate economic revival.

Meanwhile, political-level integration has faced much more essential problems, since despite official announcements, member states have not managed to unite in order to be able to represent a strong common position toward the region. The EU has not managed to build a real strategy for the integration of these countries. It has continued to deal with individual countries, which has led to a fragmented integration process.

While Croatia managed to get to the doorstep of the EU after nine years and accession talks could be opened for Montenegro, other states like Bosnia and Herzegovina, Albania and Macedonia could hardly improve their position because of external factors (e.g. the name dispute between Greece and Macedonia) or domestic ones (e.g. domestic political stalemate in BiH and Albania). Serbia was granted candidate status in March 2012 but is clearly stuck in the debate with Kosovo on its status, which will inevitably postpone the start of negotiations on accession. In the case of Kosovo, the EU is still working with temporary solutions since some member states continue to refuse recognition of the newly established state's de facto independence.

According to the most recent Communication of the European Commission on enlargement strategy and main challenges, published in October 2012, the "enlargement process of the EU got into a new phase with the successful completion of accession negotiations with Croatia which also vindicates [...] the policy adopted in the aftermath of the devastating Balkan conflicts of the 1990s, which aims to bring peace, stability, democracy and ultimately EU membership to the whole region". (European Commission, 2011, p. 2)

Nevertheless, it should be mentioned that the general approach of the EU has not changed comprehensively, and has not been upgraded to meet all the new challenges of the region stemming from its relationship with the EU. None of the Commission's communications manages to provide a strong EU standpoint on how to resolve bilateral disputes (as in the case of Serbia and Kosovo, or Greece and FYRoM), though their resolution is a prerequisite of EU membership. The Commission (2012, pp. 2-3) expresses concerns about the crisis of the eurozone and notes that the enhanced level of integration should also be taken into account in the enlargement process, as well as tackling the deteriorating effects of the economic downturn. However, it should be noted that negotiations mainly proceed in the form of sectoral policy agreements (energy policy, transportation, trade issues, visa liberalization).

The crisis put extreme pressure on the governments of member states and under such conditions these states handle enlargement issues moderately, rather easing their commitments. In a number of areas the situation is even worse, since some member states question the advancements already reached. A good example of this is visa liberalization. Among others, Germany, Austria and Sweden warned Western Balkan countries that they would restrict their visa system because of the increased number of asylum seekers coming from the region.

However, the stick and carrot method of negotiations on accession is still in place and is likely to continue. Nevertheless, it might be questionable whether such an integration process with its controversial and deteriorating effects on acceding countries can remain attractive enough in the long run to encourage the relevant governments to proceed with reforms. Recently, it has also been a great concern as to the direction in which the EU will further develop, and whether the EU and its member states will manage to overcome the crisis. Since the beginning of the crisis, the new Europe 2020 Strategy has been adopted, and new EU-level mechanisms to ensure fiscal and monetary stability in the EU have been initiated.

Under such circumstances the question should be raised concerning which factors are determinant for the EU and its member states as well as for the Western Balkans to commit themselves to the integration process.

Why is it necessary to carry on? – an EU perspective

In 2003 at the Thessaloniki European Council meeting, the EU explicitly confirmed that the future of the Western Balkan countries would be in the EU. With this the EU integration of that region became an explicit target of EU foreign policy, and the policy tools of democratization and institution-building were broadened with the perspective of EU membership. Consequently, the EU became politically interested in a successful EU integration and accession process, since failure would lead to a great loss of credit with the international community which, accompanied by the inability to overcome the challenges of the economic crisis, could negatively impact the EU's position in world politics.

In 2006 the European Council – based on the Commission's communication on enlargement – agreed on a renewed commitment to continue the enlargement process and reaffirmed "that the future of the Western Balkans lies in the European Union." (Presidency Conclusions, 2006, par. 8). This renewed consensus has become a reference point for the Commission, though it seems that EU Member States have remained rather reluctant to accept new "problematic" members that could further complicate the internal conditions of the EU.

The Commission continued to foster enlargement and this has been expressed by its subsequent communications on the subject. In 2008 the Commission's strategy paper started with the following words:

> Enlargement is one of the EU's most powerful policy tools. It serves the EU's strategic interests in stability, security, and conflict prevention. It has helped to increase prosperity and growth opportunities, to improve links with vital transport and energy routes, and to increase the EU's weight in the world.
>
> The present enlargement agenda covers the Western Balkans and Turkey, which have been given the perspective of becoming EU members once they fulfill the necessary conditions. The European perspective has contributed to peace and stability, and enabled partners to cope with major challenges, such as Kosovo's declaration of independence, while maintaining regional security. It provides in both the Western Balkans and Turkey strong encouragement for political and economic reform. It is in the EU's strategic interest to keep up the momentum of this process, on the basis of agreed principles and conditions. (European Commission, 2008, p.1)

Beyond emphasizing the importance of the EU's normative power and its enlargement policy, in this strategy paper the Commission (2008, p. 7) already referred to the possible negative effects of the crisis and noted that "the Commission stands ready to assist the authorities in the enlargement countries in managing its financial and economic consequences". The European Commission, the European Bank for Reconstruction and Development and the EU member states belong to the most important donors of the Western Balkan countries, which will rely on these supporters to a large extent. It is, however, difficult to sustain or strengthen the commitment of governments of other countries while they are suffering from austerity measures and budgetary restrictions.

Nevertheless, it seems that the EU cannot ignore its "obligations" to integrate the Western Balkans. As has been mentioned already, the linkages with the Balkans are so strong that mutual path dependence has been created. If the EU is eager to preserve its status as an international actor supporting stability, peace and democracy, it has to balance the negative spillover effects of the integration process. Another reason for not leaving the region behind is that that loss of former achievements would further increase the costs of the integration process. Furthermore, it should be noted that economic stability and growth in the Western Balkans would also benefit the EU. It could demonstrate the success of its policy tools as well as ensure security in its closer neighborhood. Thus the EU should work on encouraging commitment both within its borders and among Western Balkan countries. Accordingly, the European Commission continues to communicate in favor of the enlargement process, and plays an important role in fostering proceedings of the accession process, even though member states sometimes express their concerns about enlargement.

This necessitates, however, a more general, regional level approach that can surpass bilateral disputes which otherwise undermine the integration process. Such a regional strategy should strengthen the commitment of political parties and their leadership in the region to EU accession, because in the long run strong political determination will be essential to overcome difficulties stemming from the economic crisis.

Credibility of EU membership

From the point of view of the Western Balkan countries, the judgment of the possibility of a common future in the EU requires another approach. The most essential question is whether the promise of EU accession is credible. Credibility regarding EU membership depends on several factors, among others on the fulfillment of political conditionality, and possible ways of resolving bilateral disputes and essential challenges; the expected time of joining; and EU integration in party politics.

The EU opened accession talks with Croatia in 2005, two years after the country submitted its application, and Croatia is likely to join the EU club in July 2013. Thus approximately ten years are necessary for a country which is, from various perspectives, on higher level than other acceding countries were in 2006. What does this indicate for other potential candidate and candidate countries? Montenegro applied for membership in 2008 and the accession talks were opened in June 2012. Serbia applied for membership in December 2009 and was offered candidate status in March 2012. Similarly, Albania submitted an application in 2009 but it is still doubtful whether the Council will agree with the Commission's opinion regarding granting candidate status. In November 2005 Macedonia managed to obtain candidate status within twenty months following its application, but since then no step has been taken as a consequence of the name dispute with Greece, though the European Commission recommended the start of accession talks in October 2009. In the case of BiH and Kosovo formal application is still in question.

If the timing of accession remains unchanged, the majority of Western Balkan countries can hardly expect to be an EU member before 2020. In view of the crisis, this period of time increases uncertainty about that what kind of EU prospective members wish to join. This seriously affects credibility EU membership. Schimmelfennig and Scholtz (2008, p. 207) argue that "[…] the effectiveness of political conditionality depends on credible membership perspective for the target countries". Accordingly, it can be assumed that fulfillment of political conditionality will further slow down.

Such a tendency might be even challenging in the light of the Commission's recent *Communication on enlargement strategy and challenges* (2012) which points to the increased significance of political conditionality:

> Strengthening the rule of law and democratic governance is central to the enlargement process. The lessons learnt from previous enlargements highlight the importance of an increased focus on these areas and further improving the quality of the process. This underpins and further promotes stability in a region recently scarred by

conflict and supports the creation of an environment in south-east Europe conducive to growth and attracting investment, increased regional cooperation and dealing with common challenges such as the fight against organized crime and corruption. It addresses issues of direct concern to citizens in both the EU and the enlargement countries of justice, security and fundamental rights. With the Council's endorsement in June of the Commission's proposed new approach to judiciary and fundamental rights and justice, freedom and security as part of the negotiating framework for Montenegro, the rule of law is firmly anchored at the heart of the accession process, laying the foundation also for future negotiations." (p. 2)

Schimmelfennig and Scholtz (2008, pp. 207-208) also point out that the impact of EU political conditions varies across levels of democratization, and EU political conditionality is most effective in promoting democratic consolidation in countries that have already experienced some democratization. This finding allows us to conclude that a higher level of democratization should be accompanied by a better EU perspective.

The tables below summarize Freedom House scores on democratization for the Eastern enlargement countries a year before their accession, as well as the most recent scores of the Western Balkan countries. The Freedom House scores have been also analyzed by Schimmelfennig and Scholtz (2008).

Table 2: Freedom House Scores of countries joining in 2004 (scores in 2003)

Freedom House scores in 2003	Democracy score	Electoral process	Civil society	Independent media	Judicial frameworks and independence	Corruption	Governance
Czech Republic	2.33	2.00	1.50	2.25	2.50	3.50	2.25
Hungary	1.96	1.25	1.25	2.25	1.75	2.75	2.50
Slovakia	2.08	1.50	1.50	2.00	2.00	3.25	2.25
Poland	1.75	1.50	1.25	1.75	1.50	2.50	2.00
Estonia	2.00	1.75	2.00	1.75	1.75	2.50	2.25
Latvia	2.25	1.75	2.00	1.75	2.25	3.50	2.25
Lithuania	2.13	1.75	1.50	1.75	1.75	3.50	2.50
Slovenia	1.79	1.50	1.50	1.75	1.75	2.00	2.25

Source: *Freedom House*

Table 3: Freedom House Scores of countries joining in 2007 (scores in 2006)

Freedom House scores in 2003	Democracy score	Electoral process	Civil society	Independent media	Judicial frameworks and independence	Corruption	National Democratic Governance	Local Democratic Governance
Romania	3.39	2.75	2.25	4.00	4.00	4.25	3.50	3.00
Bulgaria	2.93	1.75	2.75	3.25	3.00	3.75	3.00	3.00

Source: *Freedom House*

Table 4: Freedom House Scores of Western Balkans (scores in 2012)

Freedom House scores in 2003	Democracy score	Electoral process	Civil society	Independent media	Judicial frameworks and independence	Corruption	National Democratic Governance	Local Democratic Governance
Croatia	3.61	3.25	2.50	4.00	4.25	4.00	3.50	3.75
Bosnia and Herz.	4.36	3.25	3.50	4.75	4.25	4.50	5.50	4.75
Serbia	3.64	3.25	2.25	4.00	4.50	4.25	3.75	3.50
Montenegro	3.82	3.25	2.75	4.25	4.00	5.00	4.25	3.25
Kosovo	5.18	5.00	3.75	5.75	5.50	5.75	5.75	4.75
FYRo Macedonia	3.89	3.25	3.25	4.75	4.00	4.00	4.25	3.75
Albania	4.14	4.25	3.00	4.00	4.75	5.00	4.75	3.25

Source: *Freedom House*

These tables underline the difference between countries acceding in 2004 and 2007, as well as the Western Balkan countries. According to these data, Croatia, Serbia, Montenegro and Macedonia are approaching the level of Romania while John E. Ashbrook (2010) provided much evidence concerning how Croatia, for example, performed better than Romania and Bulgaria.

Though these numbers should not be considered in absolute terms, they rather imply that distinction among candidate and potential candidate states in many cases depends on political decisions. The recent state of the enlargement process is better reflected by the 'Freedom in the world scores', which show a more diverse picture. Recently this score is 1.5 for Croatia, 2.0 for Serbia, 2.5 for Montenegro, 3.0 for Albania and Macedonia, 3.5 for Bosnia and Herzegovina, while Kosovo is lagging behind with a score of 4.5 on a ranking from 1 (best) to 7 (worst).

However, it can be noted that the difference between the status of the forerunners (Croatia and Montenegro) and those like Serbia and Macedonia hindered by bilateral disputes might be questioned by their democracy scores. In the case of Serbia the scores are even more controversial, since its freedom and democracy scores are better than those of Montenegro.

The advanced position of Croatia is rather underlined by its economic performance (its GDP per capita is above 60% of the EU-27 average). Croatia's GDP per capita is higher than those of Romania and Bulgaria whose results are similar to that of Montenegro, which reached the 43% level, while Serbia and Macedonia could only climb to 35-36%. Albania and Bosnia and Herzegovina are around or below 30% (Eurostat, 2012b).

From this perspective, the expected time for accession seems to be decisive. Unjustifiable differences among expected times for acceeding countries can be harmful for EU membership credibility. Therefore, the EU should define a much clearer position on bilateral disputes and what it considers a threshold for EU accession.

In the case of countries like Kosovo, particularly Bosnia and Herzegovina, which are significantly behind the rest of the regions, the problems are more essential. In the latter case, the domestic forces are unwilling to agree on the status of the state and the common vision within the EU. While in other Western Balkan countries major political parties having a powerful role in formulating the future of the countries internalized the EU perspective into their party politics, major forces in BiH still benefit from ethno-politics, which endangers the EU perspective.

Is there any alternative to the EU?

It can be assumed that Western Balkan countries will be dependent on the path of EU integration as long as there is (are) no other actor(s) which could provide political and financial support for these countries' development and political stability. Below four countries' relationship with the Western Balkan region will be examined: the United States of America, Russia, China and Turkey.

These countries either play a traditionally important role in the region, like Russia and the USA, or have intensified their foreign policy toward the region in the last few years and have a significant role in world politics. These big powers have major resources and political influence that could enable them to play a determinant role in the region's future. However, two dimensions of these policies need to be considered in order to decide whether these countries could take over the role of the EU in the region. First, the scope of the relations (political, economic or even tighter, focusing on 1-2 policy areas), and second, the geographic extension of relations (targeting the whole region or focusing on some specific countries). These two dimensions have to be considered as they are indicators of the political will and the interests of these four countries determining their foreign policy toward the region. If both the scope and the geographic extension are broad enough, we can claim that there is another actor which contests (or there are other actors which contest) the role of the EU in general, but recent analysis can highlight other ways too, how these countries might challenge the region-wide aspirations of the EU.

Jacques Rupnik (2011, pp. 18-20) briefly examined three of the above-mentioned international actors (Russia, the USA and Turkey) and concluded that the EU had a position as "the only game in town", since the presence and policies of these international actors did not weaken the EU's position. I believe that recent developments make it necessary to provide a more sophisticated picture about the "network" of the Western Balkans, and in this way detailed and nuanced conclusions can be outlined regarding the EU's role in the region.

United States of America

Despite the important US participation in military intervention and conflict resolution in the Balkans, the last decade was marked by a strengthening EU presence in the region. As a consequence of the terrorist attack in 2001, the two military interventions in Afghanistan and Iraq followed by the Arab Spring turned the attention of the US to other challenges and it withdrew from the Western Balkans. (Rupnik, 2011; Sakellariou, 2011) Since then the US has mainly followed developments in the Western Balkans from a distance while promoting these countries' Euro-Atlantic integration.

Despite criticism formulated within the Obama administration regarding the EU's achievements in the region and voices recalling the "unfinished business" in the Western Balkans, President Obama has acknowledged the EU's role as a transformative power in the Western Balkans and has continued to rely on the EU's presence and resources. (Bugajski, 2010; Sakellariou, 2011) Although the appointment of Joe Biden as Vice President and the legislation passed by the US House of Representatives to appoint a special envoy for the Balkans temporarily implied some changes, these did not come into effect. The special envoy has never been appointed and US involvement decreased mainly to the level of diplomatic visits and backing the Euro-Atlantic integration process headed by the EU, as is noticeable from the statements of Ambassador Philip Reeker, Deputy Assistant Secretary of State for European and Eurasian Affairs, made in the Washington Foreign Press Center on March 9th, 2012. (U.S. Foreign Policy: Western Balkans Update) It also shows the lack of motivation of the US Administration to re-engage with the Balkans that the EU representative is taking over supervision in areas from which the High Representative in Bosnia and Herzegovina is withdrawing.

Obama's administration further decreased the amount of aid targeting the Western Balkan region similarly to his predecessor. In 2002 this amount was USD 621 million, which decreased to USD 284.8 million in 2010. (Poulin & Teleki, 2010, p. 32)

In addition, the United States does not represent an outstanding trade partner in the region. In 2010, among the import and export partners of Croatia it accounted for just 2.2% and 2.7% of trade, respectively. The figures for Albania were 1.7% and 1.6%, for Macedonia 1.9% and 0.4%, for Montenegro 1.8% and 0.2%, and for Serbia 0.7% and 1.9%. Thus the US has a relatively low share in these countries' foreign trade relations. Its position is particularly weak in BiH, where its share in trade does not even reach a level of 1%. (See, in the order of the countries listed, DG Trade, 2012c, 2012a, 2012d, 2012e, 2012f, and 2012b)

Considering these tendencies, most scholars agree that the US has decreasing aspirations in the region. Nevertheless, they also recognize that the US is recognized as a more credible actor than the EU in countries where US intervention played an important role to end bloodshed. (Bugajski, 2010; Rupnik, 2011; Sakellariou, 2011) In the case of Kosovo Gross and Rotta (2011, p. 7) go even further by noting that US influence contributes to controversial decisions by Kosovo institutions which can weaken EU conditionality and allow the authorities in Pristina to play their international sponsors against each other to their own advantage. In addition, they point out that some specific policy advice and technical assistance of the US in relation to crucial areas (such as border management, the judiciary and law-making) rather contest than contribute to EU efforts in the same areas.

In view of the above, it can be concluded that though the USA played a significant role in stabilization of the region, and is still active to some extent in some countries, the Western Balkans lags behind other US foreign policy priorities and it is unlikely that such a tendency will change in the coming years.

Russia

Russia has always represented a counter pole of the EU and the United States in world politics, as well as in the Western Balkans. As a traditional ally of Serbia, it could take advantage of the contradictory positions of Serbia and the EU in vital issues. This position has not changed, but the significance of Slav Orthodox brotherhood in the rhetoric has decreased while issues related to territorial integrity and non-intervention policy remained strong, especially regarding Russia's policy toward Republika Srpska and Bosnia and Herzegovina, as well as non-recognition of Kosovo.

Russia actively supported foreign policy coordination with Serbia in order to block the recognition process of Kosovo. Though the decision of the International Court of Justice and the Belgrade-Pristina dialogue under the auspices of the EU took the edge off this policy to some extent, Russia still continued to promote the policy direction. In 2012 the former pro-Milosevic politician Timoslav Nikolic was elected President of Serbia, and it was expected that there might be a turn in the country's foreign policy. This was partly underpinned by the fact that the first official visit of the newly inaugurated president targeted Russia, but it should be added that President Nikolic has reaffirmed the country's engagement toward EU integration. Since then, Serbia's foreign policy messages have remained similarly double-faced. While the dialogue between Belgrade and Pristina continued with high-level meetings between the parties, the President further refused recognition of Kosovo's independence and Russia reaffirmed its support for Serbia over this issue. The pro-Russia policy is strengthened by the strong refusal of NATO membership and increased emphasis of partnership with Russia. Economist Intelligence recent analyses (e.g. EIU Country Report: Serbia, 2012, p. 3) point out that such a tendency increases the risk for the EU to have a prospective member which might become "Russia's corner in the EU".

Beyond its political role, Russia's presence in Serbia is also enhanced by its economic policy. At a summit in September 2012 Serbia and Russia strengthened their commitment to their international economic relations, especially in the field of energy policy. Russia also provides resources for budgetary support, as well as infrastructure and various investment projects. (EIU, 2012f, p. 3)

Apart from Serbia, Russia gains political benefit from disagreements relating to the domestic situation in Bosnia and Herzegovina. It often steps up in defense of Serbs living in the Serbian entity of Bosnia and Herzegovina. Vitaly Churkin, representing Russia during the presentation of the report of Valentin Inzko, the High Representative to Bosnia and Herzegovina, in May 2012 said that the High Representative in his analysis had been not objective and had presented a biased criticism of the Bosnian Serbs, though Republika Srpska had managed to make further progress. (UN Security Council, 2012 May 15) The divisive role of Russia is again supported by its aspirations vis-à-vis energy policy. Gazprom generated contradictions within Bosnia and Herzegovina by signing an agreement on the South Stream with Republika Srpska without having consulted the leadership of the state-level government. (EIU, 2012b, p. 2)

The promotion of South Stream and Russian expansion in the field of energy policy has further regional implications. Beyond Serbia and Bosnia and Herzegovina, Russia took and is taking steps to involve all the Western Balkan countries with the exceptions of Kosovo and Albania. This is the most strategic and quasi-regional-wide action of Russia in the region. The most advanced candidate country, Croatia, also took several steps to get more involved with the Russian South Stream, but its plans contradicted its candidacy aspirations since the European Commission handles Croatia as a priority area of its own integrated regional, European energy policy. Negotiations between Russia and Croatia were surrounded by diplomatic games and atmosphere-making, (Socor, V. 2011) but no contract was signed between the two parties. The Croatian government emphasized that it would not make a deal with Russia which could jeopardize its accession to the EU. The European Union considers the South Stream project as a competitor of the Nabucco project and its efforts to strengthen energy independence from Russia. (Balkan Insight August 13, 2012 based on Jutarnji List)

According to DG Trade factsheets (2012a-f), Russia also has intensive trade relations with the region. As an import partner it plays an important role in Croatia (9.1%), BiH (5.1%) and Macedonia (10.2%). In the case of Serbia, while Russia's share of imports is lower (1.6%), it is a more important export partner (6.4%). Albania and Montenegro are both trade partners of Russia, but Moscow's share in their trade is less significant.

Accordingly, considering its regional-level role Russia can be characterized as having a strong focus on energy policy. Otherwise it is unlikely that Russia will be a regionally integrative actor as it rather masters its political influence to take advantage of tensions in the region, especially the conflicts between Serbia and other countries in the region, and tensions relating to Serbs living outside Serbia. Hence Russia needs to be considered as a disruptive actor which might hinder the EU in remaining an attractive alternative for the whole Western Balkan region. Nevertheless, this role might improve together with expanding international economic relations and investments which Russia might transform into political influence. There are already some signs of such a tendency in Macedonia.

China

Throughout the last decade China experienced great economic growth that established a strong basis for political and economic influence in various part of the world. This tendency was further strengthened by the economic and financial crisis, which generated increased demand on the part of EU countries for Chinese investment and financial resources. As pointed out by Eurostat, the EU-27's international trade in goods with China grew significantly over the last decade. EU-27 exports to China rose from 26 billion euros in 2000 to 136 billion in 2011. EU-27 imports from China rose from 75 billion in 2000 to 248 billion in 2008, and after a downturn it reached a level of 293 billion in 2011. (Eurostat, 2012a)

China's presence in the region has similarly strengthened since the end of the war in the Balkans. It is the second most important trade partner of Albania and Montenegro. China is also present in Macedonia and Croatia, as well as – though with a lower share – Bosnia and Herzegovina and Serbia. China's efforts aim at developing trade networks through the Balkans to Western Europe. It has been building Chinatown centers promoting trade with these countries, while also investing in building manufacturing bases to benefit from the region's resources. China also supports infrastructural investments (railways, bridges) in Serbia.

In addition, China invests in the energy policy sectors of these countries. China's Exim Bank is providing a soft loan of one billion euros to Elektropivreda Srbije to upgrade Serbia's electricity networks and build a new thermal power plant in Kostolac. It is also funding the construction of a 300 MW coal-fired plant in Bosnia and Herzegovina, and 12 hydropower plants in Macedonia. (Poulain, 2011)

In contrast with the EU, China doesn't make political demands relating to the domestic affairs of these countries. In terms of political influence, China uses its leverage mostly in its relations with Belgrade. In August 2009, Serbian President Boris Tadic agreed to a strategic partnership with China, through which both countries committed themselves to defend each other's basic national interests. (Poulain, 2011, p. 6.) Accordingly, China is one of the main opponents of Kosovo's independence in the UN. On the other side, Serbia adopted a policy not to join any initiatives criticizing China in international forums. This has already caused tensions between Belgrade and the EU, as Belgrade has refused and blocked all actions criticizing the human rights situation in China, including the award ceremony of 2010 Nobel Peace Prize given to Liu Xiaobo.

China's role in the region is comparable to that of Russia. Though China has extended its presence to the whole Balkans, this tendency is mainly encouraged by China's intention to build a network toward the EU and its markets. However, China – similarly to Russia – represents a contradicting standpoint vis-à-vis the EU in world politics, and it can be presumed that China will gain political allies for its economic investment. From this perspective, Serbia seems to be the highest risk for the EU.

Turkey

Probably Turkey has the broadest relationship with the Balkans in terms of both policy scope and geographic extension. While the EU and the developed countries have been suffering to overcome the challenges stemming from the economic and financial crisis, Turkey managed to gain a new momentum and launched an active foreign policy both in its neighborhood and in the Middle East during the Arab Spring. Bugajski (2012) and Poulain and Sakellariou (2011) assign this active foreign policy to Ahmet Davutođlu, Foreign Minister in the government of Erdođan. It is also known as "Neo-Ottomanism".

This term appeared after the speech of the Foreign Minister in Bosnia and Herzegovina in 2009. He stated that "the Ottoman centuries of the Balkans were a success story. Now we have to reinvent this… Turkey is back" (Poulain, & Sakellariou, 2011). Though the return of the "image of the Ottoman Empire" was not welcomed by all the countries because of the historical background, Turkish presence indeed entered a new phase in 2009. This was enhanced by the opportunity presented by the chairmanship of Turkey in the South East European Co-operation Process.

Concerning the geographic scope of Turkish foreign policy, it is clear that Turkey intends to play a significant role at the regional level. Initially it naturally focused on culturally linked countries like Bosnia and Herzegovina (mainly the Muslim community), Kosovo and Albania, but gradually it strengthened ties with Croatia, Serbia and Macedonia as well. This could be underpinned by the improvement of bilateral relations with these countries (reflected by, for example, the promotion of Macedonia's NATO membership, and the diplomatic visit of Turkish President Abdullah Gül to Belgrade – the first official visit from a Turkish head of state in 23 years) as well as by involvement in (quasi-)regional issues such as mediating among conflicting parties. Thanks to Turkish mediation, in March 2010 the Serbian Parliament adopted the Declaration of Srebrenica in which Serbia officially apologized for its role in the 1995 Srebrenica Massacre, and the trilateral Istanbul Declaration on Peace and Stability in the Balkans was adopted by BiH, Croatia and Serbia in April 2010. Turkey furthermore supports Belgrade-Pristina dialogue.

Beyond its political role, Turkey has put enormous effort into increasing its economic and trade presence in the Western Balkans region. It has been particularly active in the transportation (airlines) and telecommunications sectors, as well as the bank system. Since the crisis Western European banks and companies have withdrawn and Turkey might be able to take their role, though the EU's share is still overwhelming. Nevertheless, the vacuum appearing as a consequence of the crisis might create a gap for Turkey to fill. Though Turkey's share is hardly comparable to that of the EU, it can be noted that it could become a partial, non-exclusive alternative to the EU. Nonetheless, as is pointed out by Poulain and Sakellariou (2011), the Western Balkans is unlikely to become a high priority for Turkey's economic investment due to lack of resources and limited, poor markets.

Attention directed to Turkey's recent role in the Western Balkans has increased because of the changes in EU-Turkey ties and the balance of power in the past few years. The strengthening international role of Turkey and economic stability have established a more balanced negotiation position between the EU and Turkey. After many decades of EU dictate, Turkey turned against its never-ending candidacy and Turkish Prime Minister Recep Tayyip Erdođan warned the EU that it would lose Turkey if it could not accede until 2023. (EurActiv, 2012b) Though the Western Balkan countries could hardly achieve any unilateral turnover without significant external help, the fact that Turkey demonstrates that there is life outside the EU might undermine other potential candidate and candidate countries' convictions regarding EU integration.

Costs and benefits of reorienting economic and political networks

From a rational point of view, the response to the question whether it is worthwhile for the Western Balkan countries to reorient their external relations would simply rest on a cost-benefit analysis. However, the answer is very complex and can hardly be measured by numerical data.

Although in the short run economic problems will represent concerns, it is unlikely that Croatia or Montenegro would give up the political advantages of EU membership perspective. The question is more relevant in the case of countries for which EU membership might be a target forever. In the long run, the costs of developing new or reforming former institutions can be better distributed and do not necessitate any sudden action that might cause a negative reaction on the part of the international community. In particular, the lack of credibility of EU membership if accompanied by an alternative assisting actor that expects less political compliance could increase competition for the EU.

From this perspective Serbia seems to be the most "vulnerable". Will it become the "black sheep" of the Western Balkans? The political price is that Serbia or other countries like Macedonia could become stuck in permanently unresolved debates, engaging with international actors representing contradictory positions vis-à-vis the EU in international forums. This has two important political implications. On the one hand, it would further weaken the fragile regional approach of the EU toward the Western Balkans and would undermine reform initiatives of the EU. On the other hand, if finally membership of these countries would be achieved, they might create a group of states whose foreign policy is not in line with that of the EU.

What kind of other security concerns might the EU have? The region, though burdened by tensions, is unlikely to fall back to war-level conflicts. The situation in Northern Kosovo has raised concerns, but the fact that Serbia did not intervene in 2011, as clashes arose when control of border checkpoints was given to the Kosovo Albanian administration, implies that the use of open aggression would not serve the political aims of Serbia. It is also promising that after the last Communication of the Commission Serbia continued a constructive policy and Ivica Dacic met Hashim Thaci in the framework of the EU-mediated Pristina-Belgrade Dialogue. At the same time, as underlined above, Tomislav Nikolic emphasized the limits of such a dialogue and reaffirmed that recognition of Kosovo as an independent state is unacceptable. The EU will need to find the right way to resolve this conflict in order to avoid a black hole in its closer neighborhood.

Conclusion

The analysis of this chapter is based on the assumption that the Western Balkan countries have a real promise of EU membership and it concludes on that basis. The EU's position is strong in the region as a consequence of the high-level integration with the Western Balkans achieved throughout the last decade. Recently none of the actors examined in this chapter can compete with the high share of the EU in trade, financial sector and foreign direct investement in the Western Balkan countries but this status quo seems to be vulnerable in view of the impacts of the economic and financial crisis.

The long-lasting crisis diverts valueable attention and resources from the Western Balkans while through the strong linkages built with EU, the negative impacts of the crisis spread over the region. In the long run these two parallel tendencies might weaken governments' engagement toward EU integration in the Western Balkans and strengthen the demand for diversification of economic and political relations which would open doors for other international actors seeking opportunities to improve their positions in the region. The strengthening position of Russia, China and Turkey could change the balance of powers to some extent (especially in relation to Serbia, BiH and Macedonia), which might cause serious challenges for the EU and its regional role and undermine policy initiatives being efficient at a regional level, like fighting against organized crime.

Furthermore, as these international actors often represent counter poles in other international issues against the EU, their increased political and economic influence can easily become a dividing factor in the region which would further stabilize existing division lines among and within Western Balkan countries. Particularly, Russia and China could benefit from this situation and develop their own interest groups within the region. The US seems to have the least ambitious aspirations in the region, which is the result of the new priority agenda of the United States. The role of Turkey in the Western Balkans cannot be isolated from the recent changes in the relations between Turkey and the EU. Though its policy does not contradict the plans of the EU, Turkey's competing behavior might strengthen doubts about the attraction of EU membership.

Thus the EU cannot afford wasting time and should increase efforts to re-engage both EU member states and the Western Balkan countries with EU enlargement and related reforms. EU member states will need to formulate a more strategic approach toward the region in order to ensure that no black hole will appear which could jeopardize the regional level achievements. Among others it will need to facilitate the resolution of bilateral disputes which do not simply hamper the EU enlargement process but seriously undermine the credibility of

EU membership perspective by abolishing achievements and political benefits of already implemented reforms.

EU strategy should pay more attention to the fact that the eurozone crisis has severely hit the region's economy and threatens former achievements in economic growth and democratization. Though social security was already a great challenge in the Western Balkans before the economic crisis, the worsening situation might increase the risk of migration toward the EU, which is already seen as a concern by several member states. In the long run the negative economic impacts can also decrease the public support of EU accession and can weaken political interest of local parties engaging themsleves to reform processes. Thus EU will have to balance such tendencies and build strategic partnerships with political parties in the Western Balkan countries that are in favor of EU integration and represent influential political power.

Strengthened political commitment to and public support for EU accession in the Western Balkan countries could at least partly balance the political influence of other international actors stemming from their recent economic investments in the region and could give time for the EU to address economic challenges and member states to re-engage with the Western Balkan countries' integration.

Bibliography

Altmann, F.-L. (2005). EU und Westlicher Balkan. Von Dayton nach Brüssel: ein allzu langer Weg. *SWP-Studie. January 2005.* Retrieved from http://www.swp-berlin.org/fileadmin/contents/products/studien/2005_S01_alt_ks.pdf, 10.08.2012

Ashbrook, J. E. (2010). Croatia, euroskepticism and the identity politics of EU enlargement. *Problems of Post-Communism, 57(3),* 23 ? 39.

Balkan Insight (2012). Russia Pushes Croatia to Sign Gas Deal. *BalkanInsight.* August 13, 2012 Retrieved from http://www.balkaninsight.com/en/article/russians-pushes-croatia-to-sign-a-gas-deal, 09.09.2012.

Barbulescu, I. G., & Troncota, M. (2012). The ambivalent role of the EU in the Western Balkans – "Limited Europeanisation" between formal promises and practical constraints: The case of Bosnia and Herzegovina. *Romanian Journal of European Affairs, 12(1),* pp. 5 ? 26

Bechev, D. (2012). The periphery of the periphery: The Western Balkans and the euro crisis. European Council on Foreign Relations, No. 60, August 2012. Retrieved from http://ecfr.eu/page/-/ECFR60_WESTERN_BALKANS_BRIEF_AW.pdf, 19.09.2012

Bugajski, J. (2010, September). *Western Balkans Policy Review 2010.* Retrieved from the website of CSIS http://csis.org/files/publication/100917_Bugajski_WesternBalkans_WEB.pdf, 10.08.2012

Calic, M-J. (2004). Der Stabilizierungs- und Assoziierungsprozeß auf dem Prüfstand. Empfehlungen für die Weiterentwicklung europäischer Balkanpolitik. *SWP-Studie. January 2004.* Retrieved from http://www.swp-berlin.org/fileadmin/contents/products/studien/2004_S33_clc_ks.pdf, 10.08.2012.

DG Trade (March 21, 2012). *Croatia.* Retrieved from http://trade.ec.europa.eu/doclib/docs/2006/september/tradoc_113370.pdf, 11.09.2012

DG Trade (March 21, 2012a). *Albania.* Retrieved from http://trade.ec.europa.eu/doclib/docs/2006/september/tradoc_113342.pdf, 11.09.2012

DG Trade (March 21, 2012b). *Bosnia and Herzegovina.* Retrieved from http://trade.ec.europa.eu/doclib/docs/2006/september/tradoc_113358.pdf, 11.09.2012

DG Trade. (21 March 2012d). *Macedonia.* Retrieved from http://trade.ec.europa.eu/doclib/docs/2006/september/tradoc_113381.pdf, 11.09.2012

DG Trade. (21 March 2012e). *Montenegro.* Retrieved from http://trade.ec.europa.eu/doclib/docs/2008/august/tradoc_140030.pdf, 11.09.2012)

DG Trade. (21 March 2012f). *Serbia.* Retrieved from http://trade.ec.europa.eu/doclib/docs/2008/august/tradoc_140028.pdf, 11.09.2012

Economist Intelligence Unit. (2012a). *Country report — Albania.* Retrieved from http://country.eiu.com/FileHandler.ashx?issue_id=519740836&mode=pdf, 14.11.2012

Economist Intelligence Unit. (2012b). *Country report — Bosnia and Herzegovina.* Retrieved from http://country.eiu.com/FileHandler.ashx?issue_id=39635588&mode=pdf, 26.10.2012

Economist Intelligence Unit. (2012c). *Country report — Croatia.* Retrieved from http://country.eiu.com/FileHandler.ashx?issue_id=569621841&mode=pdf, 24.10.2012

Economist Intelligence Unit. (2012d). *Country report — Macedonia.* Retrieved from http://country.eiu.com/FileHandler.ashx?issue_id=249381809&mode=pdf, 26.10.2012

Economist Intelligence Unit. (2012e). *Country report — Montenegro.* Retrieved from http://country.eiu.com/FileHandler.ashx?issue_id=29699787&mode=pdf, 26.10.2012

Economist Intelligence Unit. (2012f). *Country report — Serbia.* Retrieved from http://country.eiu.com/FileHandler.ashx?issue_id=839714868&mode=pdf, 26.10.2012

EurActive (2012a) Ghost of Yugoslav bank haunts Croatia's EU path. EurActiv 25 July, 2012. (Retrieved from http://www.euractiv.com/enlargement/ghost-yugoslav-bank-haunts-croat-news-514115, 12.09.2012)

EurActive (2012b). EU will lose Turkey if it hasn't joined by 2023, Er-doďan says. *EurActiv* 31 October, 2012. Retrieved from http://www.euractiv.com/enlargement/eu-lose-turkey-hasnt-joined-2023-news-515780, 05.11.2012

European Commission (2011). *Communication from the Commission to the European Parliament and the Council. Enlargement strategy and main challenges 2011-2012*. Retrieved from http://ec.europa.eu/enlargement/pdf/key_documents/2011/package/strategy_pape r_2011_en.pdf, 31.07.2012

Eurostat (2012a). EU-China Summit. *?EU27 deficit in trade in goods with China down to 67 bn euro in the first six months of 2012*. Retrieved from epp.eurostat.ec.europa.eu/cache/ITY_PUBLIC/6-18092012-AP/EN/6-18092012-AP-EN.PDF, 19.10.2012

Eurostat (2012b). *GDP per capita in PPS. Data from 1st December 2012*. Retrieved from http://epp.eurostat.ec.europa.eu/tgm/table.do?tab=table&init=1&plugin=1&language=en&pcode=tec00114, 01.09.2012

Eurostat. (2012c). *Harmonised unemployment rate by sex*. Retrieved from http://epp.eurostat.ec.europa.eu/tgm/table.do?tab=table&language=en&pcode=teilm020&tableSelection=1&plugin=1, 01.09.2012

Eurostat. (2012d). *Real GDP growth rate – volume*. Retrieved from http://epp.eurostat.ec.europa.eu/tgm/table.do?tab=table&init=1&plugin=1&language=en&pcode=tec00115, 01.09.2012

Eurostat. (2012e). *Pocketbook on the enlargement countries. 2012 edition*. Luxembourg: Publications Office of the European Union.

Gross, E., & Rotta, A. (2011). The EEAS and the Western Balkans. *IAI Working Paper* Vol. 11, No. 15. (Retrieved from http://www.iai.it/pdf/DocIAI/iaiwp1115.pdf, 20.09.2012)

Jović, D. (2011). Turning nationalists into EU supporters: The case of Croatia. In J. Rupnik (Ed.) (2011). The Western Balkans and the EU: 'The hour of Europe'. *Chaillot Papers*, No. 126, June 2011. (Retrieved from http://www.iss.europa.eu/uploads/media/cp126-The_Western_Balkans_and_the_EU.pdf, 15.07.2012)

Noutcheva, G. (2009). Fake, partial and imposed compliance: The limits of the EU's normative power in the Western Balkans. *Journal of European Public Policy*, Vol. 16, No. 7, pp. 1065 ? 1084

Ordanoski, S. (2011). The story of Macedonian populism: 'All we want is everything!' In Rupnik, J. (Ed.) (2011). The Western Balkans and the EU: 'The hour of Europe'. *Chaillot Papers*, No. 126, June 2011. Retrieved from http://www.iss.europa.eu/uploads/media/cp126-The_Western_Balkans_and_the_EU.pdf, 15.07.2012

Poulain, L. & Sakellariou, A. (2011). Western Balkans: is Turkey back?, *CSIS, 25 April, 2011*. Retrieved from http://csis.org/blog/western-balkans-turkey-back, 20.19.2012)

Poulain, L. (2011). China's new Balkan strategy. *Central Europe Watch*,

CSIS, 1(2). Retrieved from http://csis.org/files/publication/110829_CEW_China_in_Balkans.pdf, 20.19.2012)

Radulović, M. (2011). Montenegro's journey towards EU accession. In J. Rupnik (Ed.) (2011). The Western Balkans and the EU: 'The hour of Europe'. *Chaillot Papers,* No. 126, June 2011. Retrieved from http://www.iss.europa.eu/uploads/media/cp126-The_Western_Balkans_and_the_EU.pdf, 15.07.2012

Rüma, Ý. (2010). Turkish foreign policy towards the Balkans: New activism, neo-Ottomanism or/so what? *Turkish Policy Quarterly, 9(4),* pp. 133 ? 140.

Rupnik, J. (2011). The Balkans as a European question. In J. Rupnik (Ed.) (2011). The Western Balkans and the EU: 'The hour of Europe'. *Chaillot Papers,* No. 126, June 2011. Retrieved from http://www.iss.europa.eu/uploads/media/cp126-The_Western_Balkans_and_the_EU.pdf, 15.07.2012.

Rupnik, J. (Ed.) (2011). The Western Balkans and the EU: 'The hour of Europe'. *Chaillot Papers,* No. 126, June 2011. Retrieved from http://www.iss.europa.eu/uploads/media/cp126-The_Western_Balkans_and_the_EU.pdf, 15.07.2012.

Sakellariou, A. (2011, April 11). *Obama's Policy in the Western Balkans: Following Bush's Steps.* Retrieved from http://csis.org/blog/obamas-policy-western-balkans-following-bushs-steps

Sarajlić-Maglić, D. (2011). BiH after the elections – a tale of disillusioned optimism. In J. Rupnik (Ed.) (2011). The Western Balkans and the EU: 'The hour of Europe'. *Chaillot Papers,* No. 126, June 2011. Retrieved from http://www.iss.europa.eu/uploads/media/cp126-The_Western_Balkans_and_the_EU.pdf, 15.07.2012

Schimmelfennig, F., & Scholtz, H. (2008). EU democracy promotion in the European neighbourhood: Political conditionality, economic development and transnational exchange. *European Union Politics, 9(2),* pp. 187-215.

Socor, V. (2011). Croatia hesitates between EU and Russia on energy policy. *Eurasia Daily Monitor, 8(71),* published on April 12, 2011. Retrieved from http://www.jamestown.org/single/?no_cache=1&tx_ttnews[tt_news]=37782, 30.10. 2012

Surroi, V. (2011). The unfinished state(s) in the Balkans and the EU: the next wave. In J. Rupnik (Ed.) (2011). The Western Balkans and the EU: 'The hour of Europe'. *Chaillot Papers,* No. 126, June 2011. Retrieved from http://www.iss.europa.eu/uploads/media/cp126-The_Western_Balkans_and_the_EU.pdf, 15.07.2012

Teokarevic, J. (2011). Ten years of post-Milosevic transition in Serbia: problems and prospects. In J. Rupnik (Ed.) (2011). The Western Balkans and the EU: 'The hour of Europe'. *Chaillot Papers,* No. 126, June 2011. Retrieved from http://www.iss.europa.eu/uploads/media/cp126-The_Western_Balkans_and_the_EU.pdf, 15.07.2012

United States Department of State. (2012). U.S. Foreign Policy: Western Balkans Update. Retrieved from http://fpc.state.gov/185514.htm#

UN Security Council. (2012). *High Representative for Bosnia and Herzegovina tells Security Council country on track for "breakthrough year" if progress sustained.* Retrieved from http://www.un.org/News/Press/docs/2012/sc10650.doc.htm, 08.08.2012

Vasconcelos, Álvaro de (ed.) (2011). The agenda for EU-US strategic partnership. France: EU Institute for Security Studies.

The forever candidate – Turkey and the EU

Fruzsina Tófalvi

The literature on the accession of Turkey to the European Union has been dominated by questions weighing the advantages and disadvantages of Turkish membership, assessing EU conditionality, and evaluating Turkish efforts to fulfill those. The discussion has therefore been highly focused on the point of view of the European Union concerning Turkish membership. However, this chapter will embark on a different track, believing that the current geopolitical reality and the relative strength of the accession candidate in question induce us to treat the two sides on a more equal footing and consider the Turkish perspective in depth. Thus, the current study will deconstruct this half-century-long relationship with regard to the domestic changes in Turkey.

Until the late 1990s both the domestic and foreign policy of Turkey were dominated by mostly conservative Kemalist values. The modernization plans of Kemalism fostered the Westernization of the country and later facilitated the EU accession process. However, the subsequent interpretations of the Kemalist norms also encompassed the undemocratic guardian role of the Turkish Armed Forces (TAF) and the Constitutional Court against Islamization, the demands of the Kurdish minority, furthermore the protection of the republic and Turkish "democracy", which were in stark contrast with the political criteria and the reforms demanded by the European Union. In the early 2000s the reforms guided by the EU opened the way for the upcoming center-right Justice and Development Party (AKP), as right-wing, religious parties were mostly "sabotaged" by the secular establishment and the guardian institutions in the previous decades. The democratization process, which was boosted by the AKP, eventually led to the slow and steady reduction of the power of the institutions guarding Kemalist principles.

The study argues that the fundamental characteristic of the Turkish domestic scene, Kemalism, entailed two contradictory norms that could not be reconciled as the Europeanization plans moved forward. These two opposing norms originated in republicanism/secularism, and modernization. Although republicanism and secularism *per se* did not challenge the Europeanization plans, the guardian role of the TAF over the republic and also for the preservation of secular values soon became a norm in its own right. Those siding with the secularists believed that their methods were securing the modernization of the state and the conservation of democracy, and did not realize that the modus operandi of the guardian institutions (such as military coups and the banning of parties) were inconsistent with the values of democracy. The principle of modernization, however, pointed towards the opposite direction. Modernization, that developed into a wish to Europeanize the country and later became manifest in EU accession plans as an ultimate destination of modernity, was supported by the same groups as the guardianship. However, the "unexpected" side-effect of this process was the necessity to truly democratize the county according to European standards. Eventually, Kemalism became one of the greatest obstacles to Europeanization.

However, the list of contradictions has not ended just yet. Although in parallel with the weakening of the enforcers of Kemalism, the democratization process could be intensified. It turned the field of foreign policy upside-down: actually, the democratization of foreign policy, namely giving full control over foreign policy to the government in place of military control, resulted in decreasing the EU orientation. Therefore, the reform process not only resulted in the removal of decade-long taboos on domestic norms and institutions, but also liberated the field of foreign policy from military control and caused the immediate reconsideration of foreign policy interests. Turkey reassessed its friends and foes in its region, and began the reconstruction of its role in a new framework. Such a transformation of foreign policy was the necessary result of the significant economic interest that Turkey acquired in the neighboring regions from the mid 2000s, coupled with the new, unrestrainedly expressible Islamic/Turkic identity of the leadership, furthermore the significant change in the public opinion concerning the EU accession plans. (Bank & Karadag, 2012, p.14)

The new foreign policy of Turkey in its neighborhood included détente with the leaders of the Arab world and the neighboring countries, a pre-emptive approach towards the challenges in the area, and active diplomacy in the Balkans and Central Asia, transforming Turkey into a true regional power. The hard times that the European Union faced, being occupied primarily with its internal problems, was coupled with a strong, self-confident Turkey becoming a member of the G20, aspiring to regional leadership, and pursuing its own foreign policy interests, instead of merely following Europe. Therefore, my argument would entail that, all in all, the reform process carried out under the flag of Europeanization transformed the institutions of the Turkish domestic arena, which subsequently also distanced Turkey from the European Union.

In general, the effects caused by the domestic changes in Turkey are overlooked by the literature, as the efforts of most authors are highly EU-centered. (Buhari, 2009, p. 97) Even those considering the domestic factors have failed to give primacy to them. (Narbone & Tocci, 2009; Müftüler-Baç, 2005) However, if the adoption of laws and harmonization of policies is a one-way street where the domestic determination to join the EU is treated as a default point of departure for Turkey, explaining phenomena such as the lack of implementation of the adopted reform laws and generally the recent widening distance between Turkey and the EU is problematic. Ziya Öniş (2003) is one of the authors who have highlighted the importance of domestic factors, claiming that without the domestic will for accession it would have been impossible to even start discussing the effects of Europeanization. (p. 9) Public opinion, as well as coalitions within the ruling and the economic elite had the ability to speed up or hinder the reform process. He concludes that institutional changes alone would not have produced the expected results in Turkey. (Öniş, 2003, p. 22)

In agreement with Öniş, this study argues that by broadening the definition of institutions into the realm of norms can better explain the motives that guided the actors to support or obstruct the reforms. Therefore, the study will apply the sociological institutionalist theory as outlined by March and Olsen to the domestic changes in Turkey. (March & Olsen, 1984; 2006) Sociological institutionalism explains political acts by the institutional background they exist in, though institutions in this interpretation are not only explicit, formal rules, but also implicit norms and beliefs.(March & Olsen, 1998, p. 948.) Accordingly, the study will argue that the institutions of the Turkish political arena have shown rigidity over time: although the EU provided incentives for change, and reforms were introduced, due to the contradictory norm of Kemalism the actors adapted slowly. The legislative background and to some extent the normative background of the institutions became transformed only when the unsustainability of the institutions became evident due to the rejection received from the European Union concerning membership.

Based on this idea, the relationship of Turkey and the EU, and the consequent democratic development of Turkey, can be divided into three consecutive eras: the Kemalist modernization/Westernization period (1923-1999), the subsequent Europeanization period (2000-2007) and finally a period of "autonomization" (from 2008), where Turkey is seeking its own way of development, while pursuing a more pragmatic relationship with the EU and the West. There is no strict division between these three periods. At certain times they overlapped, but their effect on the reforms and Turkey's approach towards the EU is distinct. The analysis will focus more on the last two eras of the relationship, as these periods contain the most positive, active times of the relationship, and the swift turn in the relation soon after the start of the accession negotiations.

The overall contribution of this study to the understanding of the topic is firstly that it applies a neo-institutional explanation without being EU-centric, and without focusing on the influence of the European Union on domestic changes, but ascribing importance to the effect of domestic changes themselves. (See, for example, Müftüler-Baç& McLaren, 2003) Secondly, and more generally, this study recognizes the necessity to apply established theories of political science and international relations to the events in Turkey in order to produce a structured debate, instead of cause and effect accounts or descriptive analyses. (SoleriLecha, 2008, p. 3)

The first section outlines the analytical framework of the study, briefly introducing sociological institutionalism. Secondly, the domestic institutional and normative context of EU-Turkey relations will be examined. This process will be broken up into three parts: the Kemalist modernization period introducing the institutional background of the EU accession process; the following transitory period, when most of the legal alignment with European expectations was carried out; and finally the period of autonomization will be discussed, explaining how the reform process led Turkey on a road towards becoming a powerful actor on the international scene, resulting in a changed dynamic between the EU and Turkey. The study concludes that Turkey has undergone a deep transformation process, which to some extent democratized the country, but mostly it liberated the field of foreign policy from military influence. As a result Turkey gained an ambitious role in the international environment with defined interests in its neighborhood, sometimes different from that of the European Union. Therefore, the current environment (both domestic and international) is not conducive to Turkey's EU accession process. Consequently, the EU will have to prepare scenarios counting with an increasingly independent Turkey, where areas of cooperation are likely to be found outside the regular framework connected to the accession process.

A sociological institutional framework

The analytical framework of the chapter will rely on new institutionalist theory, more specifically the sociological institutionalist account of March and Olsen. Common to all forms of institutionalism is that they all place institutions in the center of attention, although the theory itself has branched out into a series of interpretations about how institutions matter. (March & Olsen, 1984; 2006; Evans, 1985; DiMaggio & Powell, 1991; Moravcsik, 1993; Hall & Taylor, 1996) Institutions in the understanding of sociological institutionalism are

> A relatively stable collection of practices and rules defining appropriate behavior [...]. Such practices and rules are embedded in structures of meaning and schemes of interpretation that explain and legitimize particular identities and the practices and rules associated with them. (March & Olsen, 1998, p. 948)

There are two assumptions of institutionalism that are common to most interpretations of the theory. One of them is that institutions provide the state with *"elements of order and predictability"*. The second is that

> The translation of structures into political action and action into institutional continuity and change, are generated by comprehensible and routine processes. These processes produce recurring modes of action and organizational patterns. (March & Olsen, 2005, p. 6)

The question is then, how these patterns are disrupted and altered over time, which is exactly the puzzle in the Turkish case. (March & Olsen, 2005, p. 6) The activity of the guardians in the framework of Kemalism produced such patterns: Turkish military coups and the laws the military passed in the following rebuilding periods in order to secure its policy objectives through control over the "democratic" processes caused the institutionalization of the Kemalist norms. Several authors suggest that the guardians pursued a self-interested behavior in these periods and wanted to secure their power for the future. (Belge, 2006; Varol, 2012) Although such an interpretation of the events seems plausible, it fails to explain changes over time: why did the military finally allow reductions in its power? Why did it not intervene when Turkey modified its foreign policy to pursue strong ties with its neighborhood and move towards a détente with the leaders of the Arab world recently? And lastly, why was there no push for the swift implementation of reforms under the cover of EU demands?

Sociological institutionalism has a strong explanatory power in this case. March and Olsen propose that the *"logic of appropriateness"* guides the actors in the political arena. This means that the actors probably weigh the possible consequences of their actions, but they also follow norms that are thought to be appropriate in the given situation, and they relate to previous decision-making practices, identities, and so on. (March & Olsen, 1998, p. 951-952) The logic of appropriateness, therefore, overwrites rational or strategic calculation, which is the key element of both historical and rational choice institutionalism. (Hall & Taylor, 1996, p. 949) Therefore, it is understandable that the pressure for a reduction in the power of the guardians appeared only slowly, due to the assumption concerning the embeddedness of Kemalism in both the political system and society, and also because of the fear of intervention. In addition, the TAF, which could have intervened at any time in order to save its power and influence, did not do so, and the Constitutional Court, which could have hindered this process, also abandoned attempts to hinder the reforms of the AKP government. The reason is that they were guided by the norms provided by Europeanization. Therefore, norms enjoyed primacy over rational choice when the guardian institutions gave in to the reduction of their power.

Naturally, critics of the previous proposition could argue that the change in Turkey took decades, which is indeed true. However, when examining institutional change, we need to take the so-called policy *"lock-in"* into consideration. (Pierson, 2000) This term describes the institutional inefficiency in adapting to a change in the environment: the more accustomed the actors become with institutions, the more rigidly they respond to change. Therefore, institutions, norms and practices are usually still in use when they are not particularly efficient any more ("sticky institutions"). (March & Olsen, 1998, p. 965) In the neo-institutional accounts, change generally occurs when old practices and institutions are showing the signs of failure, usually in critical times (for example historical institutionalism). Sociological institutionalists propose that the decline of the legitimacy of an institution or the norms underlying the institution also leads to change. (March & Olsen, 1998, p. 966) The idea fits the Turkish case: the primacy of the objectives of the guardian institutions as compared to the decisions of the democratically elected authorities was sustainable until the idea of the necessity to guard the republic became a generally accepted norm. When the democratization process and the continuously postponed EU accession destroyed the aforementioned norm, reconsideration of the role of the guardian institutions was possible. In the following sections the process of norm transformation and adaptation will be examined further.

The modernization project (the Kemalist era: 1923-1999)

In Turkey the idea of EU accession has been a domestic, elite-imposed venture. From 1923 Mustafa Kemal proposed the establishment of a secular republic on the ruins of the Ottoman Empire, based on the adoption of Western values. Although there was an initiative for modernization and Westernization already in the Ottoman era, the forced and inorganic Westernization of Turkey in the early years of the republic still came as a shock to most people: women's suffrage, the strict expulsion of religion from public life, the new alphabet, and other reforms changed the domestic landscape of Turkey in a short period of time. (Goldschmidt & Davidson, 2010, p. 222) But the Turkish elite wanted to join the rest of Europe and were willing to make sacrifices, often against the will of society.

The early years of the new republic brought about the formation of a Western-oriented secular elite, protective of the achievements of the modernization process, and willing to defend the republic against reactionary, conservative and Islamist forces. The project of Westernization initially did not equal democratization, the establishment rather resembled an *"authoritarian (…) unitary state"*. (Joseph, 2006, p. 1) As the TAF was an integral part of the secular, Europe-oriented elite, its influence on politics was immense. The four coup d'états that the TAF performed in 1960, 1971, 1980 and 1997 showed that the preservation of the values of Kemal and security issues enjoyed priority over actual transition, the building of a true democracy and societal demands. Evidence of this contradiction can be easily found in the election results: after the transitory, mostly single-party period of Turkey (1923-1946), at the first multi-party election in 1950 Kemal's Republican People's Party (CHP) already lost out to the right-wing Democratic Party. The CHP has had a hard time in the competition with the religious, right-wing forces ever since. Although the secular institutions did not stop these parties from forming a government, the governments were overthrown by the military if they were accused of Islamism, authoritarian attempts, or seeking ties with states in the Middle East, and/or due to the perceived inability to provide security in times of political unrest. As such, modernization and Westernization soon became more a norm than a tool for the political elite. To what extent society agreed with the acts of the TAF is open for debate. However, the military was the most trusted institution in Turkey according to Eurobarometer Survey, therefore its activity was generally legitimized by its popularity, if not by its content. (European Commission, 2011) All in all, election results, public opinion and the ideas of the secular elite were in constant asynchrony in Turkey during the modernization period.

The military not only influenced politics and decision making through direct interventions, but attempted to secure the results of these interventions via institutions: political measures and the imposition of new constitutions were the tools to establish the political influence of the military after returning to civilian governance. Most of the channels of influence of the TAF were institutionalized after coup d'états, mainly the ones in 1960 and in 1980. The National Security Council (NSC) was the body where the political influence of the armed forces was manifest, with control over most of the foreign and defense policy areas. The Council was established as a civil-military advisory group that gained more power over the years, with the number of military-affiliated members also rising. The power of the NSC was large enough for it to be able to enforce the submission of information by institutions, organizations and legal persons, whether it was unrestricted or confidential. (European Council, 2004 p. 22) From 1982 the government was forced to follow the instructions of the NSC. (Aydinli, Özcan & Akyaz, 2006, p. 82) It would be false to claim that governments had no space at all to maneuver in the area of foreign policy. For example, President Turgut Özal achieved the participation of Turkey in the Gulf War, although the NSC objected to it. (Bank & Karadag, 2012, p. 9) But generally speaking, foreign (and security) policy was the domain of the military that did not trust politicians handling such issues, and accordingly it was a strongly controlled area. In addition, the TAF also exercised (and continues to exercise) influence through its informal opinion-shaping power. The leaders of the military regularly announced their opinions on questions within the competency of the government, usually concerning security and foreign policy issues, and often beyond that. (Konijnenbelt, 2006, p. 189)

The Constitutional Court also acted as a severe guardian of secularism, nationalism and Kemalism in general. Any (assumed) attack on secularism was treated as a threat, not to mention the establishment of political parties related to the Kurdish minority. The Court has often operated under the hands of the TAF, banning political parties and certain popular politicians from the political arena. This was not surprising considering the fact that the Constitutional Court was established after the first coup, precisely in order to prevent severe deviations from Kemalist values on the part of the government and the National Assembly. (Varol, 2012, p. 329) The Court banned 25 parties during its existence over fifty years, for example the popular Welfare Party (Refah Partisi) of Erbakan in 1997 and its successor, the Virtue Party, and most recently the Kurdish Democratic Society Party. Furthermore, it attempted to ban the ruling Justice and Development Party (AKP) in 2007. (Kuru & Stepan, 2012) The activity of the TAF and the Constitutional Court shows that the coalition behind the guardian institutions and the system they maintained not only consisted of secularists, but also nationalists and those fearing Kurdish demands. In addition, the supporters of this status quo could be found in the judiciary, the media and political parties. (Kuru, 2012, p. 39)

Parallel to the guardianship of the institutions "defending" the results of modernization, there were several "quasi taboos" in the Turkish political arena that could not be challenged without expecting retaliation from the guardians, thus serving as normative thresholds for the actors of the political arena. One of the taboos was, naturally, curbing the rights and powers of the guardian institutions. In addition, the strict exclusion of religious behavior from public life had to be observed. Deals with the Kurdish minority and the Kurdistan Workers' Party (PKK) were non-negotiable. According to Kemalist foreign policy, closer ties with the Middle East and Islamic countries were not regarded as desirable, while a Western orientation (and later EU accession) was a must. The first reason was that foreign policy was rooted in a rather suspicious outlook regarding the security environment of Turkey, watching out for rivals, enemies and supporters of terrorism in its neighborhood, such as Armenia, Syria and Greece. Interestingly, this approach hardly changed with the end of the Cold War, when TAF concluded that the challenges facing Turkey had become exacerbated. (Uzgel, 2003, p. 188) The second reason is that Islam and Islamism was a part of the security perception of the TAF: they believed that the religious political forces of Turkey wished to 'cooperate' with the Islamist states of the region to construct a similar political system in Turkey. (Uzgel, 2003, p. 187) Therefore, being secular-minded, Western-oriented, republican, nationalist and democratic were synonyms in the rhetoric of the secularists.

As a result, the dominant foreign policy of Turkey involved seeking closer ties with the West while mostly ignoring the Middle East. Turkey neglected its nearest strategic environment and relations with states such as Syria and Egypt, building instead friendly ties with Western states and Israel. (Tank, 2006, p. 467) Consequently, it was quite logical to pursue membership in European institutions like the European Economic Community (EEC) and the Council of Europe. Furthermore, it was also commonly perceived that membership in these institutions would have put the rubber stamp on Turkey's Western/European identity. Therefore Westernization, which manifested itself later in EU accession aspirations, was a domestic affair with normative tones, and had a solid coalition behind it. All significant parties were committed to EU membership to some extent, or at least they could not oppose it. (Öniş, 2003, p. 17)

Successful accession to the EEC seemed to be plausible at the time. There were fundamentally three reasons for that. Firstly, the Ankara Agreement of 1963 declared the possibility of Turkish accession. Secondly, the EU accession process initially focused primarily on the economic aspect of integration and lacked cultural or political criteria, such as straightforward conditions outlining the necessary level of democratization for candidates, or the discussion over the common cultural values behind the Community, such as Christianity.[1] Therefore, doubts concerning the ability of Turkey to join the Community did not arise at the time. Thirdly, even when political conditionality became more definite, the Turkish political elite did not perceive it to be a burden in relation to accession, as the general idea in Turkey was that the country more or less satisfied the criteria by being a secular multi-party democracy: a misperception that set them up for a major disappointment. (Narbone & Tocci, 2009, p. 24)

What the elite did not want to face was that the secular institutions kept guard over the republic using undemocratic methods. Thus Kemalism contained

---

1   The *Declaration on Democracy* of 1978 was the first document focusing on the importance of safeguarding democracy and human rights in the member states, motivated by the foreseeable southern enlargement of the EU. (Sedelmeier, 2003, p. 10) Democracy and the protection of human rights only became an actual conditionality when the East-Central European states began their accession process. The Copenhagen Criteria of 1993 listed a series of political criteria, including a democracy with stable institutions and the rule of law, furthermore respect for human rights and granting minority rights. (Verney, 2009, p. 3.)

an immense contradiction. It entailed an aspect that forced its defending institutions on a track that destined them to reduce, or even destroy their own power. The Western orientation of the Kemalists and their support for EU accession was in stark contrast with the political criteria that the EU laid out for Turkey, including democratization through the establishment of civil control. The influence of the TAF over the executive, the judiciary, culture and public opinion, the lack of accountability, and the constant danger of intervention was repeatedly criticized once Turkey started the accession process. If the Turkish secular elite insisted on the Westernization process, eventually they had to loosen their grip on power. One could hardly find more adequate words than those of Henri J. Barkey (2011):

> Turkey began the process of joining the European Community, the precursor to the European Union, a unique body brought together by shared values. This is where the inconsistency of the Kemalist ideology was most apparent: it pushed Turkey toward Europe, while it simultaneously rejected much of the values that the EU represented. (p. 21)

The first rejection Turkey experienced from the Community was in 1987: after order was restored following the coup d'état of 1980, Turkey applied for membership in the EEC, unsuccessfully. After a series of economic and some political reforms, such as the removal of some restrictions on the freedom of expression, the rights of trade unions and easing the ban on the use of the Kurdish language, Turkey joined the customs union in 1995, which generally could be evaluated as a success. However, that was not the case for Turkey and for public opinion, which had been expecting membership for decades and experienced rejection in the fourth enlargement wave, as well. (European Commission, 1998) Clearly, the reforms did not cause a breakthrough and it soon turned out that for the time being joining the customs union was the temporary alternative to membership.

In 1997 at the Luxembourg summit, just a couple of months after Turkey's last military coup overthrowing an Islamist government, the EU announced its next enlargement wave. However, Turkey was again not selected to be a candidate. After the rejection, the Commission submitted a progress report criticizing the standing of human rights and freedom of expression, the treatment of detainees, the death penalty, the excessive role of the military in politics including the National Security Council, and the restrictions on the Kurdish language, not to mention the still unsatisfactory quality of the relationship of Turkey with Greece and Cyprus. (European Commission, 1998, p. 9)

As a result of the Luxembourg decision, Turkish decision-makers and society in general experienced a major disappointment: the institutions they believed to be mostly aligned with democratic principles were failing the test. Indeed, as the World Values Survey results illustrate, Turkish respondents were almost equally split on the issue as to whether they believe that a military takeover in the case of *"an incompetent government"* is an *"essential part of democracy"*, albeit those believing that a military takeover is part of democracy were in a slight majority. Furthermore, the majority of respondents believed that the country was more democratic than not. This means that Turkish society's definition of democracy was largely different from that of the European Union. The result, which was understood as a discriminatory approach, caused Turkey to temporarily turn away from the EU and announce that all dialogue with the EU would be suspended. The idea of being "European without being in the EU" started to gain popularity. (Kohen & Robins, 1998) Interestingly, candidacy was finally granted in the Helsinki summit of 1999, despite the fact that no significant improvement had happened in the previous two years, and that the memory of the coup of 1997 was rather recent, as was the ban on the former governing party, Refah, which happened merely a year before the announcement of the candidacy.

All in all, the Westernization period in Turkey was the era when the modernization of Turkey began, but also the era when the political actors and society internalized the undemocratic, guardian norms. The following section on the Europeanization era will introduce the launch of Europeanization and the phenomenon of the lock-in of institutions, as well as the process through which the norms gradually broke down.

Transition (the Europeanization period: 2000-2007)

The period beginning with 2000 marks a significant turn to Europe on behalf of Turkey. Interestingly, this era was also the time when, due to the war in Iraq, it became evident that the interests of Turkey and the West will not always be compatible in the post-Cold War security environment: Turkey did not favor the idea of turmoil in its neighborhood, and consequently the increased opportunities for the PKK. The cooling of relations with the US was coupled with growing attention towards Europe and increased discourse over the necessity of Europeanization as compared to the preservation of the undemocratic and damaging practices and policies deriving from Kemalism.

In the late 1990s it became clear for Turkish decision-makers that Europe's resistance towards Turkish membership was larger than had been assumed. Furthermore, the progress reports showed that without de facto institutional changes membership would never be achieved. In addition, the role of the military in decision making and its human rights records as outlined by the progress report resulted in a more vivid civil society discourse over its legitimacy. The powerful TUSIAD (Turkish Businessmen's and Industrialists' Association) questioned the direction and usefulness of the military-controlled foreign policy of Turkey, and a general dialogue formed over these issues in the opposition. (Uzgel, 2003, p. 210) The normative foundations of Kemalism were shaking and it was becoming clear that if Turkey wanted to keep up its bid for EU membership, the modernization project had to turn eventually into a true Europeanization project. Europeanization, however, meant more than modernization: Turkey had to reform its institutions and policies to match *"the requirements of the systemic logic, political dynamics and administrative mechanisms"* of the EU. (Joseph, 2006, p. 2)

According to most branches of institutionalism, a crisis of institutions of such significance should have resulted in their transformation. What actually happened was somewhat different. Indeed, in the positive atmosphere following the Helsinki decision a series of reforms occurred in the area of civil liberties and human rights. However, the sobering experience for both parties was that the walls of Kemalism could not be broken down easily merely by laws, and not until the actors within these institutions had internalized the norms of democracy, or until the members of the elite were replaced by a new generation, just as sociological institutionalism would predict.

After a series of short-lived governments, in 1999 a coalition government formed made up of the Democratic Left Party, the center right-wing Motherland Party and the nationalist right-wing National Action Party. Although the cohesion within the coalition was relatively weak due to the apparent ideological differences among its members, the emergence of this weak government luckily coincided with the Helsinki decision, which restored the optimism towards the chances of EU accession, thereby causing a positive change in public attitudes regarding the demanded reform process. The optimistic atmosphere enabled the coalition to launch a series of reforms, previously unimaginable. The foundation of the reform process was provided by the 2000 Accession Partnership (AP), where the priorities of reforms were listed, such as improvements in the resolution of the Cyprus question, the issue of the freedom of expression and association, the prevention of torture, the functioning of the judiciary, the abolition of capital punishment, handling the discrimination of minorities, and curbing the power of the NSC. (European Commission, 2001, p. 16, 19)

In response, Turkey presented the National Program for the Adoption of the Acquis (NPAA) in 2001. The NPAA was, however, unfit to properly address the issues proposed by the AP and the reforms did not approximate the expectations of the EU. (Öniş, 2003, p. 13) Between 2001 and 2006 a new Civil Code was introduced, and constitutional amendments and nine harmonization packages were accepted by the Grand National Assembly (TBMM). In the meantime, banning the Virtue Party led to the emergence of two parties of similar orientation: the Felicity (Saadet) and the Justice and Development Party (AKP), representing a religious right-wing and a center-right ideology, respectively. In 2002, the AKP won a majority in the early elections, so from then on it continued the reform process with a two-thirds majority in the TBMM, enabling it to speed up the reform process. It is beyond the scope of this analysis to discuss the reforms in detail. What is important from the perspective of this study is that the reforms marked the launch of a true democratization process in Turkey on the institutional level. The reforms abolished the death penalty, restored the advisory nature of the NSC, enabled its president to be selected from the civilian members of the Council, and increased the number of civilians in the Council. Conventions such as the International Covenant on Civil and Political Rights and the International Covenant on Social and Cultural Rights were signed and ratified, and efforts were made to resolve the Cyprus issue by supporting the Annan Plan. (Narlý, 2006, p. 85; Ministry of Foreign Affairs, 2007; European Commission, 2004)

However, the actual implementation of the political reforms in several areas, mainly in connection with the role of the military in the political institutions, was lagging behind. The reforms made it apparent that although there was a will to adapt to the Copenhagen criteria, the secularist elite was resistant to the actual implementation of many of the institutional changes. To be fair, the authorities also showed modesty in pushing for the implementation of the laws, which was a strategically wise decision: the reforms at this point did not mean a devastating threat to the secularists, they could still retain some of their influence on foreign policy and over governance, but the legal framework for change was already outlined at this point.

We could, therefore, characterize the years following the Helsinki decision as an era of immense de jure institutional reform. Given the nature of the reforms two things became clear: firstly, deep and meaningful legal reforms were introduced, but the embedded norms of the institutions did not show a complete transformation. Although signs of the withdrawal of hard-core Kemalism became apparent, the TAF continued to play a significant role in the political arena - albeit with a gradually shifting emphasis towards informal influence - and the Constitutional Court still stood by the secular opposition, thereby weakening the democratically elected government. The second observation is that the reforms were carried out by governments that contained parties condemned as Islamist. This already signifies that a regrouping had begun within the party system, where the secular institutions and parties observed the changes with a growing fear of Islamization, mostly because the governing AKP was the successor of the truly Islamist Fazilet Party. (Tocci, 2005, p. 80) According to the critics, the reforms and therefore democratization potentially entailed a series of measures that aid Islamism: democratization would not only destroy the power of the guardian institutions, but would also introduce civil liberties, such as the freedom of religion and the freedom of speech, creating space for Islamism (for example by aiding religious schooling). Furthermore, the enforcement of only justified detention and fair trials would make it more difficult to get rid of potentially dangerous elements of society. Lastly, and most importantly, democratic foreign policy making would entail the danger of building ties with Islam-majority and Islamist states. Naturally, these issues were not explicitly stated by the secularists.

The question rightfully emerges: why did the military or the Constitutional Court not intervene to save the state from an institutional blind flight? First of all, the phenomenon can be explained by path dependency: Europeanization, at this point, was one of the guiding principles of the Turkish political elite and sabotaging the reform process would have jeopardized the accession process. Secondly, technically the political influence of these institutions remained intact for the time being, the reforms were mostly legal, and their practical adoption still remained unfinished. This was confirmed by the Progress Reports of the European Commission (2008), which repeatedly criticized the government for "not pursuing a consistent and comprehensive programme of political reforms". (p. 7)

All in all, the interval of 2000-2007 was when the path of the underlying norms of the Turkish political system divided into two seemingly contradictory, yet in fact complementary paths: one following the path of Europeanization, democratization and liberalization as expected by the EU, and one sticking to the idea of a guarded democracy with a fear of the destruction of the secular Republic. "Yesterday's conservatives have become today's reformers," and vice versa. (Tocci, 2005, p. 80) The doubts of those worrying about the reforms should have been at least weakened: as a result of the reforms, the EU opened accession negotiations with Turkey on October 3, 2005.

The final showdown and the new Turkey (the Autonomization period: from 2008)

The previous section showed that a series of reforms began the transformation of Turkey into a more democratic system, and the release of the guardians' grip on the decisions of the government. Nevertheless, a shadow of doubt continued to linger over the head of the AKP concerning whether the party was pursuing Islamist goals. And even though the reform process significantly slowed down following the announcement of the opening of the accession negotiations, the approach of the AKP towards religion and the reforms curbing the power of the TAF, together with the resistance of the secular institutions in adapting to the norms of Europeanization, led to the final showdown between the TAF and the government, leading to a completely transformed Turkey, not only domestically, but also regarding its role in the international arena.

Although the AKP had already irritated the secularists with some of its initiatives, from 2007 the AKP with its significant majority in the TBMM started to break even more taboos. Among these there was a significant institutional norm: in 2007, for the first time in the history of Turkey, a right-wing politician, Abdullah Gül, was elected by the TBMM to the seat of the President.[2] Breaking this taboo seemed to threaten secularism to the extent of evoking the traditional routines as the chief of staff, Mehmet Yaţar Büyükanýt, threatened intervention. However, the intervention never happened in a classical form. Instead, the Constitutional Court annulled the result of the election. In the event, the AKP made a strategic step calling for early parliamentary elections, where they gained even larger support than previously. The guardians started a final attack on the AKP in 2008, trying to ban the party through the Constitutional Court by accusing them of threatening the secular system. In the end, the attempt narrowly failed.

The events indicate that in 2007 and 2008 the guardians still evoked old patterns of behavior. However, an actual military coup continued to be excluded from the toolbox of the TAF since 1997. Interestingly, the Constitutional Court made two contradictory decisions in the matter of a year (one about annulling

---

2   The president in Turkey appoints the members of the Higher Education Committee, the heads of the universities, the chief of staff, and judges; therefore, he or she has power over the army, education and judiciary, the three bulwarks of secularism.

the result of the presidential election, and one about banning the AKP), although the composition of the Court remained secularist in majority during this period. On the one hand, this phenomenon can be attributed to some extent to the democratic norms strengthened by the Europeanization process, according to which banning a governing party is rather unjustifiable. On the other hand, the unshakable popularity of the AKP demonstrated by the early elections proved that an attack on the party would have backfired on the institutions initiating it, due to the ever-growing popularity and legitimacy of the governing party and the shrinking legitimacy of the guardians. In this period, the mobilization in civil society and in the media against the undemocratic practices of the TAF continued, and the AKP could also strengthen its front due to its strong ties to socially active and influential business circles. As Bank and Karadag (2012) note, the AKP achieved the formation of an "anti-Kemalist counter-elite". (p. 11)

By 2008, therefore, we had arrived at the second identifiable breaking point, where the reforms of the Europeanization process became implemented on the institutional level. As for the Constitutional Court, it seemed to begin to align with the idea of government primacy. Furthermore, as time passed, the judges could be continuously replaced by new ones under the AKP government. However, it seemed that as long as the government could not enforce the appointment of generals supportive of, or at least less resistant towards the government, reducing the role of the TAF was almost an impossible mission. Although the reforms slowly decreased the formal influence of the TAF, such as the obligation of the government to implement certain policies proposed by the National Security Council, the informal influence remained largely intact. The Ergenekon case provided an occasion to start the process of eliminating it. The case, which is probably one of the greatest scandals in Turkey, began in 2007. Ergenekon is claimed to be an ultranationalist organization whose aim was to force the military to intervene in politics by creating domestic turmoil in Turkey. Its members were also accused of planning to overthrow the AKP government by a military coup in 2003. During the investigation journalists, scholars, high-ranking bureaucrats, but most importantly, active military officers and generals were arrested.

Whether the Ergenekon case is real or not has been questioned by many, mainly due to lack of transparency. With this process, however, the AKP has finally begun the establishment of real civil control. The fact that hundreds of the military staff were accused of participating in the coup plot and Ergenekon meant that they could not be promoted for the time being, enabling a cleansing process inside the TAF. The reason is that military promotion procedures in Turkey are very definite: as the generals line up for the stars, the line of succession becomes predictable for years ahead. The commander of the army, usually the commander of the First Army, is promoted to be the Chief of Staff. Therefore, as long as the government could not exert influence on the promotion procedures, or could not remove the leadership of the military, little change could be expected in the behavior of the TAF. A new generation of leaders was necessary, willing to accept the primacy of the government and the establishment of civil control. The Ergenekon investigation, however, removed several candidates from the line of succession and the AKP could fill up the positions with less hostile candidates. This was a serious step towards the introduction of civil control outside the realm of institutional changes.

The (apparently) final defeat of the generals was admitted in the Supreme Military Council of 2011, where the force commanders and the chief of staff, Iţýk Koţaner, resigned, the latter due to his inability to protect his staff. Therefore, the government assumed the power to appoint the commanders and the Chief of Staff. (European Commission, 2011, p. 13) The process clearly contained some irony, and accordingly the reaction of the European Union was also ambivalent: the progress report supported the Ergenekon case as an "opportunity" for Turkey to prevent actions against democracy, and it also welcomed the events at the Supreme Military Council of 2011 as a road towards the establishment of civil control. However, it also condemned the lack of transparency attached to the Ergenekon case. (European Commission, 2011, p. 15)

All in all, the autonomization period completely transformed Turkey and its relationship with the EU. The fact that the AKP government could achieve change was related to the path-dependency of the institutions. The argument behind the reform process, Europeanization and democratization was supported by the guardian institutions. Putting direct obstacles in the way of the reforms would have created the image of maladjusted institutions. Furthermore, according to the World Values Survey (2001), army rule was regarded rather negatively by 65% of the respondents, not to mention that the AKP government was not one of the weak coalition governments of the 1990s anymore, but enjoyed increasing trust and support from society, as compared to the military and also the European Union, which, according to the Eurobarometer Survey, was trusted by only 18% of Turkish respondents. (European Commission, 2011, p. 46) Therefore, one could argue that the autonomization period brought about a transformed Turkey, whereby the underlying norms of the system became transformed and there was profound change in the elite, in terms of the norms as well as in relation to the people occupying key positions.

Although the AKP successfully removed the guardian institutions as obstacles to its ability to govern, it was rather inattentive regarding other aspects of democratization, such as fundamental rights, for which they are continuously criticized by the EU. Therefore, the accusation that some self-interest can be detected on behalf of the authorities has to be taken seriously. Yet giving primacy to the self-interested behavior of the AKP in explaining the reforms would be bold, as the reform process itself was not initiated by the party. It is safer to say that the AKP exploited the normative background of the process and the institutional change already underway. In addition, its ability to stay in power for a decade enabled the AKP to enact personnel changes in the guardian institutions, which further enabled it to pursue its own goals. For example, the majority of the Constitutional Court judges as of 2012 have been appointed during the AKP period. Naturally, the fact that AKP could stay in power was already the result of the normative change within Turkey.

At this point not all areas of influence of the TAF were put under strict control. For example, their economic power remained somewhat unrestricted, but those are minor issues as compared to their role in governance.[3] The immediate effect of this process was, however, that the government was finally gaining a primary role in several policy areas previously controlled by the guardian institutions: foreign policy, which was previously a military-controlled area, started to be taken over by the government. *(Çarkodlu, 2003, p. 246)* In earlier times, the obligatory Western orientation of Kemalism forced governments to ignore their immediate neighborhood and the Arab world, which was generally regarded as an important area of interest by the right-wing parties. As the NSC has been deprived of its executive power on foreign policy, and as the number of its military members shrank, its ability to represent a strong military opinion and pursue a security-oriented policy has declined. (Aydin & Acikmese, 2009, p. 55) Thus the time for a less security-based, more proactive foreign policy had arrived.

From 2009 the government adopted its own, autonomous foreign policy approach led by Ahmet Davutodlu which, as a result of the democratization of the foreign policy decision-making process, became more responsive to the demands of society. It thus recognized the growing disinterest of the population concerning the EU accession process, a trend that ran parallel to the growing economic interest of Turkey outside of the EU: according to OECD data, Azerbaijan, Bahrain, Bosnia and Herzegovina, Egypt, Iran and Kazakhstan were on the top-list of Turkish outward FDI destinations.

Davutodlu proposed the necessity of "strategic depth" in the foreign policy arena, which meant more than normalizing Turkey's relations with its long-ignored neighborhood and freshening up trade relations: this policy signified the beginning of a proactive foreign policy approach rooted in realpolitik. In the framework of the "zero-problem policy" Turkey restored its relationship with its neighbors: Abdullah Gül visited Armenia, by which he broke one of the biggest taboos of Turkish foreign policy. Turkey improved relations with Syria and Iraq, concluded economic agreements with the Gulf states, and generally pursued positive relations with the Middle East states, the Caucasus, Central Asia and the Balkan region. (Kanat, 2010, p. 211)

Turkey's international relations now meant more than merely following Europe. Although previously there had been improvement in Turkey's relationship with Greece and Cyprus due to the expectations of the EU, Turkey's relations with Cyprus were degrading again, aggravated by the bilateral agreements that Cyprus concluded about gas exploitation on the continental shelf. In line with EU and US policy, Turkey had fostered a positive relationship with Israel, including recognition of the country and concluding military agreements. However, as the AKP government, which was sympathetic towards the Palestinians, came to power, and as Israel was accused of helping the Kurds in Northern Iraq,

---

3   The TAF enjoys freedom in defense planning and budgeting with limited civilian oversight, has a share in the defense industry, and OYAK, the pension fund of the TAF, has a major role in the national economy, for example in the building industry and the banking sector, with market-distorting privileges, such as exemption from certain forms of taxation. (Akay, 2010; Akça, 2010; Tófalvi, 2011)

their relationship took a negative turn. (Aydin & Acikemse, 2009, p. 59) When Turkey assumed a role in the Israeli-Palestinian question the events ended up in a complete breakdown of relations between Turkey and Israel due to the incident of the Gaza peace flotilla.[4]

Turkey also assumed a role in the Arab Spring, an analysis of which, however, lies beyond the scope of this analysis. What is important from our perspective is that Turkey stood up in a self-confident and proactive manner, implementing a soft power approach (Nye, 1990; 2004; 2008), hosting a series of consultations and conferences, mediating between the parties, etc. For a long time it has been one of Turkey's aims to position itself as a mediator between the East and the West, a role in which Turkey can already account for some success, for example in connection with Iran's nuclear program.[5] However, some analysts go even further and claim that Turkey is aspiring for a global role (Barkey, 2010; Wright, 2011): Turkey as a regional player has an impact on a region where events have an immediate global significance. Furthermore, Turkey started to establish ties even beyond the continent, for example in Latin America and Africa, and gained observer position in regional organizations such as the Arab League, the African Union and the Organization of the American States. (Kanat, 2010, p. 216; Brzezinski, 2012)

All in all, Turkey pursues an autonomous foreign policy, which often aligns with the policy of the EU. Nevertheless, satisfying the EU in this respect is less of a goal; it is rather rooted in shared interests. Turkey, therefore, became more a "policy producer" instead of merely being a "policy implementer" in its region. (Kanat, 2010, p. 213) Hence, regarding the question whether Turkey would exert more influence through membership in the EU, or it would only limit its room to maneuver, and would necessarily re-prioritize its foreign policy goals in a less advantageous manner, the answer seems to be the latter. Although the importance of the EU accession agenda is sometimes confirmed by the Turkish leadership, one could witness a complete standstill in the field of reforms. Furthermore, Turkey's influential appearance on the regional scene resulted in self-confident comments such as Prime Minister Erdođan's statement: "Europe needs Turkey more than Turkey needs Europe." (Spiegel Online, 2011) And discussing the full membership of Turkey by 2023 he said: "They won't keep us waiting that long, will they? ... then the EU will lose, at least it will lose Turkey." (Spiegel Online,

---

4   In 2010 six ships of the Freedom Flotilla carrying humanitarian aid to the Gaza Strip were attacked by Israeli security forces in international waters, due to the intention of the Freedom Flotilla to break the blockade of Gaza. The raid resulted in nine casualties; all of them were Turkish citizens. The incident led to the breakdown of relations between Turkey and Israel due to the reluctance of the government of Israel to apologize for the event. The Report of the Secretary-General's Panel of Inquiry on the incident issued by the UN is available at: http://www.un.org/News/dh/infocus/middle_east/Gaza_Flotilla_Panel_Report.pdf

5   Turkey and Brazil mediated the nuclear fuel swap deal between Iran, France and Russia in 2010. They would turn Iran's uranium into fuel outside its borders.

2012) Furthermore, Turkey threatened to freeze relations with the EU if Cyprus assumed the presidency in 2012.

This is the reason why the post-2008 era is called an "autonomization period" in this study: Turkey seems to act in its "own way", enabled by a transformed institutional landscape, where finally the government and the National Assembly are in charge. The changes in foreign policy also prove wrong those who attributed the gradual alignment of Turkey's foreign policy to the EU to the Europeanization of the country. However, there is some truth to it. What the relapse in this process indicated is that the process was guided partly by the logic of appropriateness in the domestic area, namely alignment to Kemalist foreign policy directions, and partly by the logic of consequences, that is, the fear of intervention from the TAF. When these two factors were safely ruled out, and when the institutional background of the foreign policy decision-making process changed, the modification of foreign policy was almost immediate. It is, however, rather ironic that it was the Europeanization process itself that resulted in changes in Turkish domestic life that enabled the government to initiate a new foreign policy and decreased interest in EU membership.

Whether the environment outlined above is conducive to further negotiations and the adaptation of the acquis, which requires serious unilateral concessions from the candidate, is still questionable. (Schrijvers, 2007, p. 33) Turkey, at the moment, does not seem to be ready for the highly asymmetrical relationship and seems to aspire to the role of a partner instead. Considering the new reality, it is necessary to consider what are the possible ways of development in the relationship of Turkey and the EU.

Ideas concerning how to integrate Turkey into the Union without taking on the burden of its membership deriving from its size and culture have provoked thinking among scholars and politicians alike. The idea of a "privileged partnership" has gained popularity among those who do not support Turkey's full membership. The content of the concept is yet undefined; however, a good guess would probably include economic and institutional cooperation, inclusion in the CFSP, support for further reforms, and would probably exclude Turkey from structural and regional funds, and the free movement of people and workforce. However, without power in decision-making, the relationship would remain highly uneven. (Ýçener, 2007, p. 425) Naturally, if a state is adopting the legislation of an organization, it is highly unfair and undemocratic to exclude it from the decision-making process. Furthermore, if membership is not guaranteed, what will be the actual incentive for reform and adaptation in the future? (Ýçener, 2007, p. 426) Declining the membership of a country that went through all the trouble of reforms would cause great damage to the credibility of the EU and it is highly unlikely that Turkey would accept this solution. (Eriş, 2007, p. 218) As Turkey's chief negotiator Egemen Bagiş claimed in an interview, the idea of privileged partnership is an insult to the country. (Gotev, 2009) Currently Turkey regards itself more as a partner of the EU than being able to accept such a degrading solution. Nevertheless, one should not equate this with Turkey turning its back on Europe. Whereas membership in the EU is a binary variable, cooperation and alliance are not. Europe and the United States were and continue to be the most important strategic partners of Turkey.

Taking all aspects into consideration, the current security environment would invite the parties to seek areas of common interests and treat this relationship as a strategic advantage. A coordination of foreign policy issues would be an area where the advantages of this relation could be further exploited. Turkey is active in its neighboring regions which are important parts of the foreign policy of the EU, as well; although it is clear that the methods and the activism of the two parties are somewhat different. Areas of mutual interest can be clearly determined in, for example, Central Asia, the Western Balkans and the MENA region, where Turkey has a significant cultural and economic influence. (Balcer, 2009; Grabbe & Ülgen, 2010; Barysch, 2011) Whether the institutionalization of such a relationship would be possible is still questionable, though two things are clear: first, in terms of foreign and security policy, Turkey has the potential to enhance both the soft and the hard power of the EU. Second, if the accession process is to come to a halt and new areas of cooperation are not exploited, then EU-Turkey relations will be threatened with a breakdown and the result might be a negative approach in Turkey towards the EU and even towards the coordination of responses concerning issues of mutual interest.

Conclusion

In the past decade Turkey has undergone a deep transformation partly due to its domestic commitment to the EU accession process and partly due to the emergence of a party enjoying the support of the majority of voters for a long period of time. However, Turkey is a warning example of the phenomenon that the reforms demanded by EU conditionality go only as far as domestic actors enable them to go: although the government was able to decrease the power of the guardians, it was less eager to improve the human rights record of the country. The phenomenon was analyzed through the lens of sociological institutionalism, according to which processes should be studied taking norms and institutions into consideration instead of merely seeking rationality in actions and looking for the transformative power of historic turning points and shocks.

Sociological institutionalism resonates well with the domestic background of the EU accession agenda of Turkey, which had a strong normative undertone: the Kemalist traditions envisioned the modernization of the country looking for models of development and partners in the West. In this framework, governments were under constant scrutiny by the Kemalist guardian institutions. At the beginning, EU accession was centered more on economic criteria than political or cultural ideas. However, when the EU began to formulate explicit political conditions, the reaction of the Turkish political elite was rather path-dependent: in theory they adapted to the new criteria instead of abandoning the idea of EU accession, but in practice they followed old patterns of action, creating a tension between the two processes. It took years after legally curbing the powers of the TAF to actually withdraw them from politics. However, due to the overall commitment of the TAF to Westernization, EU membership and Europeanization, the imposition of civil control was an outcome directly deriving from the norms of the institution. The path that they had chosen decades earlier put them on a trajectory that curbed their power.

The fact that real intervention was out of the toolbox meant that the AKP could stay in power and stabilize its position, something mostly unimaginable to the right-wing governments in the past. Therefore, the room for maneuvering back to power was reduced for the institutions the leaders of which pulled the strings in the background during the previous decades. The removal of the armed forces from politics also resulted in the democratization of policy making. The Turkish governments became able to pursue a foreign policy independent of the TAF, resulting in the opening of new horizons. As a result, Turkey started to pursue a pre-emptive, active foreign policy based on a soft-power approach in its broader neighborhood, normalized relations with the old enemies of the Republic, for example Armenia, and opened new lines of cooperation with formerly ignored states in the Middle East.

However, despite the Turkish economic growth and the reform process, no change occurred on the front of membership on behalf of the EU. Many pose the question whether the spell on Turkish membership will be broken after one of the biggest opponents of Turkey's EU accession, President Sarkozy, lost the elections in France, but that is a doubtful scenario, as the general public of the EU is still not welcoming towards the idea of Turkish membership, mainly because of identity issues and the fear of the inclusion of Turkey in the free movement of labor. The general perception regarding the double standards of the EU concerning the Copenhagen Criteria, together with the constant rejection of Turkish membership, did not help to foster the credibility of the EU in Turkey, either. So what advantages are left for the new Turkey in EU accession?

Turkey has already profited from most of the economic benefits of the EU through its membership in the customs union. If the accession remained important from any perspective, it would be only a political and normative perspective. But domestically, the coalition behind more political reforms has been diminishing, whereas the political importance of the accession itself is also decreasing due to Turkey's newfound role in the Middle East. Whether in this situation it is possible to provide Turkey with proper incentives to overcome the costs of further adoption to the expectations of the EU is questionable. And as long as Turkey fails to adopt the Additional Protocol of the Ankara Association Agreement to Cyprus, the negotiation will remain at a standstill; therefore, the majority of the work is still ahead of Turkey. (European Commission, 2012)

All in all, what the future holds for Turkish EU membership remains an open question. At present the commitment or enthusiasm is not visible, either on behalf of Turkey or the EU. What is clear is that Turkey has been through a long process of transformation resulting in a modern, more democratic Republic. However, Europe is too occupied with its internal problems to deal with the issues and disputes arising from Turkish accession. Turkey at the same time is basking in global attention and economic success, which is in stark contrast with the constant rejection received from the EU. Thus, now it is not only the EU that does not welcome the concept of full Turkish membership: Turkey does not seem to embrace the idea of continuing the long journey either, posing the danger that Turkey will be truly a forever candidate.

Bibliography

Akay, H. (2010). *Security sector in Turkey: Questions, problems and solutions.* TESEV. Retrieved from http://www.tesev.org.tr/UD_OBJS/PDF/DEMP/ENG/ENGguvenRaporKunyaDuzelti10_03_10.pdf

Akça, Ý. (2010). *Military-economic situation in Turkey: Present situation, problems and solutions.* TESEV. Retrieved from http://www.tesev.org.tr/UD_OBJS/PDF/DEMP/ENG/gsr-2-eng.pdf

Aydin, M., & Acikmese, S. A. (2009). Europeanization through EU conditionality: Understanding the new era of Turkish foreign policy. In S. Verney & K. Ifantis, *Turkey's road to European Union membership: National identity and political change.* London: Routledge.

Aydinli, E., Özcan, N. A., & Akyaz, D. (2006). The Turkish military's march towards Europe. *Foreign Affairs, 85(1).*

Balcer, A. (2009). *Heading for the strategic partnership EU-Turkey in the foreign policy.* Warsaw: demos EUROPA – Centre for European Strategy. Retrieved from http://www.demoseuropa.eu/files/W%20strone%20strategicznego%20partnerstwa%20UE%20i%20Turcji%20w%20polityce%20zagranicznej%20EN.pdf

Bank, A., & Karadag, R. (2012).The political economy of regional power: Turkey under the AKP. GIGA Working Papers, 204/2012. Retrieved from http://www.giga-hamburg.de/dl/download.php?d=/content/publikationen/pdf/wp204_bank-karadag.pdf

Barkey, H. J. (2010). *Turkey's new global role.* Carnegie Endowment for International Peace. Retrieved from http://carnegieendowment.org/2010/11/17/turkey-s-new-global-role/2dd2

Barkey, H. J. (2011). Coordinating responses to the 2011 Arab revolt: Turkey and the Transatlantic alliance. In H. J. Barkey et al. (Eds.), *Turkey and the Arab spring: Implications for Turkish foreign policy from a Transatlantic perspective.* Washington: The German Marshall Fund of the United States.

Barysch, K. (2011). *Why the EU and Turkey need to coordinate their foreign policies.* Carnegie Endowment for International Peace. Retrieved from http://carnegieendowment.org/2011/08/31/why-eu-and-turkey-need-to-coordinate-their-foreign-policies

Belge, C. (2006). Friends of the court: The republican alliance and selective activism of the Constitutional Court of Turkey. *Law & Society Review, 40(3),* 653-692.

Brzezinski, Z. (2012). The West and Turkey: Their role in shaping a wider global architecture. Discussion at The Brookings Institution, Washington D.C. Retrieved from http://www.brookings.edu/~/media/events/2012/5/02%20turkey%20west/20120502_turkey_west

Buhari, D. (2009). Turkey-EU relations: The limitations of Europeanisation studies. *The Turkish yearbook of international relations, (40)*, 93-121.

Çarkođlu, A. (2003). Conclusion. In A. Çarkođlu & B. Rubin (Eds.), *Turkey and the European Union: Domestic politics, economic integration, and international dynamics*. London: Frank Cass.

DiMaggio, P. J., & Powell, W. W. (1991). *The new institutionalism in organizational analysis*. Chicago: University of Chicago Press.

Eriş, Ö. Ü. (2007). *The European Neighborhood Policy and Turkey. In E. LaGro & K. E. Jorgensen, Turkey and the European Union: Prospects for a difficult encounter*. New York: Palgrave Macmillan.

European Commission. (2011). *Eurobarometer surveys*. Retrieved from http://ec.europa.eu/public_opinion/cf/index.cfm?lang=en

European Commission. (1998). Regular report from the Commission on Turkey's progress towards accession. Retrieved from http://ec.europa.eu/enlargement/archives/pdf/key_documents/1998/turkey_en.pdf

European Commission. (1999). Regular report from the Commission on Turkey's progress towards accession. Retrieved from http://ec.europa.eu/enlargement/archives/pdf/key_documents/1999/turkey_en.pdf

European Commission. (2001). Turkey: 2000 Accession partnership. *Official journal of the European Communities*, 24. 3. 2001. Retrieved from http://www.avrupa.info.tr/fileadmin/Content/Downloads/PDF/1_08520010324en00130023.pdf

European Commission. (2004). Regular report on Turkey's progress towards accession. Retrieved from http://ec.europa.eu/enlargement/archives/pdf/key_documents/2004/rr_tr_2004_en.pdf

European Commission. (2008). Turkey 2008 progress report. Retrieved from http://ec.europa.eu/enlargement/pdf/press_corner/key-documents/reports_nov_2008/turkey_progress_report_en.pdf

European Commission. (2009). Turkey 2009 progress report. Retrieved from http://ec.europa.eu/enlargement/pdf/key_documents/2009/tr_rapport_2009_en.pdf

European Commission. (2011). Standard Eurobarometer 76: Tables of results. Retrieved from http://ec.europa.eu/public_opinion/archives/eb/eb76/eb76_tablesresults_en.pdf

European Commission.(2011). Turkey 2011 progress report. Retrieved from http://ec.europa.eu/enlargement/pdf/key_documents/2011/package/tr_rapport_2011_en.pdf

European Commission. (2012). *Enlargement: Turkey*. Retrieved from http://ec.europa.eu/enlargement/countries/detailed-country-information/turkey/index_en.htm

Evans, P. et al. (Eds.). (1985). *Bringing the state back in*. New York: Cambridge University Press.

Goldschmidt, A., & Davidson, L. (2010). *A concise history of the Middle East*. Boulder: *Westview* Press.

Gotev, G. (2009). *Turkey's chief negotiator: 'Privileged partnership' is an insult*. EurActive. Retrieved from http://www.euractiv.com/enlargement/turkey-chief-negotiator-privileged-partnership-insult/article-186179

Grabbe, H., & Ülgen, S. (2010). *The way forward for Turkey and the EU: A strategic dialogue on foreign policy*. Carnegie Endowment for International Peace. Retrieved from http://www.edam.org.tr/eng/document/turkey_eu_policy1.pdf

Hall, P. A., & Taylor, R. C. R. (1996). Political science and the three new institutionalisms. *Political studies, XLIV*, 936-957.

Ýçener, E. (2007). Privileged partnership: An alternative final destination for Turkey's integration with the European Union? *Perspectives on European politics and society, 8(4)*, 415-438.

Joseph, J. S. (2006). Introduction: Turkey at the threshold of the European Union. In J. S. Joseph (ed.), *Turkey and the European Union: Internal dynamics and external challenges*. New York: Palgrave Macmillan.

Kanat, K. B. (2010). AK party's foreign policy: Is Turkey turning away from the West? *Insight Turkey, 12(1)*, 205-225.

Kohen, S., & Robins, P. (1998). Turkey and Europe: Integration or alienation? *Policywatch 329*. The Washington Institute. Retrieved from http://www.washingtoninstitute.org/policy-analysis/view/turkey-and-europe-integration-or-alienation

Konijnenbelt, B. (2006). The role of the military in Turkish politics: An analysis of public statements made by the Turkish General Staff. In *Governance and the military: Perspectives for change in Turkey*. Groningen: CESS.

Kuru, A. T. (2012). The rise and fall of military tutelage in Turkey. Fears of Islamism, Kurdism, and Communism. *Insight Turkey, 14(2)*, 37-57.

Kuru, A. T., & Stepan, A. (Eds.). (2012). *Democracy, Islam, and secularism in Turkey*. Retrieved from http://cup.columbia.edu/book/978-0-231-15932-6/democracy-islam-and-secularism-in-turkey/excerpt

March, J. G., & Olsen, J. P. (1984). The new institutionalism: Organizational factors in political life. *American Political Science Review, 78(3)*, 734-749.

March, J. G., & Olsen, J. P. (1998). The Institutional dynamics of international political orders. *International Organization, 52(4)*, 943-969.

March, J. G., & Olsen, J. P. (2005). Elaborating the "new institutionalism". Working paper (Center for European Studies), No. 11. Oslo:

University of Oslo. Retrieved from http://www.cpp.amu.edu.pl/pdf/olsen2.pdf

Ministry of Foreign Affairs. (2007). *Political reforms in Turkey*. Ankara: Ministry of Foreign Affairs. Retrieved from http://egemenbagis.com/wp-content/uploads/2011/09/prt.pdf

Moravcsik, A. (1993). Preferences and power in the European Community: A liberal intergovernmentalist approach. *Journal of Common Market Studies, 31(4)*, 473-524.

Müftüler-Baç, M. (2005). Turkey's political reforms and the impact of the European Union, *South European Society and Politics, 10(1)*, 17-31.

Müftüler-Baç, M., & McLaren, L. (2003). Enlargement preferences and policymaking in the EU: Impacts on Turkey. Journal of European Integration, *25(1)*, 17-30.

Narbone, L., & Tocci, N. (2009). Running around in circles? The cyclical relationship between Turkey and the European Union. In S. Verney & K. Ifantis, *Turkey's road to European Union membership: National identity and political change.* London: Routledge.

Narlı, N. (2006). Transparency-building in the defence sector and the EU reforms in Turkey. In S. Faltas and S. Jansen (Eds.), *Governance and the military: Perspectives for change in Turkey* (p. 129-155). Groningen: CESS.

Nye, J. S. (1990). *Bound to lead: The changing nature of American power*. New York: Basic Books.

Nye, J. S. (2004). *Soft power: The means to success in world politics*. New York: Public Affairs.

Nye, J. S. (2008). Public diplomacy and soft power. *The ANNALS of the American Academy of Political and Social Science, 616(1)*, 94-109.

Öniş, Z. (2003). Domestic politics, international norms and challenges to the state: Turkey-EU relations in the post-Helsinki era. In *Turkey and the European Union: Domestic politics, economic integration and international dynamic.* London: Frank Cass.

Pierson, P. (2000). The limits of design: Explaining institutional origins and change. *Governance, 13(4)*, 475-499.

Schrijvers, A. (2007). What can Turkey learn from previous accession negotiations? In E. LaGro, & K. E. Jorgensen, *Turkey and the European Union: Prospects for a difficult encounter.* New York: Palgrave Macmillan.

Sedelmeier, U. (2003). EU enlargement, identity and the analysis of European foreign policy: Identity formation through policy practice. *EUI Working Papers, RSC, 2003 (13)*. Retrieved from http://www.eui.eu/RSCAS/WP-Texts/03_13.pdf

SoleriLecha, E. (2008). Literature review on the relations between the EU and Turkey. EUPROX State-of-the-art reports, 4. Barcelona: Institut Universitari d'Estudis Europeus. Retrieved from http://www.iuee.eu/pdf-projecte/10/lRICPmd7gMnxKhQKevlf.PDF

Spiegel Online. (2011). Turkey and Europe need each other. *Der Spiegel*. Retrieved from http://www.spiegel.de/international/europe/spiegel-interview-with-turkish-foreign-minister-turkey-and-europe-need-each-other-a-767432.html

Spiegel Online. (2012). Erdogan visit to Berlin betrays tensions. *Der Spiegel*. Retrieved from http://www.spiegel.de/international/europe/turkish-prime-minister-erdogan-sets-deadline-for-eu-admission-a-864579.html

Tank, P. (2006). Dressing for the occasion: Reconstructing Turkey's identity? *Southeast European and Black Sea Studies, 6(4)*, 463-478.

Tófalvi, F. (2011). Lefegyverzett török gazdaság (The disarmed Turkish economy). *Nemzet és Biztonság, 2011(6)*, 35-43.

Uzgel, Ý. (2003). Between praetorianism and democracy: The role of the military in Turkish foreign policy. *The Turkish Yearbook, Vol. XXXIV*, 178-211.

Varol, O. O. (2012). The democratic coup d'état. *Harvard International Law Journal, 53(2)*, 292-355.

Verney, S. (2009). *National identity* and political change on Turkey's road to EU membership. In S. Verney & K. Ifantis (Eds.), *Turkey's road to European Union membership: National identity and political change*. London: Routledge.

World Values Surveys. Retrieved from http://www.worldvaluessurvey.org/

Wright, R. (2011). Turkey becomes a global player. *The New York Times*. Retrieved from http://www.nytimes.com/roomfordebate/2011/10/07/is-egypt-losing-its-regional-power/turkey-can-be-a-challenge-to-egypt

The Muslim Courtyard:
The European Union in the Maghreb

Péter Rada, Ph.D

Two years after the beginning of the Arab Spring[1] we still cannot have readymade answers concerning how the European Union should reconsider its strategy towards the Maghreb[2] countries. One thing is sure: the recent status quo and the continuation of the stability-seeking policies of the European Union will backfire in the long term. The situation is complex and the transformation of the region is an unconventional process which needs a new and unconventional approach from the European Union. The goal of the Union is to openly assist the democratic transitions, which would be a strategic shift from engaging with the authoritarian regimes for maintaining stability and security. However, from the perspective of European foreign policy the Maghreb is difficult to handle as a solid unit of similar political entities. The real challenge is that the European Union would need separate, single strategies towards each of the countries of the region.

The challenges stemming from the region are interconnected with the general security concerns of the European Union. Security threats which were considered traditional, such as terrorism and illegal migration, are still in the forefront, but new headaches have obviously appeared on the scene. "Turbulent democratization", lack of social progress, lack of regionally integrated economies, and lack of a tradition of responsive political systems and good governance are only a few of the problems which need a joint cure if the goal of the European Union – as it clearly is – is to support smooth democratic development in the region in order to avoid further security challenges and the deterioration of economic and trade relations with the region. As the title suggests the Maghreb countries are indeed the courtyard of the European Union on the Southern shore of the Mediterranean; thus these countries are connected to the European Union

---

1   Using the expression Arab Spring we refer to the term given to label the revolutionary wave of demonstrations, protests and even war which spread across the Middle East and North Africa after the self-immolation of Mohamed Bouazizi in Tunisia in December 2010. The causes of the events were complex and several factors, such as human rights violations, relative deprivation of living standards and corruption, contributed to the wave which swept through the region.

2   The traditional definition Maghreb refers to the countries in North Africa to the West of Egypt. In this analysis the expression refers to Libya, Tunisia, Algeria, Morocco and Mauritania. With the foundation of the Arab Maghreb Union in 1989, the label Maghreb became a political expression, too.

in terms of political, economic or social traditions. The region has always been fragile, but the recent events of the Arab Spring again called attention to the distinctive combination of interconnected, serious security challenges. Decades-long, frozen inter-state conflicts, such as the question of Western Sahara or the closed borders between Morocco and Algeria, have made effective regional cooperation remain on paper. The new phenomenon since the beginning of the pro-reform movements, and unrest and civil war (in Libya) proved that the inter-state character of security challenges gained a new dimension in the form of intra-state dynamics of transformation. The global, regional inter-state and regional intra-state problems appear simultaneously on the agenda for those who try to find a possible and effective response for the European Union. The effects of the global financial crisis paired with high inflation, rising unemployment, lack of political freedoms, and rampant corruption. The outcome was sweeping social unrest which demanded a fundamental change of existing political, economic and social systems. The unprecedented dynamics of the process also represents a new security challenge as the unemployed but educated youth of the Maghreb countries are impatient, thus the suggestions and recommendations that the democratization processes needs time to unfold will not work here.

Consequently, the European Union needs a new "grand strategy" [3] towards the region incorporating all the dimensions of democratization and development. Clearly, the goal of the European Union is to expand its sphere of stability and development in the neighborhood in order to increase the security of the Union. It is beyond doubt that the traditional Mediterranean policies of the European Union will not work in the future due to the significantly changed situation. The challenge also involves an opportunity for the European Union to take a lead in the events, at least to be able to minimize the risk of negative spillover; but without a coherent grand strategy the European Union will rather be pulled by the events and will follow a minimalist reactive strategy which is not in line with the general goals of building stability and supporting development.

In a traditional sense the European Union is not a coherent superpower, but it is beyond doubt that the European Union is a civilian or soft superpower (Duchęne, 1972; Nye, 2004; Simms, 2012) in the Maghreb region. Thus the European Union needs to seek a grand strategy in line with these characteristics: the Union needs to develop, so to say, a "soft grand strategy"[4] towards the Maghreb. The relation to-

---

3   Grand strategy refers to the employment of all instruments of power available for a given political entity (traditionally a state) in order to achieve an explicitly expressed political goal. Today the literature of grand strategy is widely developed; see for instance the works of Liddell Hart, John Lewis Gaddis, or Colin Gray. (Gaddis, 1982; Gray, 2011; Hart, 1991)

4   A concept increasingly used recently that refers to the need for a grand strategy of the European Union, considering that the means of the Union are more limited compared, for instance, to those of the United States. István Balogh has published a useful study on the possibilities of a European soft grand strategy. (Balogh, 2011)

wards the region and the future of cooperation will be more easily understood through this strategy. The challenges are multidimensional and the different dimensions interact. Thus the strategy itself needs to be multidimensional and needs to take into account the interconnections.

The analysis will recommend a model of how to incorporate all the challenges into a single framework in order to assist in elaborating such a comprehensive strategy. In order to do that, the study needs to understand and explain the challenges the Union faces in the Maghreb, the local dynamics of events, and the existing relations and tools the European Union has. The analysis also combines local demands and expectations regarding cooperation with the European Union with the Union's goals and interests in the region. The analysis will incorporate six dimensions: the security challenge; the challenge represented by political transformation and democratization; the challenge of economic development; the challenge of societal development; the challenge of regional and local cooperation; and finally the challenge of global processes and the presence of other international interests and actors in the region. In order to be able handle all the different dimensions in a dynamic way we employ the Rubik's Cube solution analogy[5] to explain the simultaneous interconnectedness of the different dimensions during the democratic transition processes in the Maghreb which the European Union is seeking to assist and protect. Furthermore, the study will assess the existing goals and obviously the tools, initiatives and instruments of the Union. A successful "soft grand strategy" presumes an understanding of the interconnected challenges in the Maghreb, clear and coherent goals on the part of the European Union, an assessment of the tools, and bridging the goals and means in the current security, political, economic and societal environment.

The European Union's strategic culture and the Rubik's Cube analogy

The European Union intends to become the leading regional actor in the neighborhood. This may be supported by the fact that the European Union is one of the most widely accepted international actors in North Africa and the Middle East after the Arab Spring. (See Aragall et al., 2012) In order to achieve this goal the Union needs to reassess existing policies and instruments, and develop a soft grand strategy towards the region which would provide a framework for policy actions, despite the differences in the member states' foreign policy positions. The European Union clearly lacks traditional instruments of high politics, most importantly military power, but as a normative power (Duchęne, 1972; Simms,

---

5   The Rubik's Cube solution algorithms provide a useful analogy for analyzing multidimensional processes in a single model. It helps in understanding the interconnections among the different dimensions and explaining the effects of the simultaneous processes on each other. (For more see Rada, 2010; 2011)

2012) the Union has substituted it with, for instance, "soft solutions"[6] in the framework of the Neighbourhood Policy.

In the last two decades the European Union has developed a visible common foreign and security policy, and despite the many instances of disagreements among the members – as with the case of Iraq, or recently Libya – the foreign policy thinking of the 27 in the face of direct challenges is similar. During the Balkan Wars the European Union was incapable of implementing a decisive and coordinated intervention. Today, despite divergent views about the Libyan intervention, the European Union positions itself as the leading interlocutor in the North African events and the most important external player in assisting the democratic transition of the region. (Ryninng, 2011, p. 541) It is another question whether the European Union is able to significantly influence the political development of the Middle East and North Africa. The European Union has become a close security community in which the otherwise different foreign policies converge in terms of the threat perceptions, and attitudes towards international events and conflicts – the assumptions and beliefs that drive foreign policy decisions related to security. Due to the convergence of strategic frames of thinking and attitudes regarding action, it is possible to speak about the European Union's strategic culture. The perceptions become part of the (strategic) culture and the identity normatively informing the social actors concerning the possible "right" foreign policy decisions. There is indeed a renewed effort in the literature to apply the theory of strategic culture in analyzing the foreign policy of the European Union. (Krotz et al., 2011; Norheim-Martinsen, 2011; Rynning, 2011; Schmidt et al., 2011) This effort clearly stems from the constructivist logic in examining a country's behavior in its external relations. Today it is not surprising if one notes that foreign policy is influenced not only by rational factors, but that the norms, history, or political culture are equally important. However, in the case of the European Union the difficulty is not the inclusion of these factors, rather the dilemma concerning how the European Union can be regarded as a single actor in foreign policy. On the other hand, the argument according to which integration in the field of foreign and security policy is less likely has become decreasingly convincing due to the predominantly national strategic cultures of the member states converging. (Krotz et al., 2011; Norheim-Martinsen, 2011; Rynning, 2011; Schmidt et al., 2011) The core threats and challenges in the field of foreign and security policy are the same and the security perceptions of the different members are getting closer and closer.[7]

If we approach the European Union from the aspect of norms, ideas or cultural preferences, there are several indications that there are common guiding lines. This is especially true if we do not analyze the European Union as a global actor but we try to assess the European Union's role in smaller regions, such

---

6   Conditionality in forms of pressures for political, economic and social reforms in exchange for deeper relations and financial assistance.

7   Fight against terrorism, the proliferation of weapons of mass destruction, illegal migration, organized crime, energy security, etc.

as in the neighborhood. The close neighborhood and any events here are clearly the most serious concern for the Union and in terms of perceptions the member states share similar views.[8] The goal in the neighborhood is to expand the sphere of security, stability and prosperity. (European Commission, 2012a) When it comes to disagreements they are mostly about implementation of the policies. Nevertheless, there is little controversy on the desired future for the Maghreb. For the European Union as a whole it is important to assist the region during the democratic transition in order to avoid the negative effects of a "turbulent democratization". (See, for instance, Mansfield et al., 2005)

With regards to real deeds, the experience is more sobering. Even if in rhetoric the goal of the European Union was the promotion of democracy, good governance and strengthening the respect for human rights, the real goal has been the maintenance of security and stability. (Similarly to the argument of Popescu, 2011) The result was a realist pact with the dictators of North Africa who "promised" to protect the European Union from terrorism and masses of illegal migrants. However, the Arab Spring proved that this policy had reached a dead end and the societies of the Maghreb needed change. And the demand for change was clearly demonstrated. The change is tangible, which has forced the outside world to revise former strategies. The same is true in the case of the European Union. The Union needs to find new ways of assisting the democratic transitions whilst maintaining security and stability.

The changed external environment in the last decade brought the threat perceptions closer in line with the clearly shared interests, values and norms. (Krotz et al., 2011, pp. 557-566) After the failures in the Balkans during the 1990s, the European Union became more serious in shaping common foreign policy strategies and placing more emphasis on political influence in addition to its commercial and economic leverage in its neighborhood. (Krotz et al., 2011, p. 555) A specific European strategic culture clearly evolved with the adoption of the European Security Strategy in 2003.

The specificity of the strategic culture of the European Union is that it coexists with national strategic cultures, more importantly it stems from them and their convergence. However, there are still factors which warn us not overestimate the pace of this convergence process. 2003 was a year of fortunate constellation of several factors which helped the member states to create the tangible product of strategic thinking in the European Security Strategy. This is shown by the failure to adopt a new strategy four years later. Although the mandate existed for writing a new strategy, the outcome was a rather modest document, the

---

8   However, we have to take into account that there are significant differences between the instruments of the Eastern Partnership and the Euro-Mediterranean Partnership, or the Union for the Mediterranean. Despite this, in general the goals are similar in the sense that the European Neighborhood Policy intends to expand the sphere of stability and prosperity towards the neighbors in order to decrease the negative spillover due to political instability, economic challenges and societal pressures.

Report on the Implementation of the European Security Strategy. However, this does not mean that common security thinking has not developed. Today there is clear evidence that the comprehensive logic of security in foreign policy thinking has gained prominence in European Union documents and is reflected in actual policy recommendations or review documents, for instance in the Euro-Mediterranean Partnership Programme. (Norheim-Martinsen, 2011)

In the face of the threats the Union's decision-making elites share the same perceptions and interests. Most importantly, the foremost common interest of the member states is internal security and prosperity. The pursuit of internal security can be seen in the process whereby the European Union step by step, clearly after 2001, externalized its internal security mechanisms[9] and programs. (Bosse, 2011, p. 443) However, the security threats to the European Union come from different dimensions and not only traditional "hard security" is needed to be taken into account but challenges regarding the economy, social development, energy, regional conflicts, state failure, or negative environmental effects. The dimensions many times overlap. Consequently any change or process in one dimension automatically affects the other dimensions. The ultimate challenge in interpreting such a complex model is the enormous number of variables that influence each other. The present study uses an alternative schema of thinking which better helps in understanding, explaining and forecasting EU-Maghreb relations. The model builds on the analogy of the solution methodology of Rubik's Cube. The cube can be solved despite the fact that the six faces and the "cubelets" can be oriented independently, while each move affects all the faces and "cubelets" at the same time. Obviously, in the model the faces are the different dimensions which have to be taken into account when analyzing the Union's options in the Maghreb. The solution methodology, or at least the way which leads to the solution, shows striking similarity with the interconnected system of development of a state during democratic transition where several dimensions and different steps jointly determine the outcome while mutually influencing each other. The dimensions represent sets of factors. These sets are important in themselves, but also contribute to the outcome of any process in the other dimensions. Differentiating among the dimensions is not always easy as they are overlapping, but on the theoretical level we can differentiate six dimensions: security-military, political, economic, societal, domestic and external. (See Rada, 2011)

In the future, EU-Maghreb relations will center around the question of how the countries in the region are able to develop during the process of democratic transition. A smooth and mutually beneficial relation is inevitably dependent on the success of democratization. In fact, democratic transitions are mostly turbulent, and evaluating the Arab Spring so far, it is clear that the stability of the whole region is at stake. In this sense the security of the European Union and its relations with the region will be influenced by the complex matrix of interdependent processes in the six different dimensions.

---

9   Fight against terrorism and organized crime, or supporting stability in the neighborhood.

First, the security-military dimension is overwhelmingly mentioned as the basic and most important dimension in the literature as the sine qua non of successful democratization. In the case of the Arab Spring it is a timely question, especially in Libya, how the Maghreb can progress along the long and exhausting road of democratic transition without falling (back) into violence and civil turmoil. The goal in this dimension is to avoid future violence and civil conflict, and maintain security by using military solutions if necessary, as was the case in Libya.[10]

Second, the institutions determine the design of the state, the economy and society. Thus they help the development of factors in other dimensions. The most important goal for the European Union here is to assist in building up institutions which help the state to be the effective and legitimate agent of development. Third, the economic dimension means the material basis for the democratic transition. The realization of achievements in this dimension helps maintain development in the other dimensions. In the case of significant failure of economic development, this dimension undermines the development in other dimensions. Fourth, the society carries the given societal differences among groups, religions, ethnicities, or cultures. The diversity in this dimension can represent a serious challenge for the future of democratic transition. On the other hand, it is also true that the given characteristics of a certain society represent a resource and opportunity for the transition. Fifth, the domestic conditions are as important as the other dimensions. This dimension indicates what the European Union has to add something for the whole process to be successful. The domestic dimension covers and represents the historical cornerstones of local development, the ways how the country organizes its economic activity, governance, or the attitudes towards peace and development. Finally, none of the democratic transitions has happened in a closed laboratory. The interaction of international processes with the domestic conditions is very influential in relation to the final outcome of the process. External processes can help or hinder the development of other dimensions.

The Union's role in the Maghreb is not to act as a "new trustee" or build narrow state functions, but the European Union is responsible for supporting the development of an environment which secures the sustainable presence of state functions by managing a healthy balance between legitimacy and effectiveness of the functions and institutions that the state has to be able to influence in order to provide opportunity for development.

---

10 We refer here not to a demand that the European Union must become a military power, since the Union can rely on NATO in case military solutions are needed. Cecile Wendling published a deep analysis on NATO's comprehensive approach, which also explains NATO-EU relations in detail. (Wendling,

How can Rubik's Cube be solved in the Maghreb?

When solving Rubik's Cube there are general algorithms, lists of well defined instructions for implementing the process from a given initial state, through well defined successive states to a desired outcome. Each of the algorithms takes into account the beginning situation and describes the effect of the steps and forecasts the success of the way applied in bringing the cube closer to the desired outcome. The originality of the algorithms lies in the fact that they are strategies for transforming only the necessary parts without scrambling the already solved parts. Accordingly, during the democratic transition of the Maghreb the European Union may be able to follow certain strategies bearing in mind that a change in one dimension will affect other dimensions. A "soft grand strategy" for the Maghreb has to take into account this characteristic of the interconnected dimensions.

Figure 1. The beginning and the end situation of the solution process for Rubik's Cube.

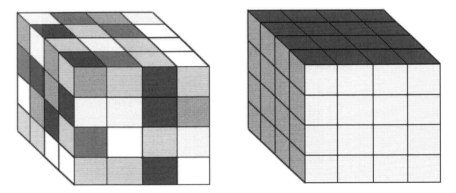

Source: *Hardwick, n.d.*

The beginning situation in the different Maghreb countries is not the same, but the relation among the dimensions is similar. Moreover, the development in Libya, Tunisia, Algeria, Morocco or Mauritania also influences the development of the other countries through the external dimension: the "different Rubik's Cubes" are connected to each other. In every different development process certain dimensions are in a closer relation with each other, and this is also true in the case of the Maghreb. In today's volatile geopolitical environment in the Maghreb it is understandable that the security dimension is closely related with the external dimension because negative spillover effects easily influence the security of the given country. It is also obvious that during a significant political change the dimension of the political institutions, the society and the domestic opportunities are also closely related. Finally, it makes sense to handle the economic dimension separately, it being the most important dimension of cooperation between the

European Union and the Maghreb.[11] However, it is worth taking into account that in the long term the economic performance of the countries will seriously impact the development of the other dimensions.

The security and external dimensions

It was several times mentioned in security assessments (see Elder, 2011) that the final security challenge for the European Union is represented by the existing terrorist cells in the Maghreb. The authoritarian rulers of the Maghreb countries were able to persuade the European Union about their importance in fighting against the Union's "real enemy", the terrorists. Consequently, the European Union as a "realist actor in normative clothes" (Elder, 2011, p. 433) moved from the goal of creating a "ring of well governed countries" (European Commission, 2003) in the Maghreb to engaging with the existing regimes in order to avoid the negative security consequences of a "turbulent democratization".

Cristoph Zürcher (2011, p. 81) mentions in his recent article about the relation between democracy and peace that since the end of the Cold War building peace has meant building democracy at the same time. The belief in the success of this foreign policy goal is built on the assumption that democracy will bring stability by creating peaceful and reliable partners. The problem is that the success rate of democratic transition has subsequently not been encouraging. The record rather proves that even in situations where international intervention was able to achieve peace, democracy did not follow, or at least not in the sense of how it had been planned originally, such as in Liberia and Sierra Leone after 2003, or in Cambodia after 1993. It is a commonly cited statement (see, for instance, Dobbins et al., 2004; 2005; 2008) that the local societies after a destructive war do not possess the resources for establishing functioning democratic institutions. On the one hand, this is true but, on the other, the reality is more complex. The external actors have been weak in pushing local elites towards more democratic and more risky reforms due to the fact that the democratic transition per se challenges the fragile peace, and the peacebuilders rather favor stability over democracy. (Call et al., 2003) The unpredictability of interim periods during democratization provides the hope for opponents of democratization that the process will fail. The characteristics of the interim period are that the domestic central institutions are not stable enough; peaceful channels of conflict management among the groups is not institutionalized; the demand of society for a better life already stresses the system; and groups with incompatible interests try to mobilize the accumulating energy of society. Therefore, democratization is even more dangerous in such situations because democracy is a marketplace for ideas where different groups have to compete. Without functioning peaceful mechanisms, competition may lead to violent conflict. (Henderson, 2002; Mansfield et al., 2005; Mansfield et al., 2007; Zürcher, 2011, p. 83)

The local stakeholders and those who are in power take advantage of the unstable situation by convincing the external actors about their exclusive ability

---

11   At least thinking in terms of the economic influence of the European Union.

to maintain peace. The Union's relation towards the Maghreb countries has experienced similar patterns. On paper the most important goals of the European Union were emphasized in the policy documents of the several instruments towards the Maghreb, more importantly in the Euro-Mediterranean Partnership or in the European Security Strategy. Fighting against terrorism, countering illegal migration, and avoiding regional conflicts, especially in the immediate neighborhood, overshadowed the liberal goals of promoting democracy, good governance and respect for human rights. Trade relations with the Maghreb are undoubtedly the cornerstone of the partnership. Developing trade relations necessitates stability and avoiding the above-mentioned security challenges, considerations which all led to the realist foreign policy wherein the European Union overlooked the dictators.

Democratization is clearly not a one-size-fits-all process. In recent decades we have experienced that new democracies are less effective in terms that they are not able to distribute rights equally, the executives are centralizing power contributing to the failure of checks and balances, the accountability of the government is low, or the rights of the minorities are in danger. Similarly to the argument of Jack Snyder and Edward Mansfield (2005), we have to see that democratic transitions are conflict prone. Due to the background dynamics, those groups and elites who feel their level of security decreasing are more prone to use radical means. Transition also weakens pre-existing structures of rules and the new uncertainty is a security threat for local stakeholders and consequently the outside world. (Henderson, 2002) The turbulent events of the Arab Spring definitely threaten the interests and indirectly the security of the European Union. Stability has been the Union's goal in the Maghreb which, as mentioned above, many times collided with the values of freedom, the rule of law and respect for human rights. Now, democratic opening may bring new scenarios in which the new democracies may not be in line with Western values and in which the new governmental structures create unpredictability and insecurity for the European Union.

The regional interconnectedness of the events during the Arab Spring appeared clearly in 2011. However, we also have to note that behind the common threads there were several different causes and obviously the outcomes will be not the same either. The events which began in December 2010 generated positive feelings about democracy, but the reality proved that general geopolitical factors should not been neglected. As Zsolt Rostoványi (2012) argues in his recent article, the Arab Spring altered the general political constellation in the region. The 21st century began with the strong presence of the United States and the emergence of non-Arab countries on the peripheries – Turkey and Iran. Due to the Arab Spring the United States lost its strategic position. Some allies – such as Saudi Arabia – initiated a more independent foreign policy, while others – such as Egypt – even changed completely. The last two years have also witnessed the emergence of Russian influence and interests in the region, whilst Iran is getting weaker. The situation is even more complex because Israel needed to step back to a defensive position, but on the other hand Turkey gained new momentums to increase its influence. Returning to domestic politics, the danger of becoming a failed state is critical in many countries of the region, and the spillover of failure will be quick due to the tangible interconnectedness of the societies. The Arab Spring let some kind of reemerged pan-Arab identity be born, which is paired with the strengthening of a new organized force of Islamism.

Even though, as Katerina Dalacura mentions (Dalacura, 2012, p. 63), the comparison between the Arab Spring and the system changes and the end of communism in Central and Eastern Europe was rather premature, the events since December 2010 have irrevocably transformed the Middle East and North Africa. In the external dimension we need to overcome looking only for common threads because that would prevent us from understanding the different causes and consequences of democratic changes from country to country. Or it would prevent us from putting the events in a different context. Support from external players such as the European Union is crucial, but making the new governments overly dependent on the European Union or too much internationalization would aggravate the existing problems and may strengthen the position of the extremists. (Tisseron, 2012, pp. 20-21) When analyzing the external context we also need to pay attention to the external consequences of the Arab Spring in the Sahara and Sahel regions. The war in Libya and the flow of arms to other countries made the security situation in the Sahara considerably worse. Radicalism and terrorist activities are spreading south. Al-Qaeda in the Maghreb infiltrated Mali and Niger. The sad but clear and not too surprising evidence is the death of democracy in Mali. The military coup in spring 2012 was a linear consequence of the deteriorated security situation. What was otherwise promising democratic development in the political dimension was undone by the security dimension. The returning Tuareg fighters from Libya posed an unsolvable challenge for the government, and the Northern independence movements merging with the new fighters launched attacks on the Malian military from January 2012 on. Although Mali presents an extreme example of the effects of negative spillover, the entire region is unstable and the future of Niger is not optimistic, either.

The political, societal and domestic dimensions
The greatest challenge in the political dimension is the expected appearance of those Islamist groups which were not held to be part of the opposition or which were even banned. Now it is their turn to prove that they are able to govern, to structure everyday life and to maintain the achievements of the democratic transitions without falling back to social turmoil or civil war, for instance in Libya. The success of the Islamist groups and parties during the elections in the region in 2011 and 2012 can be explained by several factors. The main motivation behind the mass protests and revolts was the demand for dignity. The Islamists groups were well organized locally and they could provide a real alternative for the population, promising to deliver social justice, economic development, and "Arab democracy". The mass population is disappointed with the secular opposition parties and the model which the European Union can offer. Many argue that the population now rather admires the moderate Islamist development of Turkey, and the real successes of the AKP (Justice and Development Party). (Tis-

seron, 2011, p. 7) The Islamists were organizers, or at least they had real local roots, because in most countries all not co-opted opposition groups and civil society organizations were banned except those who gathered in the mosques. It is important to emphasize here again that the different countries reflect different societal and political landscapes, and we need to make a difference between, for instance, the moderate groups and the Salafist groups that involve security rather than political concern.

Consequently, the challenge for the European Union is not the powerful Islamists groups and parties in power, but those groups which are more extreme and are willing to build states along the laws of Islam. Large parts of the population are not open to such a change, but success in terms of fundamentals will eventually depend on the ability of the governing parties to maintain development and satisfy at least the basic demands of society. There are already signs that younger people are dissatisfied with the achievements of the process and are turning more radical, feeling that the revolutions are being stolen from them – this is a real danger in Libya and less seriously in Tunisia. (Tisseron, 2011, pp. 7-8) The test of the durability of the regimes and the democratic transition in the political dimension is how old slogans like "Islam is the solution" can be translated into real deeds, how the parties in power are able to form real political programs, and how they will be able to implement them.[12] It is almost common sense that the Islamist groups and parties are not monolithic blocks and it is a question how they can reconcile Islamic identity with the wish of fulfilling the demands of the population for modernity, political participation and economic development. It is a long and difficult process. From the Union's point of view it is even questionable whether it can be labeled as the beginning of democratic transition. Nevertheless, the European Union cannot do much more at the moment in this dimension than to engage with these parties and get to know them better. On the other hand, the European Union cannot let these processes turn around and call into question the basic principles of democracy and human rights. A reversal of the processes would mean an even more turbulent and unpredictable development than the Arab Spring itself, and would confirm the fears of the pessimist voices about the "Islamist winter". (See, for example, Totten, 2012; Rostoványi, 2012) A democratic transition is obviously a complex process. It is difficult to judge at the beginning whether the outcome would be a desired democratic political and institutional constellation or a turbulent environment which rather gives space for further challenges and threats both to the domestic players and the European Union.

The immediate outcome of the Arab Spring is definitely dangerous. Democracy is in line with European values and with the Union's long-term interests, while the Arab Spring created a highly volatile political situation which is even more complicated by the different domestic events in each country. The transitions are a turbulent and messy interplay of external and domestic factors. As Michael

---

12   Today we can witness that this and similar slogans are fading away from the rhetoric due to the political pressures which necessitate pragmatic solutions.

Totten argued on the pages of *World Affairs* recently, the likelihood of the emergence of genuine liberal democracies as a consequence of the Arab Spring is close to zero, and the common feature of the processes is that all the countries are in turmoil. (Totten, 2012, p. 43) The European Union may not be able to step back to the old policies of supporting "liberal" dictators, that is those authoritarian regimes which definitely did not serve the fulfillment of Western values but at least did not threaten Western interests directly in the short term. In the case of Morocco and Algeria the Union still tries to pressure the incumbent regimes to reform their policies, mainly because it has limited resources to handle instability and foster further significant changes. An Islamist takeover was feared before the fall of the old regimes, and after the elections their gain in power was not a surprise as they were the most (if not the only) organized political forces in the region. However, the political turmoil decreases the ability of the new regimes to maintain security domestically and consequently the stability of the region.

The European Union as a "civilian superpower" (Duchêne, 1972; Simms, 2012) has long aimed at reaching out towards the civil societies of its neighbors, especially towards those which undergo deep political changes threatening the European Union with an unstable environment. The European Union also has been keen on engaging civil society organizations in the planning process of the different programs towards the neighbors. In the recent joint communication of the European Commission *Delivering on a new European Neighbourhood Policy* (2012) there is a list of the instruments the European Union has used to empower civil societies. Special emphasis is put on the Civil Society Facility, which was launched in September 2011 with an annual budget of 26 million euros. Furthermore, in the Southern neighborhood the Union intensified support for the Anna Lindh Foundation. It is a fact that all the Maghreb countries adopted promising reforms in the political sphere and allowed more space for civil society, but it is difficult to prove the causality between the rather modest support and the incremental change.

Following the revolts in North Africa and the Middle East the European Union put new emphasis on so-called "deep and sustainable democracy", which can be characterized not only by elections but also by certain other freedoms attached to political participation. Freedom of expression and association is still challenged in the Maghreb countries, yet civil society is relatively strong. The easy recipe follows: the European Union needs to empower this already strong civil society. The problem is that the European Union is reluctant to open dialogue towards those organizations, some of them already in power, which have Islamist roots. The reason is that the European Union views these groups as potential radicals threatening the Union. However, the Union needs to accept that in most of the Maghreb countries the real opposition groups which had been organized are the Islamists and they are the ones who are able to provide a viable alternative to the old regimes. Even though the outcome of the democratization process is not clear yet, we cannot hide behind the cultural-relativist standpoint anymore that claims that Islam or Arab societies are not compatible with democracy. Even though it does not originate from a religious leader of the Maghreb, the statement of Saudi Salafist hardliner Sheikh Salman al-Awdah is still remarkable: "Democracy might be not an ideal system, but it is the least harmful, and it can be developed and adapted to respond to local needs and circumstances." (Quoted by Zelin, 2012) This is surprisingly positive, given that before the Arab Spring most of the Salafis, close to power in Tunisia, regarded democracy as contrary to Islam because it would elevate humans to the level of God. On the other hand, it is also true that this change in rhetoric will not immediately turn the Islamists into liberals in a Western sense, but it still creates hope for the future, given that Islamists have become powerful political figures in the region.

The analysis of the domestic dimension shows what the European Union has to add for the democratization process to be successful. The domestic dimension covers and represents the historical cornerstones of institutional development, the ways how a country organizes its economic activity, governance, or the motivations for development. The final success of democratization obviously depends on the domestic settings. The external dimension needs to make up for the factors which are missing or temporarily not present in the domestic dimension. That is why it is so important to understand the local-regional characteristics of the Maghreb. The lack of domestic capacity is the real limit of success of the democratic transition. The institutions and democracy can only work when local stakeholders also participate in the rebuilding process from the first moment. The experience of former democratic transitions proves that pre-existing law and order, a pacific political culture, literacy, high levels of general education, moderate economic differences, general economic development, a sizable middle class, the rule of law, and a strong civil society all contribute to the sustainability of the reformed institutions. (Etzioni, 2007, p. 42)

After the Arab Spring a discourse on the irrelevance of "being Arab" emerged with the claim that the local-regional context has little influence on the development of events and future development of the countries. At first sight this seems to be a valid argument due to the experiences in the Maghreb, which show that all the countries performed differently. On the other hand, the argument of Morten Valborn and André Bank (2012) in their recent article is rather for emphasizing the domestic dimension and the influence of "being Arab" on the events in North Africa and the Middle East. The scenarios for the future are different than before, but the real turning point was rather 2003 and not necessarily the beginning of the Arab Spring, which is part of a longer process. In this context "being Arab" meant distancing from the United States, the occupier of Iraq, and Israel, and on the societal level seeking a new identity not associated with the corrupt old regimes.

In line with the above characteristics it is important to note that the local or domestic settings or dimensions have a real influence on future development. "Being Arab", however, expands the domestic dimension to the regional level, which means that the political borders do not necessarily separate the societies, and definitely not identities. By emphasizing this, the analysis of the domestic dimension necessitates a deeper understanding of the dynamics which sometimes enhances but unfortunately in many instances rather hinders regional cooperation among the Maghreb countries. The security threats, the political realities, the economic needs and the societal interconnections create a special framework.

The expression state failure region invented by Stefan Wolff (2011) aptly describes the situation in North Africa and the Middle East. State failure regions are regions where the spillover of state failure is likely due to smaller "spillover costs" and the fact that in this region the interactions are more intense than on the global level. The turbulent events of the Arab Spring definitely threaten the interests and indirectly the security of the European Union. The Union's goal in the region has been stability, which many times collided with the values of freedom, the rule of law and respect for the human rights of a liberal Western democracy. Now, the democratic opening may bring new scenarios in which the new democracies are not in line with Western values. The new opening may mean new opportunities for regional cooperation in the Maghreb where regional institutions, for instance the Arab Maghreb Union, certainly exist, but are not effective or they do not function at all due to local-regional (domestic) political differences and hostility.

The literature (for example, Dalacura, 2012, p. 64) seems to be disposed to handling the Arab world as unified because of certain strong internal bonds. This approach is based on the fact that the uprisings were contagious and spread quickly over the whole Middle East and North Africa. Behind the chain of events we need to suspect a similar mix of socio-economic problems, such as relative deprivation, the clash of expectations and reality, mass youth unemployment, rampant corruption, general inequalities[13] and, most importantly, rising food prices. The problems were not solved simply by the regime changes and the reaction of the new governments to the still present tensions will be crucial in the future. The countries of the Maghreb with more potential for success are those which can build on pre-existing institutions, such as Tunisia. Libya, however, faces an enormous challenge of simultaneous state-building and nation-building.

The economic dimension

The European Union's policies towards the Maghreb have always had a significant economic dimension. The project for economic growth sometimes overshadowed other general goals of the Union. The phenomenon can be explained by the belief in the power of modernization and the spillover effects of economic development to other dimensions. This approach is in line with one of the dominant democratization-related theories that have been present in development politics for a long time. (See Carothers, 2009) First, the political approach emphasizes the political processes, such as elections, political institutions, or political parties, and it strives to convince decision-makers to channel aid through political development as it will lead to general economic well-being in the future. The easiest way to generate development is democratic transition for which the sound tool is aiding local democrats. Second, the broader developmental approach does not simply focus on political institutions or democracy; rather it believes in the importance of

---

13   The diplomatic cables released by Wikileaks revealed the luxurious lifestyle of the ruling elite. The most scandalous example was the series of Ben Ali style parties whilst the people suffered from high food prices.

good governance and its connections to general socio-economic features. Democracy in this approach is not a value in itself, but the tool for achieving more equal economic conditions. In words the European Union follows the first approach, but as was argued before the reality rather proves that the Union's real goal is to maintain stability and foster economic development. However, the economic policies which focused on economic development and reducing inequalities in the Maghreb are expensive in the midst of the economic problems and financial crisis of the European Union, so their future is not clear. The newly emerged governments in the Maghreb estimated their needs for economic development at tens of billions of euros. (Tisseron, 2012, p. 14)

The wave of revolts was rooted mostly in changing economic opportunities for the youth as the masses on the streets demanded jobs, at the same time hoping for decreasing economic inequalities. The reaction of the European Union to the Arab Spring, similarly to that in the political dimension, has been rather modest in terms of economic assistance. The EBRD promised 3.5 billion euros to the whole Middle East and North Africa, which is mostly going to Egypt. The Maghreb lacks other sources. However, through the European Neighbourhood Policy 1.75 billion euros will help the region's development, furthermore the European Investment Bank and members of the European Union on the bilateral level are also trying to contribute, mostly in the form of cancelled debts. (Dadush et al., 2011, p. 135)

Today it is already clear that the political changes could not improve the economic situation in the Maghreb. In many places even the opposite is true. Nevertheless, we should not come to the conclusion that the changes will lead to a dead end. Today's economic problems and poor outlook are indeed the linear consequence of the failed economic policies of the former regimes and also proof of the failed development approach of the European Union. Thus the economic dimension of EU-Maghreb relations cannot be separated from the security, political or social dimensions. The economic demands of the masses also imply political consequences in the form of democratization, or at least in the wish for more equal political rights and participation in the public sphere. On the other hand, people are impatient and they cannot be calmed by theories or intangible economic forecasts. Consequently, social dissatisfaction maintains political unrest and an unstable security situation. Thus, unrealized speedy economic development is the real backdrop to political problems. As the comprehensive analysis of the Thomas Moore Institute emphasizes (Tisseron, 2012, pp. 12-16) the economies of the Maghreb countries have been fragile, and structurally associated with rampant corruption and the predatory behavior of local stakeholders in the economy. The inequality stems from the failed diversification of the economy, such as overdependence on gas or oil exports (mainly Algeria and Libya). A growing gap in development and consequently the expected incomes in different sectors has been threatening, not to mention the inequalities between certain age groups or certain job families. In all countries the unemployment rate among young people under the age of 25 is way over the general rate. Furthermore, young university graduates find themselves more easily without a job than unqualified people of the same age.

Beyond all these problems the Arab Spring provided a shock to the economies followed by an economic downturn in all countries. In those where the regime remained intact but needed to allow certain reforms, such as Morocco and Algeria, the budget deficits are multiplied due to the "social welfare" policies of the governments which subsidized basic necessities of the population such as gas, oil, rice or sugar, and created civil servant positions and increased salaries in the public sector. In those countries which were affected more by the civil turmoil the situation is even worse. Tunisia lost significant income due to a drop in tourism of 33% (Tisseron, 2012, p. 13) and the war in Libya acted as a warning for investors (not only in Libya), most of whom relocated their business elsewhere.

The development model clearly needs to be changed. The economic outlook should not depend on sectors which mostly require a large number of unqualified workers, especially because these sectors cannot cope with Asian competition, and the domestic markets are too small for development. However, the recipe is not "black or white". The entire educational system is in crisis, and the increasing number of graduates without jobs will further fuel social problems. Thus the role of those such as the European Union who want to break this "vicious circle" is important but difficult, as they do not have many options for providing solutions. The European Union has long been focusing on the fight against corruption and this is still at the heart of the expected reforms. (Tisseron, 2012, p. 15) However, the Maghreb countries have the real stakes in the matter and they can also represent the real limit of success. Less corruption would rekindle the confidence of investors and would respond to one of the demands of the people. On the other hand, fighting against corruption involves tackling a socially embedded institution stemming from traditional structures by attacking a complex equilibrium and consequently creating even more unpredictability in the economy.

Out of sequence institutional changes in the economic sector, even if they seem to bolster faster economic growth, may undo achievements in other dimensions. Globalization and the experience of the developed countries may suggest that the recipe for development is privatization of state-owned enterprises, the deregulation of currency, lowering tariffs and cutting back public expenditure, but as the spectacular failure of the "Washington consensus" showed, generalization of economic development is false. Before the economy can undergo large-scale reforms, there is a need for other institutions and conditions, such as for security, for the state's ability to collect taxes, for transparent policies, for a low level of corruption, and for functioning government. In any other situation, economic reforms may contribute to a (new) collapse of the state. (Haken, 2006) Inequality also appears in geographical terms. The centralist tradition is still strong in the Maghreb countries. It is similar to other regions of the world where the otherwise weak state was the only provider of basic social services and public goods. However, decentralization may not be the cure because tearing down the anyway weak central institutions will not serve to strengthen the local economy, rather it would hinder development.

The means: the policies and instruments of the European Union

After the Arab Spring the situation in the Maghreb is far from stable. The region is undergoing significant change, and the countries also face different realities. However, one thing is sure: the European Union needs to review its strategy towards the region according to the new parameters. The new environment demands new responses which evidently need to be comprehensive and need to take into account several interconnected factors in the different dimensions. The upheavals and social turmoil took different forms in the five Maghreb countries: in Mauritania, Morocco, Algeria and Tunisia, and most significantly in Libya. On the regional level, as the special report of the Thomas Moore Institute emphasizes (Tisseron, 2012), we can witness a turnaround in politics after the decade since 2001. The region is at the beginning of a new political cycle where the long awaited democratic change has an opportunity. It became clear to the old regimes that neglecting the political and social demands of the people is not a possibility and, on the other hand, it became clear to the European Union (or more generally to the international community) that authoritarian regimes do not do a better job in protecting the outside world from terrorists and political extremism. The Arab Spring has created an opportunity but also a challenge for the European Union, which needs to restructure its relation to the region and take a leading role, or at least be better committed in supporting democratic transitions. It is clear that the European Union has to leave behind its "traditional" position towards the Maghreb, which rather sought stability in pursuit of the Union's internal security, and revisit the liberal democracy-building agenda which was part of its foreign policy in recent decades, more specifically since the launch of the Barcelona process in 1995.

The Euro-Mediterranean Partnership already reflected a comprehensive logic as part of the Union's strategic culture, but the conditions and the goals remained rather on the level of rhetoric. The goal of the program has been similar to other foreign policy programs of the European Union. The three pillars of cooperation aimed at strengthening security, maintaining stability, and promoting good governance and respect for human rights. The partnership was sometimes seen, especially after the new Barcelona Summit in 2005, as a complementary initiative in relation to the presence of the United States in the region. The new summit added a forth pillar – justice and internal affairs – to the original political and security, economic and financial, and social, cultural and human chapters. After years giving birth to the program it became obvious that the initiative is not able to reach the originally designated goals. Thus the newly elected president of France took the lead in 2007 and sought to build up a stronger though parallel structure for the Mediterranean region. Finally, due to Angela Merkel's disapproval the plan was dropped and as a substitute the Union for the Mediterranean was created. The Union for the Mediterranean built on the Barcelona process but aimed to achieve more in maintaining peace and expanding the sphere of prosperity towards the Southern shore of the Mediterranean. Although the new initiative was ambitious at the beginning and became significantly more visible than its predecessor with, for instance, the creation of the Secretariat and the model of biennial summits of heads of states and governments of the Union's 27 member states and the Mediterranean partners, the result was sobering. Even the summits were not held after 2008 due to regional conflicts.

Another instrument of the European Union which aims to manage relations with the Maghreb is the European Neighbourhood Policy (ENP) launched by a European Council communiqué in 2003. The originally mainly bilateral model later embraced the idea of supporting regional cooperation. Thus the above-mentioned Union for the Mediterranean is also part of the ENP. The ENP aims at fostering political and economic reforms and managing development in the neighborhood more closely through detailed Action Plans and regular Progress Reports. Regarding the Maghreb, the ENP has a rather poor grade card: neither Libya nor Algeria has an Action Plan.[14] The ENP fosters cross-border cooperation; however, the political reality in the Maghreb is the real obstacle. The borders between Morocco and Algeria are still closed.

The future is still obscure, yet some experts are optimists (see Lachen, 2012; Abderrahmane, 2012) who see the opportunity for revival of the Arab Maghreb Union, which has been frozen since 1994. The optimism is not completely without basis. The Algerian minister for foreign affairs met his Moroccan counterpart in January 2012, and a meeting was held in Rabat in February 2012 in order to revitalize regional cooperation. On the other hand, the old obstacles are paired with new challenges. It is not clear how those groups will react who benefited from the stalemate, such as terrorist groups or organized crime groups. Furthermore, the border issues are still not resolved between Morocco and Algeria, and Western Sahara's denied independence is also a dark menace in the region. As we have seen, the new opening can also create instability, the pro-democratic movements are in most cases poor, and the demanded democratic practice indeed created space for the radical Islamists groups who were more organized.

The ENP's goal and more generally the Union's foreign policy towards the Maghreb was in rhetoric the export of liberal economy and democracy. Thus the European Union "full heartedly" welcomed the Arab Spring. In fact, the quick changes and the mass protests, violence and war were rather a sign of the failure of the Euro-Mediterranean Partnership, or the ENP. (For a similar argument see Hollis, 2012) This is not surprising. The European Union promised shared prosperity, a developing economy and more jobs, at least on paper, while, on the other hand, it favored dictators and the old regimes who maintained stability. According to widely accepted security perceptions in the European Union, the authoritarian leaders were not perfect but were necessary players in countering terrorism and decreasing illegal migration to the European Union.[15] Intelligence,

---

14 Algeria was asked to initiate it at the end of 2011. For more information see the official EU websites. For instance: http://ec.europa.eu/europeaid/where/neighbourhood/country-cooperation/algeria/algeria_en.htm

15 Understandably, in rhetoric the European Union always pushed the authoritarian regimes towards political reforms. Yet the conditionality of the European

counter-terrorism and border control issues were at on the top of the real agenda regarding relations with the Maghreb countries. For years the European Union prioritized its own prosperity and stability over democracy and the spread of the rule of law in the Maghreb. Indirectly, the European Union helped maintain the old regimes and increase the social tension which eventually triggered the revolts, protests and uprisings in the region. (Hollis, 2012, p. 92)

Even though the central pillar of the European Union towards the Mediterranean region and consequently the Maghreb has been the promotion of democracy, the Union has been reluctant to assist and support Islamist groups. The contradiction is obvious because, as more and more observers argued (see Pace et al., 2009), the Islamists may also be the basis of democratic development, albeit not an EU-like liberal democracy. The Union's strategy before the Arab Spring involved engaging with the autocratic leaders whilst assisting civil society and fostering economic reforms. In defense of the Union's approach we have to note that the strong regimes governed weak states, thus any change threatened stability with the menace of a turbulent and unpredictable process. However, given the events since December 2010 the European Union has needed to revisit its approach towards North Africa. A further challenge stems from the generally used practice, which needs to be changed as well. The European Union was able to reach a compromise with the old regimes while, on the other hand, supporting the secular opposition groups which were far from united. The secular opposition has "lived" from European Union support and it has been crucial for them to appear as the only viable democratic option. The alienated local population, however, has not associated itself with the "Westernized" opposition, rather they turned to the Islamist parties. A further challenge is that these Islamists parties are organized, united and are able to accept democratic rules. Being democratic for them is important, since after the Arab Spring they have to show that they are rather the exception and can reach a common platform with the external Western actors, mainly the European Union.

With all this in mind it is worth revisiting the Union's democracy promotion strategy. Based on the widely accepted liberal democratic peace theory (Doyle, 1986; Oneal et al., 1997; Ray, 1997) the European Union has promoted democracy because it has believed that this is an appropriate tool for maintaining security and stability. In recent decades the practice appeared to be controversial and the Arab Spring proved that "EU style" democracy promotion may not work and that the European Union must adapt more to the local reality with

---

Union, which was regarded as an effective tool, was not appropriate when the criticism of Brussels appeared only in rhetoric. Even though cultural ties with the Maghreb were definitely strengthened, direct assistance to real institutional and political change was rather modest in overall figures. The mixture of positive incentives, selective punitive measures and the direct funding of democratization programs was not able to create a favorable environment for the fulfillment of the Union's goals of securing political and economic stability. (See, for instance, Tisseron, 2012)

its political, economic and social settings. (For a similar argument see Pace et al., 2009, pp. 5-6) The authoritarian elites were able to convince the European Union they were the real agents of liberal reforms and that they were the only ones who could maintain stability and protect the European Union against terrorism and illegal migration flows arising due the weakness of their states. The European Union eventually fell into the trap. The choices were: further supporting the incumbent regimes and hoping for economic reforms which may bring democracy gradually in the long term; assisting the Islamists groups to gain power against the regimes along with unfolding unpredictable events; or supporting the co-opted secular opposition groups and civil society.[16] In general, the Union's policy even increased the divide between the Islamists and the secular opposition groups, making it easier for the regimes to stay in power. The goals of the foreign policy instruments such as the Euro-Mediterranean Partnership or the Union for the Mediterranean have contradicted the real practice in the Maghreb region – obviously in the greater Mediterranean region, too – because stability was preferred over real democratic change. From the Union's point of view Morocco as the main source of migrants needs to be stable in order fight against illegal migration on the Southern shore of the Mediterranean. Algeria is not democratic, but the Bouteflika regime has been able to suppress the radical Islamists and terrorism. The same was true in Tunisia, where the regime was able to maintain stability up to December 2010. Mauritania is rather far from the European Union and the military coup in 2008 and the controversial elections in 2009 did not really ignite any response besides the usual rhetoric of condemnation. Libya, in contrast, was important because of the Union's energy consumption and because the European Union reluctantly accepted Gaddafi as a partner in the 2000s after he made a commitment to dissolving Libya's nuclear weapons program. As we saw, in 2010 and 2011 everything changed.

Endemic instability and Islamic extremism were an appropriate cover for the dictators of the region. It was easier to rely on them and believe in the modernist idea that economic development will force democracy in the long term. We need to note here that eventually economic causes indeed contributed to the revolts (revolutions), but in an inverse manner because the mass public demanded better economic opportunities and jobs. The Union's approach involving top-down change and encouraging the regimes to implement political and economic reforms is now substituted by a genuine process and a bottom-up change, the driver of which is the people. The response of the European Union was extremely modest, which can be explained by the reluctance to support a process which is detrimental to the European Union in the long term. The European Union is highly dependent on the energy sources of the Maghreb. In addition, it is in the

---

16   The reality points to even more concerns regarding civil society because most of the functioning civil society organizations have been somehow created, or if not created then influenced by the government. In the literature the label for these organizations is GONGO (Governmental Non-Governmental Organizations).

midst of a financial crisis, which means that its room for maneuver has been rather limited. (Dadush et al., 2011, pp. 132-135)

After September 11, 2011, the Union's cooperation with the region intensified under the aegis of the fight against terrorism. Despite strong security-oriented policies, the European Union has not been able to impact decisively on the unresolved conflicts in the Maghreb. (Benantar, 2006) The number of institutions and initiatives constantly grew when NATO and the United States became active in the region. NATO created an intensified dialogue with all the Maghreb countries except for Libya and Algeria. Later both of them joined NATO's Mediterranean Dialogue. The European Union duplicated this initiative and through the European Security and Defence Policy (Common Security and Defence Policy) added its own programs of trust-building measures. The Maghreb felt targeted by the existing policies, therefore the more problematic issues have never been pushed by the European Union. It is clear that the Union needs to revise its strategy towards the Maghreb. The effort can be seen in official documents such as the joint communication of the European Parliament, the Council, the European Economic and Social Committee, and the Committee of the Regions entitled *Delivering on a new European Neighbourhood Policy* (2012) wherein the European Union expresses the intention to apply a comprehensive approach with the aim of reaching a common strategy.

The strategy of the European Union in relation to promoting democracy, similarly to other foreign policy objectives, reflects a mixture of high ambitions, real European experience with democracy and human rights promotion, and general knowledge regarding the nexus of democracy and human rights. The reason for the contradiction between goals and realities is rooted firstly in the ambition of general foreign policy aims; secondly, in the fact that there are no clear definitions of democracy or human rights; and thirdly, in the outcome of the bureaucratic attributes of the Union's policies, namely under-funding and incoherence in terms of linkages. The Union's commitment to promoting democracy, human rights and good governance penetrates every aspect of its foreign, security and development policy. However, the expectations are set too high in the relations with developing countries, which factor stems from the positive experiences with the enlargement in the 1990s. It is beyond doubt that enlargement has been the most successful foreign policy instrument of the European Union, but the historically, politically and geographically specific context created a different situation. Furthermore, the perspective of membership, being the engine of development, has been a stronger incentive than any other rewarding or punitive measures of the European Union. Consequently, no policies towards the Maghreb can be as effective, and similarly the Union is not able to assist the countries after the revolts, as it was able after the system changes in Central and Eastern Europe. Copying the strict conditionality in relations with other regions clearly results in different outcomes. The European Union routinely asserts that all aspects of its foreign policy consider the goals of promoting democracy and human rights. In the rhetoric the Union is keen to avoid forcing "one-size-fits-all" models on its partners and emphasizes that it promotes different models of democracy as the European Union itself is a collection of 27 distinct methods of democratic governance.

After the changes of 1989-90, the European Union became very active in the post-socialist Central and Eastern European states; and by setting up the mechanisms of conditionality it contributed to the large-scale transformation of politics, economy and society. However, the integration process is rather "member-state-building" and as such it has been the most successful among the state-building projects so far. The integration process is a complex set of different forces that together influenced the candidate states to cooperate in state-building. Conditionality and the Europeanization of these countries were completed by the persuasive pressure of the member states, the policy transfer of different NGOs and endowments from the European Union, and by the leading example of European-style institutions. All the applicant countries could be forced to implement reforms because of their hoped benefits of full membership of the community. (Zaborowski, 2003, p. 16) The Union's "member-state-building" could be successful because it prescribed concrete institutional requirements, and altered the domestic opportunity structures and the institutional context. Furthermore, it altered the beliefs and expectations of domestic actors. The European Union clearly has an advantage in Europe and especially on its own periphery, where the promise of membership has the power of attraction.

Putting things together: Conclusions regarding a soft grand strategy for the Maghreb on the part of the European Union

The European Union's goal is to take the lead in relation to the events and development in the Maghreb, and it aims at becoming the leading regional actor. The Union has the basis for it in terms of decades of experience with institutional relations; furthermore, the European Union is accepted by the local population as an international actor. (See Aragall et al., 2012) The situation in the Maghreb is highly volatile and all the countries need different treatment as they involve a different beginning situation regarding the Rubik's Cube analogy. The European Union has the task of adapting its existing policies and instruments according to the new situation, and it is willing to look at the region comprehensively, leaving behind the policies simply intended to maintain stability and security in the short term. The existing policies and instruments are a good basis for this effort; the only requirement is to rethink the interconnections among the different dimensions of development and plan the changes of the relations between the European Union and the Maghreb accordingly. The Rubik's Cube model provides some intellectual support in this effort.

The Arab Spring disproved many commonly held assumptions about the inability of Islam and Arab peoples to develop democracy, and also about the necessary conditions for democratic transitions. On the other hand, the events seem to support other theories about the characteristics of such processes. The political development in North Africa and the Middle East is indeed turbulent and not predictable, and in its present form does not seem to serve the Union's interest in stability.

Even though the European Union has twenty years of successful experience of promoting democracy in its neighborhood, the linear model of democracy promotion proved to be less and less effective, which made the European Union fall back to a post-modern realist agenda. Post-modern realism in this sense meant engagement with the autocrats of the Maghreb whilst in rhetoric the European Union emphasized the importance of liberal values, good governance and respect for human rights. Consequently, the European Union sought stability rather than real and deep structural changes, due to which it was reluctant to push too hard towards democracy. Engagement in the region features rather in major speeches than in real actions. Yet in spite of all these arguments the Union still has the potential to expand stability and prosperity because of the very reason that the attractiveness of the European Union is still very high in the neighborhood.

In our globalized world, global political, economic and social processes penetrate into local and regional relations, and there is a need to understand the new realities. In order to do so the European Union needs to have a comprehensive strategy towards the Maghreb which takes into account all dimensions, that is the presence of external players and the interests of the partner countries, whilst not having all the "hard" means which would be necessary in a geopolitical contest such as is emerging in the Mediterranean. The new strategy is in this sense a "soft grand strategy". Nevertheless, the gap between expectations and capabilities is still significant.

The conditionality of the European Union was an effective tool vis-à-vis those countries which had real a opportunity for membership and consequently it is not appropriate towards the Maghreb. Even though the cultural ties with the Maghreb have been definitely strengthened, direct assistance aimed at real institutional and political change has been rather modest in overall figures. The mixture of positive incentives, selective punitive measures and the direct funding of democratization programs has simply not been able to create a favorable environment for the fulfillment of the Union's goals of securing political and economic stability. The democratization initiatives have necessarily been sacrificed on the altar of stability and more importantly of the geopolitics of energy. The future is not clear but one thing is sure: the European Union cannot continue the weak policies towards the region because in the long run security will be at stake due to the highly volatile political situation. There is a necessity for the convergence of words and deeds in the Union's foreign policy.

As has been argued throughout this study, the situation is complex as it differs country by country. The goal of the present analysis, however, was not to analyze each country separately but to introduce the Rubik's Cube model, which helps us understand the interconnectedness of the security, political, economic, societal, domestic and external dimensions. These dimensions can be separated only in theory and any change in one dimension automatically results in change in another. Differences between countries means a different beginning situation in terms of the model, and it also means that the European Union faces five cubes in the Maghreb. The model suggests that, despite the fact that there is no general blueprint for each situation, the repetition of similar algorithms would lead to similar effects. On the other hand, the "cubes" of the countries of the region are connected to each other in the external dimension.

Due to the fact that the dimensions are separated artificially in theory, the analysis had the opportunity to restructure them according to the realities of the Maghreb countries following the Arab Spring. The security and external dimensions have a closer interplay regarding the theme of the study and the general geopolitical situation in that the external players, such as the European Union, are at least as important as domestic factors in maintaining security. The political, societal and domestic dimensions are similarly more closely interconnected, bearing in mind that the pivotal issue of the democratic transitions in the Maghreb concerns the survival of the new regimes. This survival depends on the new Islamist parties in power, their ability to handle domestic demands, to create viable political institutions, and to remain pragmatic and avoid Islamist radicalism, which would clearly tear society apart.

The European Union has always been very good at communicating its ambitions to develop democracy and promote human rights. Nevertheless, the Euro-Mediterranean Partnership and the Union for the Mediterranean were regarded as promising instruments of the ENP, but systematic action is still needed. Apart from the lack of financial resources, these suffer from the same disease as the programs promoting democracy and human rights in general. The individual policies of the member states, the trade interests, and development, migration, or agricultural questions in general involve the previously stated goals of those programs. These all result in an incoherent and not agreed narrative of democracy-building and human rights promotion in terms of different regions and situations. The already mentioned "soft grand strategy" is for channeling the existing policies towards being able to achieve the European Union's goal of increasing influence on development in the region. A new style of coherent strategy will also serve creating better relations with the individual countries in the Maghreb. One of the basic roles of those countries and alliances spreading democracy and encouraging peace is to be aware of the possibility of eruption of new conflicts, and to implement all possible measures aimed at preventing potential conflicts.

The European Union is the largest political and trade partner of the Maghreb countries, but due to the Arab Spring the Union needs to launch a new neighborhood policy, which is both a difficult geopolitical project and a new grand strategy at the same time. The situation is indeed complex and the European Union has so far issued two joint communications. Nevertheless, the space for real change is very limited. The European Union is keen to broaden its financial support for the new regimes in order to maintain security and encourage them to implement further political reforms. However, the Union itself is experiencing financial problems and the allocated funds are way below the amount expected by the Maghreb countries. Providing wider access to the European markets for the Maghreb countries would be another possibility for assisting economic and social change in the region, but as with supporting the mobility of the people it collides with the short-term security interests of the European Union. To sum up, the new strategy needs to face the extreme complexity deriving from the interconnections of the different dimensions. Each dimension itself seems to be a priority for the European Union at first sight. The Union simultaneously seeks to fight against terrorism and political extremism, supports the democratic reforms, promotes the institutions which help economic development, tries to alleviate the social tensions, and assists in the revival of regional cooperation, namely the Arab Maghreb Union, whilst playing a geopolitical game in the Mediterranean. It is clear that achieving all these goals at the same time is almost a mission impossible.

The Rubik's Cube analogy and adaptation of the solution methodology's model help us complement the theoretical findings of the securitization theory and thoughts about the European Union's strategic culture. The study did not intend to provide a deep quantitative analysis of the relations between the European Union and the Maghreb countries, it rather sought to introduce a model which aims to focus on the interconnectedness of the different dimensions. The conclusion is that the Union has an enormously difficult task in assisting the Maghreb, whilst the long-term goal is still the maintenance of the European Union's security. The European Union needs to elaborate a "soft grand strategy" which incorporates the suggestion regarding how to address the challenges of the different dimensions comprehensively. Only such a strategy will help the European Union bring together all the existing different policies, programs, initiatives and instruments in developing the Maghreb. Thus, as the Thomas Moore Institute's study (Tisseron, 2012) summarized, the European Union needs to learn to live together with the new parties in power whilst remaining insistent that democratic principles and respect for human rights are not called into question. The democratic transitions are turbulent and in the Maghreb they have just begun; thus the governments and civil society need extended support. The gap between the expectations of the people and the slow development project has put at risk the achievements so far and threaten the re-emergence of revolutionary events and the strengthening of extremist groups. Beyond the short-term goals, the strategic thinking suggests investing in the future, namely in the creation of a sound economic environment for both local and foreign investments. Maintaining the political achievements necessitates the maintenance of security and peace, thus the European Union needs to invest in the security sector, too. Finally, even though the bilateral relations between the European Union and Maghreb countries would seem to be developing without the enhanced or – to put it better – revived regional cooperation, the future of the Maghreb is not bright. At the same time, there are positive signs of a real local commitment to use the Arab Maghreb Union again, which should be encouraged by the European Union.

Bibliography

Abderrahmane, A. (2012). *Hope for reviving the Arab Maghreb Union*. Retrieved from http://www.iss.co.za/iss_today.php?ID=1425

Aragall, X., & Padilla, J. (2012). The 2011 Euromed survey: Spotlight on the Arab Spring. In Euromed Survey of Experts and Actors. Euro-Mediterranean Policies in the Light of the Arab Spring. European Institute of the Mediterranean. Retrieved from http://www.iemed.org/observatori-en/arees-danalisi/arxius-adjunts/anuari/med.2012/aragall_padilla_en.pdf

Balogh, I. (2010). Considering a "European Soft Grand Strategy". *European Security and Defence Forum Workshop*. Chatham House: London. Retrieved from http://www.chathamhouse.org/sites/default/files/public/Research/International%20Security/1110esdf_balogh.pdf

Belhaj, A. (2011). Europe's security strategies in the Maghreb. *EU External Affairs Review*, July 2011, 107-114.

Benantar, A. (2006). NATO, Maghreb and Europe. *Mediterranean Politics, 11(2)*, 167-188.

Buzan, B. (1991). *People, states and fears*. London: Harvester.

Carothers, T. (2009). Democracy assistance: Political vs. developmental. *Journal of Democracy, 20(1)*, 5-29.

Call, C. T., & Cook, S. E. (2003). On democratization and peacebuilding. *Global Governance, 9*, 233-246.

Cofmann Wittes, T. (2012). Learning to live with the Islamist Winter. *Foreign Policy, July 19*, Retrieved from http://www.foreignpolicy.com/articles/2012/07/19/learning_to_live_with_the_islamist_winter?print=yes&hidecomments=yes&page=full

Dadush, U., & Dunne, M. (2011). American and European responses to the Arab Spring: What is the big idea? *The Washington Quarterly, 34(4)*, 131-145.

Dalacoura, K. (2012). The 2011 uprisings in the Arab Middle East: political change and geopolitical implications. *International Affairs*, 88(1), 63-79.

Dobbins, J., & McGinn, J. G. (2004). *America's role in nation building from Germany to Iraq*. Santa Monica: The Rand Corporation. Retrieved from http://www.rand.org/publications/MR/MR1753/

Dobbins, J., & McGinn, J. G. (2005). *The UN's role in nation building from Congo to Iraq*. Santa Monica: The Rand Corporation. Retrieved from http://www.rand.org/publications/MR/MR1833/

Dobbins, J. et al. (2008). *Europe's role in nation building from the Balkans to the Congo*. Santa Monica: The Rand Corporation.

Doyle, M. (1986). Liberalism and world politics. *American Political Science Review, 80(4)*, 1151-1169.

Duchêne, F. (1972). Europe's role in world peace. In R. Mayne (ed.), *Europe tomorrow: Sixteen Europeans look ahead*. London: Fontana.

Elder, F. (2011). The EU's counter terrorism policy towards the Maghreb. *European Security, 20(3)*, 431-451.

Etzioni, A. (2012). The folly of nation building. *The National Interest*, Retrieved from http://nationalinterest.org/article/the-folly-nation-building-7058

European Commission. (2003). *A secure Europe in a better world. Security strategy.* Retrieved from http://ue.eu.int/uedocs/cmsUpload/78367.pdf

European Commission. (2012a). *Delivering on a new European neighbourhood policy.* Joint Communication to the European Parliament, the Council, the European Economic and Social Committee and the Committee of the Regions. 15.5.2012. Brussels. Retrieved from http://ec.europa.eu/world/enp/docs/2012_enp_pack/delivering_new_enp_en.pdf

European Commission. (2012b). *Partnership for democracy and shared prosperity: Report on activities in 2011 and roadmap for future actions.* Joint Staff Working Document. 15.5.2012. Brussels. Retrieved from http://ec.europa.eu/world/enp/docs/2012_enp_pack/pship_democracy_report_roadmap_en.pdf

Gaddis, J. L. (1982). *Strategies of containment: A critical appraisal of American national security policy during the Cold War.* Oxford: Oxford University Press.

Gray, C. S. (2011). *War, peace and international relations: An introduction to strategic history.* London: Routledge.

Hardwick, C. (n.d.). *Solving the Rubik's revenge.* Retrieved from http://www.speedcubing.com/chris/4-solution.html

Hart, B. H. L. (1991). *Strategy.* New York: Plume.

Hollis, R. (2012). No friend of democratization: Europe's role in the genesis of the Arab Spring. *International Affairs, 88(1)*, 81-94

Inbar, E. (2012). *The 2011 Arab uprisings and Israel's national security.* The Begin-Sadat Center for Strategic Studies, Bar-Ilan University. Retrieved from http://www.biu.ac.il/Besa/MSPS95.pdf

Krotz, U., & Maher, R. (2011). International relations theory and the rise of European Foreign and Security Policy. *World Politics, 63(3)*, 548-579.

Lachen, A. (2012). The Arab Spring revives Maghreb integration. *Al-Hayat*, March, Retrieved from http://carnegieeurope.eu/publications/?fa=47385

Mansfield, E. D., & Snyder, J. (2005). *Electing to fight. Why emerging democracies go to war?* Cambridge: MIT Press.

Mansfield, E. D., & Snyder, J. (2007). The "sequencing" fallacy. *Journal of Democracy, 18(3)*, 5-9.

Norheim-Martinsen, Per M. (2011). EU strategic culture: When the means becomes the end. *Contemporary Security Policy, 32(3)*, 517-534.

Novotny, D. et al. (2011). *The changing security situation in the Maghreb*. Research Paper April 2011, Association of International Affairs. Retrieved from http://www.anatem.info/articles/securite_maghreb.pdf

Nye, J. S. (2004). *Soft power: The means to success in world politics*. New York: Public Affairs

Oberpfalzerová, H. (2012). The European Union facing security challenges in the Maghreb. Retrieved from http://www.eu-review.com/articles/hana-oberpfalzerova-the-european-union-facing-security-challenges-in-the-maghreb

Oneal, J. R., & Russett B. M. (1997). The classical liberals were right: Democracy, interdependence, and conflict, 1950–1985. *International Studies Quarterly, 41(2)*, 267-294.

Pace M. et al. (2009). The EU's democratization agenda in the Mediterranean. *Democratization, 16(1)*, 3-19.

Popescu, N. (2011). Democracy promotion: now what? European Council of Foreign Relations. Retrieved from http://ecfr.eu/blog/entry/deomcracy_promotion._now_what

Rada, P. (2010). The Rubik's Cube of democratic development: Lessons from democratization and statebuilding experiences. In Robert Ondrejcsák (ed.), *Panorama 2010*. Bratislava: CENAA.

Rada, P. (2011). The Rubik's Cube of democratic development: A normative model of statebuilding. Ph.D Dissertation. Budapest: Corvinus University of Budapest.

Ray, J. Lee. (1997). The democratic path to peace. *Journal of Democracy, 8(2)*, 49-64.

Rostoványi Zs. (2012). Az "arab tavasz" hatása a Közel-Kelet geopolitikai térképének újrarendeződésére. *Külügyi Szemle, 2012(1)*, 44-71.

Rynning, S. (2011). Strategic culture and the common security and defence policy. *Contemporary Security Policy, 32(3)*, 535-550.

Schmidt, P., & Zyla, B. (2011). European security policy: Strategic culture in operation? *Contemporary Security Policy*, 32(3), 484-493.

Simms, B. (2012). Towards a mighty union: how to create a democratic European superpower. *International Affairs, 88(1)*, 49-62.

Tisseron, A. (2012). The European Union and the Maghreb. Thomas Moore Institute, Special Report, February 2012. Retrieved from http://www.institut-thomas-more.org/en/actualite/lunion-europeenne-et-le-maghreb-quel-engagement-un-an-apres-le-printemps-arabe-.html

Totten, M. J. (2012). Arab Spring or Islamist Winter? *World Affairs, Jan/Febr. 2012*, 23-44.

Wendling, C. (2010). *The comprehensive approach to civil-military crisis management*. Institute de Recherche Strategique de l'Ecole Militaire. Retrieved from http://www.humansecuritygateway.com/documents/IRSEM_TheComprehensiveApproachtoCivilMilitaryCrisisManagement.pdf

Wolff, J. & Wurm, I. (2011). Towards a theory of external democracy promotion: A proposal for theoretical classification. *Security Dialogue, 42(1)*, 77-96.

Wolff, S. (2011). The regional dimensions of state failure. *Review of International Studies, 37*, 951-972.

Youngs, R. (2010). *The European Union and democracy promotion: a critical global assessment*. Washington DC: The Johns Hopkins University Press.

Zelin, A. Y. (2012). Democracy, Salafi style. *Foreign Policy, July 20*. Retrieved from http://www.foreignpolicy.com/articles/2012/07/19/democracy_salafi_style?page=0,1

Zürcher, C. (2011). Building democracy while building peace. *Journal of Democracy, 22(1)*, 81-96.

The promises and future of the Eastern Partnership

András Rácz–Katalin Varga[1]

As the Vilnius Eastern Partnership (EaP) summit approaches increasing attention is paid to the future of the whole initiative. This chapter contributes to the debate by providing a detailed analysis of the achievements and problems of the EaP. The main research questions to answer are the following. First, to what extent was the EaP successful in terms of fostering the political and social transformation of the target region? Second, originating from an inherent methodological concern: if transformation took place in a given country, could it be clearly linked to the activities of the EaP there, or are the changes mostly results of other internal or external processes?

The chapter is composed of six main parts. Following a short historical overview of the EU's neighborhood policy, the second section will deal with the institutional setup and context of the Eastern Partnership. The third section focuses on the promises of the initiative, while the fourth one discusses its main problems, covering both structural and external issues. Thereafter, the fifth section provides a detailed evaluation of achievements of the EaP since 2009 through measuring the performance of the six target countries by using quantitative indicators. The chapter ends with a final, concluding section.

As the study focuses on the development of the Eastern Partnership as an EU policy tool, domestic developments in the six partner countries are analyzed only to the minimum necessary extent. Due to limitations of space, equally limited attention is paid to the role of Russia.

Development

The Eastern Partnership (EaP) grew out of the European Union's (EU) initiatives towards its direct neighbors. Until 2004, the main direction of these policies was the Eastern enlargement, which together with the accession of Romania and Bulgaria in 2007 highlighted that the EU reached its institutional limits. By 2004 it was clear that the EU cannot promise accession to other countries in the short

---

1 The views presented here are of the authors' own, and they in no way represent the official position of the CEU Center for EU Enlargement Studies, or of any other institution or entity.

run; this can only be a long-term goal. Nevertheless, the EU kept its normative power. All in all, the goal of the EU in relationship with its partners remained the promotion of its norms but without one of its most important policy tool, the clear promise of becoming a member state.

The first initiative targeting the neighborhood countries was the Wider Europe framework of 2003. The purpose of this instrument was to create a ring of friends around the EU, including Russia. Although, it never got a tool set, this was the first step to later policies because it first outlined the EU's approach to its neighbors. (Commission of the European Communities, 2003; Végh, 2010)

The European Neighbourhood Policy (ENP) established in 2004 grew out of this framework but showed a more differentiated approach. Most importantly the Western Balkan and Turkey were incorporated in other frameworks, signaling that they were potential member states. As Romano Prodi, the President of the Commission that time formulated it; the states participating in ENP should be allowed access to "everything but the institutions". ("The European Neighbourhood Policy (ENP) and the Eastern Partnership (EAP)", 2011) This meant that the EU was aiming to motivate the countries in its near abroad to internalize its norms and practices. In return, it promises access to the internal market. From 2004 to 2007 the first steps were taken to put ENP in practice. In this period, the Commission was the main actor and initiator pushing forward the ENP. One of the most important steps was that the Council established a separate financial instrument to support policies within the ENP. This was the European Neighbourhood and Partnership Instrument accepted for the 2007 – 2013 budget period. (Commission of the European Communities, 2012a, 2012b) The logic of the ENP was similar to the ideas of the earlier enlargements. Not only was the ENP formulated mostly at the DG Enlargement[2], but clear policy transfer and adaption were also institutionalized. The common values that the ENP is based on and whose development is targeted by many of the ENP programs are very similar to the accession conditions. Nevertheless, the coercive approach to conditionality was abandoned and the ENP rather follows a more compromising approach where conditional thinking is complemented by ideas that treat the partner countries as real partners and advocate their responsibility in the ENP's development. Hence, they involve the partner countries in the policy processes which can increase their engagement with both process and outcome. Still, the most important incentive, the clear promise of accession was abandoned; consequently the motivation of the partner countries to implement policies diverges to a large extent. (Marchetti, 2008; Tulmets, 2006; Végh, 2010)

The ENP was suffering from several weaknesses; one of the most important was the difference among the countries in South and East from the EU. In the Southern region, the main aim became to promote the rule of law and economic cooperation, while with the Eastern partners, democratization remained just as

---

2   The Task Force "Wider Europe", which was later responsible for the ENP's development, was made up of civil servants partly from the DG Enlargement, it was only later moved to the DG Relex.

important. The difference between the EU's approach to the two regions is best reflected by the names used to label them: "Neighbours of Europe" for the South and "European Neighbours" for the East. This separation has become the policy practice in the late 2000s when two different instruments were launched for the two regions. First, French President Nicolas Sarkozy proposed the idea of the Mediterranean Union at the beginning of 2008, which was followed by the Polish-Swedish initiative in May 2008 to launch the EaP. (Romsics & Végh, 2010)

In order to understand the origins of the EaP, the actions of several actors need to be analyzed. Poland has been one of the main drivers of the idea that closer cooperation with the Eastern partners of the EU is necessary. The initiative has long traditions in Polish foreign policy due to Poland's geographical proximity to the region, their common history and the considerable Polish minority living in Belarus and Ukraine. Hence, already before its accession, Poland advocated that the EU should take responsibility and be more active role in this region not only to ensure the region's stability but also because access to the region's markets means considerable economic potential for the EU. After its 2004 accession, Poland continued to be the promoter of cooperation with the Eastern neighbors, but it was only in 2007 that the general approach of the newly elected Polish government allowed it to find other supporters within the EU. (Romsics & Végh, 2010; Végh, 2011) The Visegrad 4 countries presented a joint document demanding more political attention and financial resources for the Eastern European region. During its presidency (mid-2007 to mid-2008), the Czech government circulated a non-paper in Brussels, calling for resolute democratization, access to the internal market and creation of a regional format to support the bilateral relations and to promote cooperation among the Eastern partners themselves. (Ananicz & Sadowski, 2012) Negotiations between Poland and Germany also became frequent; however, the real turning point came with the support of Sweden: the Polish and Swedish foreign ministers presented their proposal in the EU's General Affairs and External Relations Council on 26 May 2008. ("Polish-Swedish Proposal on the Eastern Partnership," n.d.)

The proposal showed that both countries were highly critical towards the EU's neighborhood policies even though their motivation was different. Sweden saw the EU as a soft power whose main role is to promote democracy, human rights and market economy in the Eastern regions. Polish politics were rather divided regarding what approach the country should represent. While the governing Civic Platform which prepared the proposal, argued that the goals formulated were the maximum possible in light of the EU's enlargement fatigue, the Law and Justice party strongly criticized the proposal for not offering a clear promise for future membership. Other member states, such as Germany, criticized the proposal because they wanted to make sure from the beginning that the Eastern countries could not use this framework as a promise for future accession. All in all, already the reactions to the proposal highlighted member states' diverse approach to future enlargement. Sweden saw EaP not as an alternative to future accession, but a tool that brings these countries closer to the EU and enhances accession if possible. Poland clearly was aiming to keep all options open; also by emphasizing that the Eastern countries are the neighbors of the EU while the Southern countries are the neighbors of Europe. (Romsics & Végh, 2010)

In spite of the differences, the EaP proposal went on, probably partly because it was a good counterpart to the Mediterranean Union launched earlier. In the Presidency Conclusions of 19-20 June 2008, the European Council gave mandate to the Commission to prepare a more detailed and comprehensive proposal to be presented by Spring 2009. ("Presidency Conclusions, 19/20 June 2008," n.d.) The process was sped up by the 2008 Georgian conflict. The Council decided to adopt the new EaP in March 2009; hence they changed the deadline of the Commission's proposal to December 2008. ("Presidency Conclusions, Extraordinary European Council, Brussels, 1 September 2008," n.d.) The Commission indeed prepared a communiqué about the issue by December 2008. (Commission of the European Communities, 2008a, 2008b) The Commission, already responsible for the ENP, was ready to take action and use its expertise from the earlier enlargement periods. However, already in this initial stage it was clear that, in line with its earlier logic, the Commission will be able to engage in low-politics issues but will not be able to ensure that higher political and diplomatic cooperation also accompanies these.

The EaP was officially launched on 7 May 2009 at the Prague Eastern Partnership Summit. Next to the EU member states, all six partners of the EaP participated in the summit which resulted in a joint declaration that laid down the EaP's main goals and mechanisms. ("Joint Declaration of the Prague Eastern Parntership Summit," 2009)

Apart from the active engagement of Poland, Sweden, the Czech Republic and other Visegrad four countries, Germany's and France's approach towards the proposal was also important for the future of the EaP. Germany has ambiguous relation to the Eastern region. It is not particularly important from the German economic point of view, but due to historical reasons, the general public as well as decision makers consider the post-soviet region more important than pure economic calculation would suggest. On the other hand, German foreign policy has several priorities that it would not risk with the cooperation with the Eastern region. First, the relationship with the big EU members, such as France and the United Kingdom is a clear priority. Second, Germany constantly tries to balance out its and the EU's relations with Russia, something that clearly could be undermined by enlargement to the post-Soviet region. Third, Germany has been aiming to take more control over the EU's decision making processes. This notion has become even stronger after the global financial crisis which also highlighted the EU's inner problems. This on one hand pushes the EaP back among the priorities of German politics. On the other hand, Germany is very careful about not having any clear preferences in issues that divide the European community, such as the EaP. Finally, the integration of the Western Balkans competes with the EaP among German political priorities. Hence, Germany has developed a middle-of-the-roader, but still committed approach to the EaP. It clearly supports non-institutional cooperation, free trade agreements and other economic cooperation, policy transfer, support for the development of government capacities as well as multilateral cooperation between the EU and the countries of the Eastern region. However, Germany clearly distances itself from any initiatives that would indicate possible accession of these countries. Even though officially it does not rule out opening membership negotiations with the countries in the far future, it frequently emphasizes that accession is unimaginable in the foreseeable future. (Romsics & Végh, 2010)

France is less supportive towards the EaP than Germany. Officially, France supports the initiative as the logical counterpart of the Mediterranean Union that France initiated. Moreover, France could see an opportunity in the separation of the two regions as it could have allowed for the 2:1 division of the available funds. However, in reality, it does see the EaP more and more as a rival policy of the Mediterranean Union, partly because the EU member states in general see less and less democratization potential in the Arab countries. There are always more voices that argue that the EU should rather support the Eastern regions, because there norm and rule transfer has more possibilities. Moreover, France is also concerned about the relations with Russia, even though their relations are not as strong as those of Germany and Russia. Nevertheless, France never clearly blocked the EaP, which probably could have made the development of the program impossible. (Romsics & Végh, 2010)

Working and Institutions

The EaP's institutions can be divided into two main groups, the bilateral and multilateral dimensions. The bilateral dimension's logic resembles the earlier enlargement logic in the sense that its programs are to help norm transfer from the EU to the partner countries. The bilateral dimension is aiming to "support reforms in three main areas: good governance; rule of law and fundamental freedoms; sustainable economic and social development, trade and investment." (European Union, 2012) Its aim is to conclude Association Agreements (AAs), and Deep and Comprehensive Free Trade Agreements (DCFTA) with all partner countries and to establish visa free travel regimes to the EU. (Commission of the European Communities, 2013a; EaP Community, 2012a) The bilateral track builds on the earlier bilateral cooperation under the ENP between the EU and the partner states ("Joint Declaration of the Prague Eastern Parntership Summit," 2009; Végh, 2011), meaning also that having a Partnership and Cooperation Agreement (PCA) with the EU in force is a precondition of starting the AA negotiations. The DCFTA is treated as part of the AA (Commission of the European Communities, 2008a), meaning that a country can only participate in DCFTA negotiations, if it is already negotiating its AA. Moreover, the precondition for starting the negotiations on the DFCTA is World Trade Organization (WTO) membership. (EaP Community, 2012a; Romsics & Végh, 2010) AA negotiations with Ukraine were already launched in 2007, during the ENP. It was a clear goal within the ENP to harmonize the agreements with the neighboring countries, to replace the AAs in the Mediterranean countries and the PCAs in the Eastern region with common Neighbourhood Agreements; the Ukrainian was set to be the first of these. (Marchetti, 2008) These negotiations were continued later within the EaP's framework. Negotiations on AAs started with Armenia, Azerbaijan, Georgia and Moldova in 2010. The only country which could not yet start the negotiations is Belarus because it does not have a PCA in force (Végh, 2011). Moreover, neither Azerbaijan nor Belarus could start the DCFTA negotiations yet. Azerbaijan is trapped because it is not a member of the WTO. Belarus cannot launch the DCFTA negotiations because it has not started the AA negotiations yet, but even if were to enter the AA phase, it still could not start negotiating a DCFTA because it is not member of the WTO. (EaP Community, 2012a)

Regarding the visa dialogue the picture is even more diverse. In order to reach a visa free regime with the EU, each country needs to first conclude a Visa Facilitation and Readmission Agreement, after that it can enter the Visa Liberalization Dialogue, whose goal is to conclude a Visa Liberalization Action Plan. After meeting all the criteria in the latter, will a partner country be able to launch the visa free regime. Up until today, the following process has been made by the individual countries (in order of the progress in this dimension). Belarus has not started any of the negotiations yet. Azerbaijan has started the negotiations and seems close to concluding them. Armenia signed the Visa Facilitation Agreement in December 2012 and the Visa Readmission Agreement in April 2013. Visa Liberalisation Dialogue with Georgia was launched in April 2012 and the Visa Liberalization Action Plan was handed to the Georgian authorities in February 2013. Ukraine has a Visa Liberalization Action Plan since December 2010; however the implementation of the first phase has not yet been successful. Moldova's Action Plan has also been in power since December 2010. The first phase was successfully implemented and it shows good process in the implementation of the second phase as well. (Stefan Batory Foundation, 2012a, 2012b)

However, there are certain factors that hamper further progress in visa liberalization. The so-called 'frozen conflicts' pose an obvious hardship as certain EaP countries do not control their whole territories, thus cannot ensure full and complete control of their borders. This is the case of Moldova due to the Transnistrian conflict, of Georgia due to Abkhaz and South Ossetian separatism, and also of Azerbaijan that has no control over the Nagorno-Karabakh region. The Georgian and Azerbaijani cases are particularly complicated, as all Abkhazia, South Ossetia and Karabakh all have borders with non-EaP countries, namely with Russia and Iran, respectively. The situation of Transnistria is slightly less difficult in these terms, because if the border control of Ukraine and Moldova (both are EaP countries) both get improved, it will automatically solve the control of the Transnistrian border as well, simply due to the geographic location of the separatist region.

Progress in the bilateral arm shows high diversity. On one end, there is Belarus, the government of which is not involved with any parts of this dimension, though the NGO sector has vivid EU connections. Next to the above mentioned administrative limits, the EU is not willing to start bilateral negotiations with Belarus because it is an authoritarian regime. As the political and civil freedoms, which give the basis of the EU's integration, are not observed in the country, the EU is not willing to sign a cooperation agreement with it. (Végh, 2011)

On the other end is Ukraine, with whom the AA was initiated on 30 March 2012, and the DCFTA on 19 July 2012. However, the EU member states are not willing to ratify these agreements yet because of shortcomings in the democratization process in Ukraine. The AA was originally set to be signed on the next EaP Summit in Vilnius in November 2013. (European External Action Service, 2013) However, this can be delayed because of problems in the three areas where Ukraine's progress is to be assessed. First, the 2012 elections showed several shortcomings and even deterioration compared to earlier achievements. Second, selective justice is still a practice, as it is clear from the political convictions of Yulia Timoshenko and other members of the earlier government. Third, the reforms included in the commonly agreed Association Agenda still need to be implemented. (Council of the European Union, 2012) Even though there are signs that even the older member states would be willing to support this, Ukraine still needs to take several steps to show commitment. (Potocka, 2013; Ukraine Monitor, 2013) Another question is whether the hastily amended laws and adopted reforms in Spring-Summer 2013 reflect to an honest commitment, or are just perceived by the Ukrainian decision-makers as compulsory exercises before the Vilnius summit. This is particularly true because in certain fields where meaningful progress is highly unlikely. For example, Ukrainian society is firmly opposed to the emancipation of sexual minorities. Hence, it is quite probable that even if a relevant law is going to be passed by the Verkhovna Rada, it would not be fully implemented – or perhaps implemented at all.

The multilateral dimension's main goal is support cooperation and stabilization among the partner countries through creating fora where different actors from different policy levels can meet and cooperate. One of the biggest assets of the multilateral track is that Belarus participates in all but one of its programs (EuroNest), thereby preventing the country from becoming completely insulated from Europe. Moreover, this way the EU can hopefully affect the system in Belarus through the dimension's socialization-based elements. (Végh, 2011) There are several institutions under this dimension that are aiming to enhance this goal in different policy areas through different instruments. They always include a common representation from the EU's side and separate delegations from each partner country. First, there are four thematic platforms in the following areas: 1) good governance, democracy and stability, 2) economic integration and growth, convergence with the EU policies, 3) energy security, 4) contacts between people. As these issues are in the front interest of all partner countries, the platforms are aiming to foster exchanges on best practices and through that help the partner countries not only to get close to the EU but also to strengthen cooperation among each other. The platforms include senior officials of the European Commission, the EU member states and the partner countries, who meet twice a year to discuss the specific issues. Hence, the platforms are not the highest level meetings in the EaP but they are among the most important because they address specific issues. Their work is supported by sector specific working panels. These consist of officials from the countries participating in the EaP and meet several times a year, more often than the platforms. The platforms report about their work at the annual meeting of the foreign ministers. (Commission of the European Communities, 2013a; EaP Community, 2012b; "Joint Declaration of the Prague Eastern Partnership Summit," 2009)

Second, the EaP's multilateral dimension contains the six flagship initiatives, which are under the platforms supervision. These are regional cooperation projects in the following fields: 1) Integrated Border Management Programme, 2) Small and Medium-size enterprise (SME) Facility, 3) Regional energy markets and energy efficiency, 4) Diversification of energy supply: the Southern Energy Corridor, 5) Prevention of, preparedness for, and response to natural and man-made disasters, 6) Good environmental governance. Within the framework of the flagship initiatives, the EU launches specific projects and distributes the financial and technical support to the partner countries. While the thematic platforms are there to set the goals, the projects within the flagship initiatives are the tangible tool in the multilateral arm. These are implemented on the ground and help realize the policy goals in practice. (Commission of the European Communities, 2013a; European Union, 2012; Végh, 2011)

There are two more levels above these two instruments in the multilateral dimension of the EaP. The highest body is the EaP summit. Here the heads of states and governments of the EU member states and the partner countries meet every two years to review the EaP's progress and define the general developmental lines and goals. The next level is the annual meeting of the foreign ministers of the EU member states and the partner countries. Here, they review and define the guidelines set on the summit. Moreover, they monitor the work of the multilateral platforms. Next to this annual meeting, other ministers of the countries also meet on an ad hoc basis. Their role is to support activities in the specific sectors they are responsible for; hence they meet only if the progress of a program requires their insight. (EaP Community, 2012b; "Joint Declaration of the Prague Eastern Parntership Summit," 2009; Végh, 2011)

Next to the meetings of government-level officials, in the multilateral track of the EaP there are several fora supporting cooperation among other actors in the EU member states and the partner countries. First, the Civil Society Forum, aiming to support cooperation between civil society organizations in the partner countries and in the EU member states. It was launched in November 2009 and has been meeting annually ever since. Next to strengthening the civil society in the partner states through dialogues with organizations from the EU member states, the Civil Society Forum's role is also to provide input and monitor the working of the thematic platforms. Hence, it has four working groups, which are functioning parallel to the four platforms. This can also help the cooperation between the members of the civil society and the public authorities both in the framework of EaP and in the partner countries as well. (EaP Community, 2012b; EU Neighbourhood Info Centre, 2013; European Union, 2012) Second, the EaP's multilateral dimension has a parliamentary component, the EURONEST Parliamentary Assembly. This is a platform where the members of the European Parliament and MPs from the partner countries meet to monitor the activities of the EaP. It was inaugurated in May 2011, without Belarus whose membership was suspended because the 2010 elections were declared flawed. Hence, the platform now has 110 members instead of the 120 planned originally: 60 delegates from the European Parliament and 10 delegates from each of the partner countries. It has a plenary, the Bureau, four standing committees and two working groups that meet during the ordinary sessions once a year. Its goal is to promote democracy in the partner countries by exchanging best practices. Moreover, it is aiming to strengthen the development and the visibility of the EaP by providing a space for parliamentary consultation, supervision and monitoring. (EU Neighbourhood Info Centre, 2013; EuroNest, 2013) Third, the Conference of the Regional and Local Authorities for the Eastern Partnership was launched in 2011 in Poznan as a platform for the local and regional authorities from all countries to meet and exchange ideas on their take of the EaP. Finally, there are several other institutions that support specific aspects of the EaP, like the Eastern Partnership Culture Program or the informal Group of Friends of the Eastern Partnership. (EaP Community, 2012b; EU Neighbourhood Info Centre, 2013)

Since establishing the EaP several new financial assistance initiatives with separate financial resources have been launched to support the development of the Partnership. Although, these initiatives are usually agreed upon bilaterally, the projects funded in their framework are related to both the EaP's bilateral and the multilateral arm. First, the Comprehensive Institution Building (CIB) program, for which the bilateral documents were signed with all partner countries between October 2010 and January 2011. Since 2011 a CIB component is included in the Annual Action Programme (the bilateral action plan) of each country. The CIB Framework Documents identify the core institutions in the key areas. These institutions need to prepare Institutional Reform Plans, from which the CIB supports selected components, where its added value is considered the biggest. The individual core institutions receive the support from the financial tool, but the partner countries are responsible for the CIB's implementation, which is coordinated by a lead institution from the given country. (Commission of the European Communities, 2013b; European Union, 2012)

Second, in the regional development framework, the EU is financing pilot regional development programs. These funds are aimed at projects, where civil society and local communities are involved. The use of funds is highly diverse among the partner countries also because of the different background and initial institutional setup in the countries. For instance, the EU funded such projects already in the past in Georgia and Ukraine but not in the other countries. Hence, Armenia and Moldova used these pilot projects to enter the regional development field for the first time. (Commission of the European Communities, 2013c; European Union, 2012) Third, the Eastern Partnership Integration and Cooperation Program is an incentive-based financial assistance program based on the principle of "more for more" introduced after the 2011 ENP review. This principle means that countries that deliver reforms faster can get more support. These are additional funds that are granted to countries, whose progress is deep in democracy and human right related issues. Progress is assessed based on the Country Progress Reports. The fund's country allocation is pre-defined, it is decided every year based on the progress the previous years. The funds can be used both for new projects and existing ones in democratic transformation, institutional development and sustainable and inclusive growth. (Commission of the European Communities, 2013d; European Union, 2012) Finally, the Neighborhood Civil Society Facility, which was also introduced only after the 2011 ENP review and covers the Southern neighborhood as well. This supports diverse projects led by civil society actors and closely related to bilateral level reform targets. (Commission of the European Communities, 2013e; European Union, 2012)

Promises

The future and the added value of the EaP were not clear ever since its launch. As it can be clear from the description of the development of the EaP, the agenda of the initiative was based on many compromises among the different actors. Poland together with the backing of the three other Visegrad countries were the ones, which really advocated that these countries are handled as potential candidate countries. All the old member states, that were supporting the initiative, were in the opinion that any cooperation with these countries should help norm and policy transfer, democratization but strictly without the near prospect of accession. Even though, most of them do not rule out that offering membership to these countries can be a long-term possibility, they still want to make clear that it is only a long-term and theoretical possibility. This notion has from the beginning put a clear limit on the EaP's possible role in the region.

Nevertheless, the EaP has also had several aspects that were promising for the participating countries. First of all, the fact that this region has got its own framework allows for more efficient engagement from the EU's side. Programs can be better shaped for the specific need of these countries than in the framework of the ENP where the means of working together were prepared in a generic way, to be fitting for all countries involved. As described earlier, the EU member states have very different approaches to the Eastern and Southern neighbors. Hence, the fact that the policies towards these two regions became separated could make the Eastern partners hopeful that the resources they receive will be better targeted towards their needs.

As described in the part about the EaP's institutions, the EaP has two main legs: the bilateral and the multilateral dimension. The bilateral dimension is important because it supports deeper cooperation between the EU and the individual partner countries. It is not new for the EU to cooperate with these six countries; however, the earlier framework given by the PCAs were rather superficial. In the framework of the EaP, the EU is aiming to conclude Association Agreements (AAs) with these countries. Earlier, AAs were drafted with the countries that were to become members of the EU. Even though this is not the goal with the EaP partner countries, negotiating and aiming to close AAs with them was a promising sign as it is the closest contractual tie that exists between the EU and third parties. (European Union, 2012) AAs and partnership agreements have common ground in the sense that Article 21.1 of the Treaty on European Union states that all external actions of the EU have to be guided by its founding principles and that the EU shall seek relations with third countries that share these principles. (European Union, 2010)

However, the Treaty on the Functioning of the European Union describes association separate from other types of relations. Concluding associations is more complicated than concluding partnership. (European Union, 2008) Moreover, association has a number of elements which are inherent to association agreements under European law: reciprocal rights and obligations; common action and special procedure; privileged links between the EU and a third country; and the participation of a third country in the EU system. (Petrov, 2011) In case of the EaP countries, the AAs are particularly beneficial for the partner countries because of the reciprocal nature of the rights and obligations. On one hand this means that voluntary legal harmonization is required from the partner countries, which in turn brings on serious internal changes in their regulatory systems. This is a considerable change from the PCAs, which did not require or even provide any incentive for the countries to adopt the acquis. On the other hand, reciprocity also means that the EU commits to providing for instance financial assistance for the reforms and access to its internal markets. (Petrov, 2011) Their goals are usually more general and do not contain clear transfer of standards and regulations. Moreover, the EU's obligations are also not clearly built in the system. (Various, 2010)

Concurrent with the AA negotiations, the EU is also negotiating and aiming to conclude Deep and Comprehensive Free Trade Agreements (DCFTA) with all countries except Belarus and Azerbaijan. DCFTAs are "a new generation of free trade areas providing for the fullest possible liberalization of not only trade in goods, but also trade in services and investment, as well as extensive regulatory convergence on issues like technical standards, sanitary and phytosanitary measures, protection of intellectual property, public procurement, energy-related issues, competition, customs etc." (EU Neighbourhood Info Centre, 2013, p. 4) Hence, even though the DCFTAs require partner countries to further approximate their laws and standards to the acquis, they also promise accession to the EU's internal markets. This creates new markets for the countries as well as possibly higher competition among these countries. Finally, the promise of visa free travel is also an essential part of the EaP's magnetism. (Petrov, 2011)

The EaP's other aspect, the multilateral leg introduces a completely new policy tool in the relations of the EU and the partner countries. For the first time, it "gathers all six Eastern partners and the EU at various levels of representation and in different arenas. The EaP's multilateral track is thus an attempt to develop a multilayered and participative institutional framework based upon a logic of socialization." (Delcour, 2011) The multilateral dimension has had several promising aspects for the partner countries. From the partner countries' point of view, one of its biggest added value is that it can strengthen relations among the countries of the region through providing a space for cooperation and for exchanging experience among the countries, hence, enhancing stability in the region. Since the relations among these countries are filled with historical conflicts that the Soviet era further escalated in some cases, having such space for cooperation can become highly important for their foreign policies. (Végh, 2011) From the EU's point of view, the multilateral dimension was the main tool for Europeanizing the partner countries and building a system with Brussels in its center of gravity. Through creating the space where these countries can cooperate, the EU may ensure that it becomes a central player even in intra-regional matters. Moreover, obviously this cooperation can help in creating a stable region and a "ring of friends" around the EU. Finally, the multilateral dimension can lay down the foundation so that the system of DCFTAs may develop into a free trade area in the future. This would obviously be beneficial for both the EU and the partner countries. (Depo, 2011; Shapovalova, 2009)

Finally, the EaP has several promising aspects in the policy areas that it is covering. One of the aspects most important for the partner countries is the possible establishment of a visa-free regime with the EU. In order to achieve this, there are several institutions both in the EaP's bilateral and the multilateral arm. The negotiations about abolishing the visa are conducted on a bilateral level. However, it is also related to the border management flagship initiative program in the multilateral arm. Another important policy issue covered by the bilateral track is energy security, which is highly important from both the EU and the partner countries. Moreover, it would also influence how much the countries are dependent from Russia. (Depo, 2011) Above these issues, the EaP programs are also aiming to strengthen the economy, democratic institutions and civil society in the partner countries. Moreover, there are several initiatives that provide direct help and opportunities to the individual citizens.

Problems

Even though the EaP has offered several promising aspects to the partner countries, it also has been suffering from diverse structural problems. First, the target countries are rather diverse. Although they all need to deal with their post-Soviet heritage, the state of their political and economic institutions at the dissolution of the Soviet Union and their development path ever since has been rather different. The institutional environment, as well as the quality of social and economic institutions is diverse. These differences can limit the efficiency of the multilateral EaP institutions. For instance, the EuroNest Parliamentary Assembly's establishment was delayed because the 2010 Belarusian elections were found to be flawed. Eventually it launched without Belarus because the negotiations about the forming the government were not successful. The diversities can partly be handled in the bilateral track through differentiation. (Végh, 2011) However, even the bilateral arm is not perfectly capable of accommodating these differences. For instance, even though Belarus was interested in the EaP's economic component and even planned several projects together with Lithuania and

Moldova, these never could be realized because the European Council excluded Belarus from the European Investment Bank's projects due to the aforementioned problems with the 2010 elections.[3] (Depo, 2011)

In addition to the differences in the internal conditions of the countries, there are other differences that limit the EaP's efficiency. As described earlier, the member states have diverse approaches to the EaP countries. This is also signaled by the wording used by the EU documents. While, at the beginning the partner countries were referred to as "(Eastern) European countries", in the final document it was changed to "Eastern European partners" or "partner countries" because the former would not have clearly eliminated accession. Moreover, many member states have more interest in the countries that are geographically closer to the EU, hence, the South Caucasian countries get less attention.

Second, the partner countries also have diverse preferences and goals. Georgia, Moldova and Ukraine have clear European aspirations. Hence, it is not acceptable for them, if the EaP becomes an alternative to enlargement, mostly because the EaP's promises are rather weak. The AAs do mean an improvement compared to the PCAs, but no fundamental changes. The DCFTA's promise to access the internal market is important but the implementation of the rules leading up to the DCFTA are costly and the reward is in the future. Moreover, some countries (e.g. Ukraine) point out that the EU is not willing to liberalize all areas, for instance it is not willing to open the agricultural market. Finally, the visa liberalization could be highly attractive but it is handled differently case by case and the member states' rhetoric regarding visa free travel is rather ambiguous. (Végh, 2011) Contrary to the cases of Georgia, Moldova and Ukraine, Azerbaijan has declared several times that it does not aspire for EU membership at all. Instead, Baku intends to pursue a balancing foreign policy between its large neighbors, such as Russia, Turkey and Iran. Armenia is also in a delicate situation due to its strong political, military and economic dependence on Russia. Even though Yerevan intends to conduct a "complementarist" foreign policy (Melikian, 2013), if Armenia joins the Russia-led Eurasian Union, as it was indicated by President Serzh Sargsyan in Moscow in September 2013, from then on the DCFTA with the EU will become impossible, because dual membership is institutionally excluded. (Panarmenian.net, 12 September 2013). These differences indeed hamper the coherence of the multilateral track of the EaP.

Third, the six EaP countries strongly differ from each other not only in terms of their foreign policy priorities, but also concerning size, political systems, religion, economic power, etc. Ukraine is far the biggest one of the six, both in terms of size and population. While five EaP countries are predominantly of Christian religion, Azerbaijan is a Muslim (though officially secular) country. While Armenia, Georgia, Moldova and Ukraine are more or less democratic, both Azerbaijan and Belarus are clearly authoritarian regimes. Last, but not least, two EaP coun-

---

3   Whenever talking about the EaP's policies towards Belarus, it is important not to forget that Belarus is an extreme case because it is the only country, which clearly is a dictatorship.

tries, namely Azerbaijan and Armenia are still in the state of war with each other over the disputed territory of Nagorno-Karabakh. These factors make it hard for the EU to handle the six EaP countries as a coherent group.

Fourth, general enlargement fatigue that has been present among the EU's member states since the accession 2004 enlargement and which can be associated with the internal problems of the EU. The general public became disenchanted with EU policies. This came at a moment when the member states' citizens already started to question their efficiency also because the EU's economic competitiveness could not be reinstated despite several policies devised specifically to that end. After 2008, these problems were further escalated by global crisis. This further highlighted the European countries' economic problems and that the EU institutions are not able to give a constructive answer to that.

Since the establishment of the EaP in 2009these problems further escalated with the Greek crisis, the constant threat of economic failure in the Mediterranean states and the slowing growth across the board. More and more voices surfaced that argued that the EU should deepen integration before thinking at all about further enlargement. The lack of resources is visible in the financing available for the EaP. Even though, the available financing was increased for the 2010 – 2013 period, the resources are still rather small. This problem has been raised several times also by the partner countries. (Végh, 2011) In addition to these issues, the Arab Spring has also taken much of the EU's attention away of the EaP since 2010.

Finally, the EaP has also suffered from the issues related to the EU's external relations. These countries are in Russia's "near abroad," to which the EU has a contradictory approach. Russia clearly perceives these countries as belonging to its own sphere of influence, and does its best to prevent them from any closer, institutionalized cooperation with the West, concerning nowadays particularly the Association Agreement/DCFTA with the EU. (Zagorski, 2012) Most EU member states do not want to clearly oppose Russia by intervening in the relations of the partner countries and Russia. This became clear through the EU's position during the Georgian – Russian conflict. On the other hand, some of the partner countries are in limbo between Russia and the EU and from time to time even like to use, at least on the level of political discourse, the possible cooperation with Russia to get more from the EU. For instance when Yanukovich was elected president of Ukraine in February 2010, the country returned to a balancing, multivectoral foreign policy. (Végh, 2013) It needs to be noted that so far the EU did not seem to be able to efficiently counter the various economic incentives used by Russia vis-a-vis the EaP countries, be it positive (cheap gas) or punitive measures (import bans).

Evaluation

Evaluating the EaP's effect in the partner countries is a highly complex issue. The EaP's main goals are to help political and economic transformation in the partner countries, to change their democratic practices and market based mechanisms.

These are policy issues that may be influenced not only by the EaP's measures but also by several other internal factors, for example elections or the relationship among key political actors; and issues relating to third parties. In order to establish a clear causal link between the steps taken within the EaP and the changes in the political and economic systems of the partner countries, we would first need to measure the internal systemic changes, and then clearly link these to the operationalized measures of the EaP. Measuring complex political and economic changes is difficult. Nevertheless, even if the changes are verified, linking them to EaP policy tools is only possible with highly detailed microanalysis which clearly traces the link between the two ends. Such analysis is not possible within the scope of the current study. Instead, this section will do the following. First, we will present and interpret quantified indices measuring political and economic changes in the partner countries. This will help us establish the internal systemic end of the problem, and give us indication in which countries we can at least suspect that the EaP had an effect at all. Second, we will select a few cases based on the quantitative indicators, which we will analyze more in detail, and try to establish if the changes were the result of the EaP's measures or of other factors.

The EaP is a rather new policy tool: it was launched only four years ago. This short timeframe constrains the effect that the EaP can possibly have in the partner countries. Moreover, the countries participating in the EaP have rather diverse historical, institutional and cultural background, and the level of their development at the EaP's launch was also different. This has an effect on their current state of affairs as well. Hence, we will put more emphasis on analyzing the changes of the individual countries than comparing them to each other.

Analyzing quantitative measures
Through interpreting the below indices, we are aiming to establish the overall changes that happened in the partner countries' political and economic systems. It is not the aim of this part of the study to establish causal link between the EaP and the policy changes. Hence, when we refer to the start of the EaP during describing changes in the indicators, it only means that change occurred concurrent with the EaP and does not mean that it occurred directly because of the EaP.

We will present measures not only for the EaP's period but overall for the 2000s. This will help us to establish whether a change occurred in a country's development trend after 2009. Such a change can be a sign that the EaP had influence in the country, since that is one of the new variables that affects the political and economic system. This method can help us compensate for the short time span of the EaP. On the other hand, such change in the trend would mean a rather fundamental change in the system. This probably will be rare, and most of the changes that we can expect the EaP to have on the partner countries will be incremental.

In order to measure the temporal changes of political freedom in the EaP region, we will analyze three different indicators. We will consider them all because they all use different definitions for identifying democratic and non-democratic regimes. Since all of these indices rely on different definitions, taking them all into consideration without directly comparing them gives us a more complete picture. Hence, we will examine several different indicators, in order to get a better understanding of the processes in the partner countries.

The first is the Polity IV Project, which provides quantitative data on countries' authority characteristics. So-called "polity scores" are given to every country, on a 21-point scale, that ranges from -10 (strongly autocratic) to +10 (strongly democratic). Under -6 regimes are considered autocracies, while over +6 they belong to democracies. Polity scores are counted based on two composite indicators measuring institutionalized democracy and institutionalized autocracy in the countries. Both of these are additive eleven-point scales. Both are derived from the coding of the following aspects of the political system: the competitiveness of political participation, the openness and competitiveness of executive recruitment, and the constraints on the chief executive to which the coding of the regulation of participation is also added in the case of the autocracy index. (Marshall, Gurr, & Jaggers, 2013)

Figure 1. Authority trends (2000 – 2012)

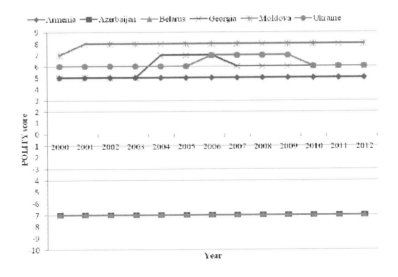

Source: *Center for Systemic Peace, 2013*

As the graphs demonstrate, the political system did not change fundamentally in any of the partner countries. Azerbaijan and Belarus remained absolutely undemocratic regimes, and Armenia also preserved its status below the level of democracies. Moldova is the only country that is clearly above 6 points, meaning that it is the only one rated as democratic. Its rating stagnated as well. Georgia and Ukraine are just on the border to be rated as democratic. In these two countries there were small improvements throughout the 2000s, however, they got reversed in Georgia before the launch of the EaP, while in Ukraine right after that (between 2009 and 2010). However, none of these changes can be called polity transition, which is defined as 3 or more points change in the polity score. All in all, according to the Polity IV scoring, the political system and the level of political freedoms in the partner countries has been stagnating since the beginning of the 2000s, and this trend has not changed since the launch of the EaP.

Second, we will analyze the Democracy Index of the Economist Intelligence Unit. This indicator has been published since 2006 first every second year and every year since 2010. The index is based on a thick definition of democracy. It is based on 60 indicators from five general categories, namely pluralism and electoral process, civil liberties, functioning of the government, political participation and political culture. These indicators are aggregated and converted to a scale from 0 to 10 points. Based on this, the 167 countries studied are divided into four categories: full democracies (8 to 10 points), flawed democracies (6 to 7.9 points), hybrid regimes (4 to 5.9 points) and authoritarian regimes (less than 4 points). (The Economist Intelligence Unit, 2013)

Table 1: Performance of the Eastern Partnership countries according to the Democracy Index (2006 – 2012)

	Armenia	Azerbaijan	Belarus	Georgia	Moldova	Ukraine
2006	4.15	3.31	3.34	4.90	6.50	6.94
	(hybrid)	(authoritarian)	(authoritarian)	(hybrid)	(flawed)	(flawed)
2008	4.09	3.19	3.34	4.62	6.50	6.94
	(hybrid)	(authoritarian)	(authoritarian)	(hybrid)	(flawed)	(flawed)
2010	4.08	3.14	3.35	4.59	6.32	6.29
	(hybrid)	(authoritarian)	(authoritarian)	(hybrid)	(flawed)	(flawed)
2011	4.09	3.15	3.16	4.74	6.33	5.94
	(hybrid)	(authoritarian)	(authoritarian)	(hybrid)	(flawed)	(hybrid)
2012	4.09	3.15	3.04	5.53	6.32	5.91
	(hybrid)	(authoritarian)	(authoritarian)	(hybrid)	(flawed)	(hybrid)

Source: *The Economist Intelligence Unit, 2013*

According to the Democracy Index, Azerbaijan and Belarus are the only clearly authoritarian regimes, while Moldova is considered to have the most democratic regime among the partner countries. The rating worsened slightly in Belarus and considerably in Ukraine, it improved in Georgia and remained stable in the other three countries. For Georgia it shows gradual decline from 2006 to 2010, which then got reversed. The latter is highly important from the EaP's point of view, because this implies that Georgia's the political system of a partner country improved since the program's launch. The Democracy Index shows that Ukraine's system got downgraded between 2008 and 2011 to the extent that the system went from flawed democracy to a hybrid regime, meaning that the change was big enough to be considered a regime change according to the terminology of the index.

Figure 2: Democracy Index
(2006 – 2012)

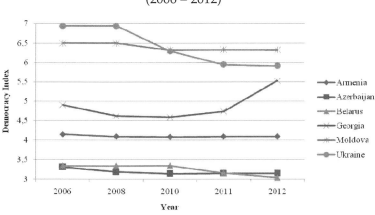

Source: *The Economist Intelligence Unit, 2013*[4]

The third indicator for political freedom is Freedom House's Freedom in the World index. The freedom ratings are counted as the average of the political rights and civil liberties ratings, both of which are given based on the annual Freedom of the World survey. They both are on a 1 to 7 scale, 1 representing the most free, 7 the least free. "Political rights ratings are based on an evaluation of three subcategories: electoral process, political pluralism and participation, and functioning of government. Civil liberties ratings are based on an evaluation of four subcategories: freedom of expression and belief, associational and organizational rights, rule of law, and personal autonomy and individual rights." Freedom in the World, 2001-2013 According to freedom ratings, countries are divided into categories: Free, Partly Free and Not Free. The dividing lines between the categories were changed in 2004.[5] Since 2003 the categories are defined as follows: Free 1-2.5 points, Partly Free 3-5 points, and Not Free 5.5-7 points. (Freedom in the World 2013, 2013)

---

4   Although, the Democracy Index is calculated on a 0 to 10 scale, for Figure 2 numbering on the vertical axis goes from 3 to 7 in order to better highlight the trends in the individual countries.

5   Before 2003, they were the following: Free 1-2.5 points, Partly Free 3-5.5 points, and Not Free 5.5-7 points. Whether a country with 5.5 points was considered Partly Free or Not Free depended on its combined raw scores in the political rights and civil liberties ratings.

Table 2: Performance of the Eastern Partnership countries according to the Freedom in the World index (2000 – 2012)

	Armenia	Azerbaijan	Belarus	Georgia	Moldova	Ukraine
2000	4	5.5	6	4	3	4
	(Partly Free)	(Partly Free)	(Not Free)	(Partly Free)	(Partly Free)	(Partly Free)
2001	4	5.5	6	4	3	4
	(Partly Free)	(Partly Free)	(Not Free)	(Partly Free)	(Partly Free)	(Partly Free)
2002	4	5.5	6	4	3.5	4
	(Partly Free)	(Partly Free)	(Not Free)	(Partly Free)	(Partly Free)	(Partly Free)
2003	4	5.5	6	4	3.5	4
	(Partly Free)	(Not Free)	(Not Free)	(Partly Free)	(Partly Free)	(Partly Free)
2004	4.5	5.5	6.5	3.5	3.5	3.5
	(Partly Free)	(Not Free)	(Not Free)	(Partly Free)	(Partly Free)	(Partly Free)
2005	4.5	5.5	6.5	3	3.5	2.5
	(Partly Free)	(Not Free)	(Not Free)	(Partly Free)	(Partly Free)	(Free)
2006	4.5	5.5	6.5	3	3.5	2.5
	(Partly Free)	(Not Free)	(Not Free)	(Partly Free)	(Partly Free)	(Free)
2007	4.5	5.5	6.5	4	3.5	2.5
	(Partly Free)	(Not Free)	(Not Free)	(Partly Free)	(Partly Free)	(Free)
2008	5	5.5	6.5	4	4	2.5
	(Partly Free)	(Not Free)	(Not Free)	(Partly Free)	(Partly Free)	(Free)
2009	5	5.5	6.5	4	3.5	2.5
	(Partly Free)	(Not Free)	(Not Free)	(Partly Free)	(Partly Free)	(Free)
2010	5	5.5	6.5	3.5	3	3
	(Partly Free)	(Not Free)	(Not Free)	(Partly Free)	(Partly Free)	(Partly Free)
2011	5	5.5	6.5	3.5	3	3.5
	(Partly Free)	(Not Free)	(Not Free)	(Partly Free)	(Partly Free)	(Partly Free)
2012	4.5	5.5	6.5	3	3	3.5
	(Partly Free)	(Not Free)	(Not Free)	(Partly Free)	(Partly Free)	(Partly Free)

Source: *Freedom in the World, 2001-2013*

Figure 3: Freedom ratings based on the Freedom on the World Survey
(2000 – 2012)

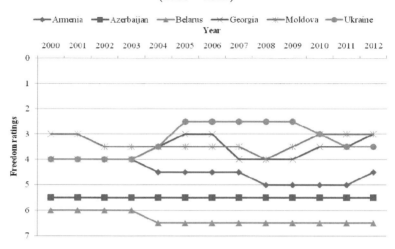

Source: *Freedom in the World, 2001-2013*[6]

Based on the freedom ratings, Azerbaijan[7] and Belarus are the only clearly non-democratic (non-free regimes) in the region. The rest of the countries have mixed political systems. The regimes of Azerbaijan, Belarus and Armenia were stable during the whole period, in line with the other two indicators. In case of Georgia, the freedom ratings show that the system improved in the first half of the 2000s but this got reversed later. More importantly, the freedom ratings support the results of the Democracy Index that the political system improved in Georgia from 2010 on. Moreover, the freedom ratings also show improvement for Moldova between 2009 and 2011. However, neither of these improvements resulted in regime change. Finally, for Ukraine the freedom ratings shows that the regime improved in the first half of the 2000s but this got reversed later on, again to the extent that it is possible to talk about regime change. Moreover, the freedom ratings suggest that the country was free between 2006 and 2010.

---

6   For Figure 3 numbering on the vertical axis is reversed to make interpretation easier. Hence, similar to the earlier two figures, here the countries represented by the lines on the top are valued as more democratic.

7   The regime change of Azerbaijan in 2004 is due to the recoding of the categories not because of changes in the political system of the country.

Table 3: Civil liberties (CL) and political rights ratings (PR) based on the Freedom in the World survey (2001 – 2013)

	Armenia		Azerbaijan		Belarus		Georgia		Moldova		Ukraine	
	CL	PR	CL	PR	CL	PR	CL	PR	CL	PR	CL	PR
2000	4	4	5	6	6	6	4	4	4	2	4	4
2001	4	4	5	6	6	6	4	4	4	2	4	4
2002	4	4	5	6	6	6	4	4	4	3	4	4
2003	4	4	5	6	6	6	4	4	4	3	4	4
2004	4	5	5	6	6	7	4	3	4	3	3	4
2005	4	5	5	6	6	7	3	3	4	3	2	3
2006	4	5	5	6	6	7	3	3	4	3	2	3
2007	4	5	5	6	6	7	4	4	4	3	2	3
2008	4	6	5	6	6	7	4	4	4	4	2	3
2009	4	6	5	6	6	7	4	4	4	3	2	3
2010	4	6	5	6	6	7	3	4	3	3	3	3
2011	4	6	5	6	6	7	3	4	3	3	3	4
2012	4	5	5	6	6	7	3	3	3	3	3	4

Source: *Freedom in the World, 2001-2013*

Analyzing the civil liberties and the political rights ratings that are behind the freedom ratings, we can say that in case of Georgia, Moldova and Ukraine, the changes in the freedom ratings were usually due to changes in both areas.

All in all, the following tendencies can be discovered for the state of political freedoms in the EaP partner countries. Although in the earlier sections we were analyzing all the trends since 2000s, here we will be concentrating on the changes that happened since 2009, during the EaP's working.

1. Azerbaijan and Belarus have clearly remained authoritarian regimes. Since the EaP's launch this has not changed. The situation even slightly worsened based on the Democracy Index.
2. Armenia's political system has been in the bottom range of the mixed systems, worst of the partner countries with mixed regimes. In line with the earlier two countries, the situation has slightly worsened since the EaP started, although the Freedom of the World survey shows a slight positive change in political rights for 2013. This improvement is however too recent to draw any conclusions from it.
3. For Ukraine all three indicators show that the improvements which happened in political freedoms were reversed after 2009. Based on the Democracy Index and the freedom ratings, this drop in the quality of the political system was so high that we can talk about regime change. However, this can be the result of measurement problems. Based on deeper analyses, it is highly questionable whether Ukraine was de facto democratic before 2009. Hence, not only did the situation of political freedoms in Ukraine worsen

since the launch of the EaP, but even improvements that happened in the system before the EaP were turned around.

4.   All three indicators show that Moldova is among the frontrunners in the region. Based on the Polity IV scores it has been the best performing country throughout the entire period but the Democracy Index and the freedom ratings also show that the state of political freedoms has been the best in Moldova, since they started to decline in Ukraine. Moreover, the freedom ratings indicate that the situation improved between 2009 and 2011 and even though the country still is in the Partly Free category, it on the threshold to be in the Free group. However, the Democracy Index shows a slight decrease in the system for the same period.

5.   Both indicators that capture the early 2000s, namely the Polity IV scores and the freedom ratings, show that in Georgia, political freedoms first improved and then dropped back before the EaP's launch. More importantly, the Democracy Index and the freedom ratings indicate that this tendency could be turned back after 2010. Based on the Polity scores, the system stayed stable during this period. Since two of the three indicators show an improvement in this period and none of the three show a decline, this is the only case that can be interpreted as a clear improvement.

After analyzing changes in political freedoms in the partner countries, we will present the situation of economic freedom. For that we use the Index of Economic Freedom, compiled by The Heritage Foundation. The index is based on ten components in four pillars. These are as follows:

1.   Rule of law (property rights, freedom from corruption)
2.   Limited government (fiscal freedom, government spending)
3.   Regulatory efficiency (business freedom, labor freedom, monetary freedom)
4.   Open markets (trade freedom, investment freedom, and financial freedom)

Each of the components is a composite measure and is graded on a 0 to 100 scale. Some of the factors measured are also connected to the broader sphere of human rights and democratic norms, such as property rights or freedom from corruption. The overall Index of Economic Freedom is counted as the average of the ten components with equal weights for each component. The Index itself is measured on a scale of 0 to 100, where bigger a number means larger economic freedom in the given country. Each year the components are measured based on several sources providing data on from one or two years before. When visualizing the data, we will use the year when the index was complied. Hence, when analyzing the EaP's effect, we will take the data points of 2010 as the starting point, because this contains the information collected in 2009, the year when the EaP was launched. ("Methodology, Index of Economic Freedom," 2013)

Figure 4: Economic freedom
(2000 – 2013)

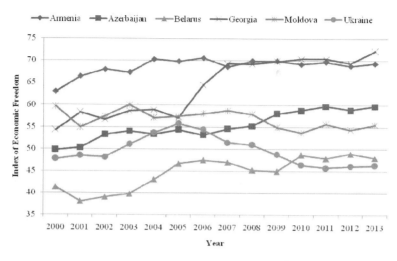

Source: *The Heritage Foundation, 2013*[8]

The Index of Economic Freedom shows a partially different picture than the indicators measuring political freedoms. Although Belarus is still among the worst performers, in Azerbaijan, which was the other clearly authoritarian system, is among the countries with higher levels of economic freedom. Armenia, which among the non-authoritarian regimes showed the worst situation in political freedoms, has had the highest scores on the Index of Economic Freedom. Georgia, after a considerable jump between in the mid 2000s, caught up with Armenia and has stably been the other best performer ever since. Moldova and Ukraine, which showed the best situation in political freedoms, are clearly performing much worse on the Index of Economic Freedom. Ukraine's situation was improving between in the early 2000s, but later this trend was reversed and the state of economic freedoms has been declining ever since to the extent that now Ukraine performs worst among the partner countries, even worse than Belarus marginally. Moldova is in a better position, however, its economic freedom slightly declined as well, and this trend could not be reversed ever since.

Even though the results of the overall Index of Economic Freedom is interesting, several areas are included in it which are not directly related to the EaP. Hence, in order to better understand the EaP's possible impact in the partner countries, we analyze some aspects closer, namely property rights, freedom from corruption and business freedom components of the overall index. Property

---

8   Although, the Index of Economic Freedom is measured on a 0 to 100 scale, the
     numbering of the vertical axis on Figure 4 runs from 35 to 75, so that the trends
     are better highlighted.

rights and the freedom from corruption indices are part of the rule of law pillar, which is an important goal under the EaP. Moreover, level of corruption is also related to good governance. Business freedom component talks to the EaP's economic freedom and economic growth targets. For high levels of growth, it is highly important that market processes can work and actors can allocate resources to the most efficient sectors. Moreover, it is also related to the SME facility, in order that SMEs can be founded and then maintained, business freedom is inevitable.

Figure 5: Property rights index
(2000 – 2013)

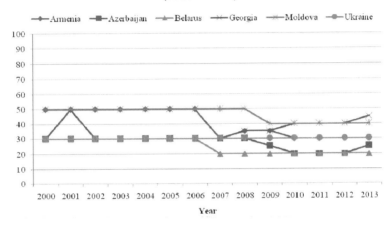

Source: *The Heritage Foundation, 2013*

The state of property rights shows a generally bad picture in the region (none of the countries reached more than half of the possible points). The trends are only partly in line with the trends of the overall index. Similar to the overall index, Belarus is among the worst performers and Georgia is among the best performers. However, property rights in Georgia started to improve later and to a much smaller extent than the overall index. In the rest of the countries, the property rights situation seems not to be in line with the overall picture. Compared to the other countries, Armenia and Azerbaijan performs much worse than in the general index, while Moldova and Ukraine performs better. Since the launch of the EaP, the state of property rights improved only in Georgia. Even that was only a slight change and in line with the earlier trends. In the remaining countries, the situation remained unchanged or even slightly declined.

Figure 6: Freedom from corruption index
(2000 – 2013)

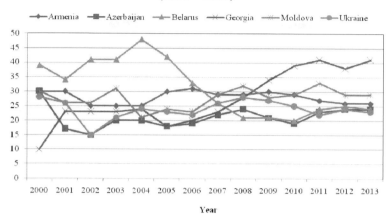

Source: *The Heritage Foundation, 2013*[9]

As with the state of property rights, the general picture regarding freedom from corruption is also unfavorable. As opposed to the overall index, by the end of the 2000s, there were no big differences among the individual countries. Moreover, there has been no clear trend throughout the last 13 years[10] except in Georgia, which clearly had outperformed the other countries by the end of the 2000s and where the state of corruption has clearly improved in the last eight years. There has been huge improvement since the launch of the EaP as well. However, this is in line with the earlier trends, thus it cannot clearly be attributed to the effect of the EaP.

9   Although, freedom from corruption is measured on a 0 to 100 scale, the numbering of the vertical axis on Figure 6 runs from 0 to 50, so that the trends are better highlighted.

10   This is not true for Belarus, where freedom from corruption is shown to have been much higher before 2004. However, from other research, we know that the state of affairs have not changed in that direction in Belarus, so the sudden worsening after 2004 can probably be attributed to measurement issues. The index is based on the Transparency International's Corruption Perception Index, which measures the perception towards corruption and not the realistic level of corruption in the countries.

Figure 7: Index of business freedom (2000 – 2013)

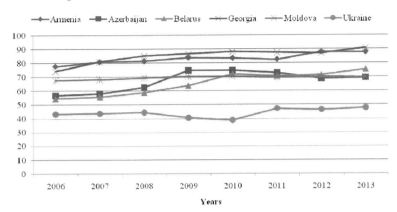

Source: *The Heritage Foundation, 2013*

Figure 8: Economic freedom (2000 – 2013)

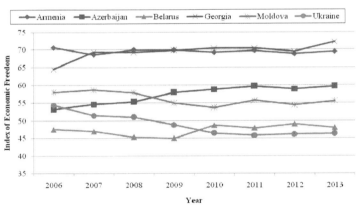

Source: *The Heritage Foundation, 2013*

All in all, based on the Heritage Foundation's Index of Economic Freedom and its subcomponents the economic freedom of the partner countries have developed as follows since the EaP's launch.[11] The situation of property rights and corruption shows a highly negative picture overall in the region, and there has not been any fundamental changes in these aspects since the EaP started.

---

11   As mentioned earlier, the years on the graphs refer to the year, when the report was complied. Hence, if we want to consider the EaP's launch, we have to look at the data from 2010 – 2011.

1. Similar to the political freedoms, Belarus performs the overall in economic freedoms but also in the property rights and freedom of corruption aspects as well. In the business freedom aspect it performs surprisingly well. Since the EaP's launch, the situation has been stable in all aspects, there hasn't been any significant changes.
2. Overall, Armenia is among the best performing countries, as opposed to the political freedoms, which showed a rather negative picture in Armenia. From the other three aspects, it also has good rating in business freedom, but the situation is much worse regarding property rights and corruption. Since the EaP started, both the overall index and the three components have been stable, no significant changes occurred.
3. In the general economic freedom index, Armenia performs much better than in terms of the political freedoms, it has the third best economic freedom rating in the region. However, the state of property rights and corruption is bad even within the region. The system has been stable, there has not been any significant changes in any aspects concurrent with the EaP.
4. After a considerable jump in its economic freedom ratings in the first half of the 2000s, Georgia has been the frontrunner in the region. It outperforms the other countries in the field of property rights, corruption and business freedom as well. However, its absolute rating in the former two is rather negative (it does not reach half of the possible score in either of them). Since the EaP's launch, the state of all aspects has been stable.
5. Compared to its performance in political freedoms, the state of economic freedoms in Moldova is rather negative, also relative to other countries in the region. This is also true for the three components analyzed separately. The system has been stable since the EaP's launch.
6. Finally, Ukraine's economic freedom rating has been constantly declining since the first half of the 2000s, until it stabilized at a comparatively low level. As opposed to political freedoms, Ukraine's performance in terms of economic freedoms has been the worst within the region. Low level performance is also reflected in business freedom where Ukraine's rating is again the worst in the region. The state of property rights and corruption has also been clearly problematic. Since the EaP started, no changes occurred in any of the three aspects or the overall performance.

Policy analysis
The discussed indicators show that the state of political and economic freedoms has changed little in the region, in many cases earlier developments were reversed during the EaP. The situation is worst in Belarus the only dictatorship remaining in the region. The country's relations with the EU are practically frozen, regardless of the EaP's presence. Moldova represents the other extreme: the country has made such a progress that most probably it will get the Association Agreement in November 2013 in Vilnius. Hence it is worth take a closer look at these two cases.

Regarding Belarus, the initial conditions were also far the worst there compared to the other EaP countries. When the Eastern Partnership launched in 2009,

Belarus was already highly dependent on Russia in terms of defense, energy and trade. As pointed out by Marin (2013), the defense sectors of the two countries are practically integrated: Russia operates two military bases on Belarusian soil, and Russia is the main market of the Belarusian defense industry, in addition to a fully integrated air defense system. In terms of energy, Gazprom has been the majority owner of the main gas transit pipeline operator in Belarus, the Beltransgaz Company since 2009, in which the Russian company took over in 2011. Russian companies are increasingly engaged to get control over the lucrative non-energy elements of the Belarusian economy and industry as well, such as chemical plants, factories, etc. This very strong dependence on Russia obviously contributed to Minsk's reluctance to participate in the Eastern Partnership, thereby essentially blocking the transformation efforts of the EU. Though Belarus is part of the EaP, it still does not participate in a number of its institutions, which further limits the EaP's possible effect. The resulting complete stagnation is well visible on the political indicators.

Contrary to Belarus, Moldova is often presented as the success story of the Eastern Partnership. However, interestingly enough, the indicators alone do not seem to justify this optimism at all. This is so despite that the new government that took office in 2009 has had a very strong pro-European agenda. They took the opportunity the EaP offered, and have been actively engaged in cooperation with the EU, in spite of a series of domestic political crises. The very fact that Moldova is ready to initiate both the Association Agreement and the Visa Liberalization Agreement in Vilnius demonstrates the progress Chisinau has made in its relations with the EU. However, what may be the reason that the indicators studied do not reflect these achievements?

One explanation may be that the lack of significant improvements in the indicators shows the skepticism of The Heritage Foundation, the Freedom House and the Economist Intelligence Unit about the implementation of the reform measures adopted by Chisinau. However, the foreseeable progress in Vilnius seems to contradict this interpretation. If the EU trusts Chisinau sufficiently enough to initial the Association Agreement and the Visa Liberalization Agreement, it is not likely that all three organizations would question this judgment.

Another, more plausible explanation may be that the indicated stagnation is connected to the very structure of the indicators, due to four main reasons. First, in Moldova there has been a practically constant crisis of governance between 2009 and 2013 which may have well distorted the indicators in terms of political stability, predictability, stability of the democratic system and rule of law. Second, the indicators themselves are too general and to register small, incremental change, even though such shifts do seem to take place. The aggregated indicators represent an average score generated of several different sub-scores. Opposite dynamics of the sub-scores may well result a stagnating average.

Third, time has an important role to play here. Political crises in Moldova have been practically continuous since 2009; it is enough to recall the most recent, March-April 2013 crisis. The next parliamentary elections will be held in 2014. If that voting will be conducted successfully, in a democratic and transparent way, most probably it will result in spectacular improvements in the 2014 political indicators. However, there is one more year left until then, and not much time has yet passed since the Spring 2013 coalition crisis. Regarding economics, when the Association Agreement (including the DCFTA) will enter into force, the economy of Moldova will get fundamentally transformed, something that will obviously be reflected in the economic indicators. Nevertheless, Moldova is not yet there at that point of breakthrough.

Fourth, the fields on which progress has taken place do not fully overlap with the fields reflected in the indicators. Indicators do not measure the rate of the adoption of the *acquis*, or the on-going legal harmonization, even though these are the most important success stories of Moldova's participation in the Eastern Partnership. Thus in short, in the case of Moldova the main reason of the lack of visibly progress in the indicators is that progress took place mostly on those fields, which are not measured by them, while on the measured ones no breakthrough has happened so far.

Paradoxically enough, the very recent Russian punitive measures against Moldova indicate that Chisinau has indeed made significant progress on the way of EU approximation. On 10 September 2013 Moscow introduced a ban on the import of Moldovan wines and spirits to Russia, officially due to quality concerns. However, Chisinau interprets the move as a clearly punitive measure aimed at derailing the country's bid for the Association Agreement in Vilnius. Just a few days earlier Russian Deputy Prime Minister Dmitry Rogozin openly said in Chisinau:"Take care not to freeze in the winter and not to lose a train in the vortex of European integration you are caught in."(Natural Gas Europe, 6 September 2013): a sentence that is hard to interpret as anything other than an open threat. All in all, Russia's concerns and blackmailing efforts indicate that Moldova has reached the point of establishing closer relations with the EU by signing the Association Agreement.

Conclusion

Since its launch in 2009, the EU's Eastern Partnership initiative has developed into a complex, multi-level structure the main aim of which is to foster the political, economic and social transformation of six neighboring countries (Belarus, Ukraine, Moldova, Georgia, Azerbaijan and Armenia) and their approximation to the EU. The EaP addresses the partner countries both in bilateral and multilateral frameworks, and uses a constantly increasing number of policy tools. The most important promises consist of conducting Association Agreements (AA), including a Deep and Comprehensive Free Trade Agreement with the best performing EaP countries. Another important incentive is the gradual liberalization of the visa regime which may lead to visa free travel in the future.

However, despite its growing inventory, the EaP has to face many challenges, both internal and external ones. Regarding the first, the EU itself is far from being coherent regarding the overall importance of the initiative. While the

Central European member states and Sweden consider the EaP to be highly important, other member states have different priorities, and pay less attention to Eastern Europe. Besides, the ongoing crisis of the EU also does not contribute to the overall attractiveness of the idea of EU approximation.

Concerning external challenges, first, the six partner countries are highly different from each other in size, population, economic power and religion. Two of them are actually still at a near-war status with each other, namely Azerbaijan and Armenia over the disputed territory of Nagorno-Karabakh. But the most important external challenge is still Russia, itself intensely opposed to any Western efforts aimed at transforming those post-Soviet countries which Moscow still perceives as integral to its own sphere of influence.

None of these structural challenges could be solved before the November 2013 Vilnius Summit of the Eastern Partnership. Moreover, as conducting Association Agreements institutionally exclude the given country's participation in the Russia-led Customs Union project, the resistance from Moscow is fiercer than ever before.

Based on all these, the answer to the research questions are the following. Concerning the first one, the intended political and economic transformation of the Eastern Partnership region produced only very modest results so far, at least according to the indicators chosen. In terms of politics Belarus, Azerbaijan and Armenia have been stagnating since 2009, trends in Ukraine have become worse, and limited progress has been visible only in Georgia and Moldova. However, concerning the latter two, late 2013 and 2014 will be of crucial importance as presidential elections will take place in Georgia and parliamentary ones in Moldova. It remains to be seen whether the positive trends will continue. Regarding the economic transformation, except Georgia that performed well in property rights and fighting corruption, no significant positive change took place in the other five countries, though their level of performance differs a lot. All in all, the lack of significant changes shows that the Eastern Partnership initiative was far from being fully successful in transforming the region between 2009 and 2013.

This leads to the second question namely to what extent the changes in 2009-2013 could be linked with the Eastern Partnership. Actually the lack of spectacular changes seem to transform the question into one of "Whom to blame?" Besides the inherent general problems of the Eastern Partnership and the economic and political pressure from Russia indeed contributed to the stagnation. So did the world economic crisis and the euro crisis as well. However, it seems to be impossible to determine which of these factors had a bigger role to play. Only the general conclusion can be drawn that the EaP has been obviously lacking the strength and attractiveness to overcome these hampering factors.

A methodological conclusion also emerges, namely that quantitative indicators need to be used with care when measuring the overall efficiency of the Eastern Partnership. The lack of spectacular progress in the indicators seems to contradict the EU's interpretation of progress at first sight. The very fact that the EU is ready to grant the Association Agreement to Moldova, Georgia and probably to Ukraine indicates that significant positive developments have taken place in these countries. What may then be the reason that almost no progress is seen in the indicators? A closer look reveals that the very structure of the indicators may distort the picture: sub-scores moving to opposite directions may result the stagnation of the aggregated average. Moreover, the indicators simply do not measure the speed and depth of adoption of the acquis and EU standards, according to which Brussels judges the progress of the partner countries. However, the current research is timed just before the breakthrough will start with the implementation of the AA and the DCFTA.

As it was already mentioned before, Vilnius and the subsequent implementation of the AAs and the DCFTAs may well change the picture particularly in Moldova, Georgia and possibly Ukraine. In these countries the widespread transfer of EU norms and practices will start bearing fruits after Vilnius, at least for those states that keep up their commitments. Hence, even though the 2009-2013 period has been characterized by the lack of significant changes, this is likely to change by the implementation of the AA and the visa liberalization.

All in all, this means that so far the Eastern Partnership has indeed been successful in the studied 2009-2013 period by *preparing the changes* that will probably take place in the near future in the cooperating countries. At the same time, the gap between the committed and non-committed EaP states is likely to get wider. Thus paradoxically enough, the foreseeable success of the Eastern Partnership in particular countries will weaken the general cohesion of the project, at least in its current form.

Bibliography

Ananicz, S., & Sadowski, R. (2012). Central Europe facing "Eastern Europe": Symphony or Cacophony? In Z. Sabič & P. Drulák (Eds.), Regional and International Relations of Central Europe (pp. 286-309). Palgrave Macmillan.

Center for Systemic Peace. (2013). Polity IV Annual Time-Series 1800–2012. Retrieved August 05, 2013, from http://www.systemic-peace.org/inscr/inscr.htm

Commission of the European Communities. (2003). Communication from the Commission to the Council and the European Parliament, Wider Europe – Neighbourhood: A New Framework for Relations with our Eastern and Southern Neighbours. COM(2003) 104 final. Retrieved from http://ec.europa.eu/world/enp/pdf/com03_104_en.pdf

Commission of the European Communities. (2008a). Communicaton from the Commission to the European Parliament and the Council, Eastern Partnership. COM(2008) 823 Final. Retrieved July 29, 2013, from http://ec.europa.eu/europeaid/where/neighbourhood/eastern_partnership/documents/eastern_partnership_communication_from_the_commission_to_the_european_parliament_and_the_council_en.pdf

Commission of the European Communities. (2008b). Commission Staff Working Document accompanying the Communcation from the Commission to the European Parliament and the Council, Eastern Partnership. Retrieved from http://eeas.europa.eu/eastern/docs/sec08_2974_en.pdf

Commission of the European Communities. (2012a). European Neighbourhood and Partnership Instrument. Retrieved August 02, 2013, from http://ec.europa.eu/europeaid/where/neighbourhood/overview/

Commission of the European Communities. (2012b). European Neighbourhood and Partnership Instrument. Retrieved August 02, 2013, from http://ec.europa.eu/europeaid/how/finance/enpi_en.htm

Commission of the European Communities. (2013a). EU cooperation with eastern neighbours in the framework of the Eastern Partnership. *Development and Cooperation – EuropeAid.* Retrieved August 05, 2013, from http://ec.europa.eu/europeaid/where/neighbourhood/regional-cooperation/enpi-east/index_en.htm

Commission of the European Communities. (2013b). Comprehensive Institution Building in the framework of the Eastern Partnership. *Development and Cooperation – EuropeAid.* Retrieved August 05, 2013, from http://ec.europa.eu/europeaid/where/neighbourhood/regional-cooperation/enpi-east/cib_en.htm

Commission of the European Communities. (2013c). Regional development in the framework of the Eastern Partnership. *Development and Cooperation – EuropeAid.* Retrieved August 05, 2013, from http://ec.europa.eu/europeaid/where/neighbourhood/regional-cooperation/enpi-east/prdps_en.htm

Commission of the European Communities. (2013d). Eastern Partnership Integration and Cooperation (EaPIC) programme. *Development and Cooperation – EuropeAid.* Retrieved August 05, 2013, from http://ec.europa.eu/europeaid/where/neighbourhood/regional-cooperation/enpi-east/eapic_en.htm

Commission of the European Communities. (2013e). Eastern Neighbourhood Civil Society Facility. *Development and Cooperation – EuropeAid.* Retrieved August 05, 2013, from http://ec.europa.eu/europeaid/where/neighbourhood/regional-cooperation/enpi-east/csf_en.htm

Council of the European Union. (2012). Council Conclusions on Ukraine. *3209th FOREIGN AFFAIRS Council meeting, Brussels, 10 December 2012.* Brussels. Retrieved August 05, 2012, from http://www.consilium.europa.eu/uedocs/cms_data/docs/pressdata/en/ec/134353.pdf

Delcour, L. (2011). The Institutional Functioning of the Eastern Partnership: An Early Assessment | EaPCommunity. *EaP Community.* Retrieved August 05, 2013, from http://www.easternpartnership.org/publication/2011-10-31/institutional-functioning-eastern-partnership-early-assessment

Depo, B. (2011). The Eastern Partnership two years on: Success or failure for the diversified ENP? *EaP Community*. Retrieved August 05, 2013, from http://www.easternpartnership.org/publication/2011-07-07/eastern-partnership-two-years-success-or-failure-diversified-enp

EaP Community. (2012a). The EaP's bilateral dimension. Retrieved August 05, 2013, from http://www.easternpartnership.org/content/eap-s-bilateral-dimension

EaP Community. (2012b). The EaP's multilateral dimension. Retrieved August 05, 2013, from http://www.easternpartnership.org/content/eap-s-multilateral-dimension

EU Neighbourhood Info Centre. (2013). Eastern Partnership and Russia Glossary Eastern Partnership and Russia Glossary. Retrieved August 05, 2013, from http://www.enpi-info.eu/files/publications/glossary East_EN.pdf

EuroNest. (2013). What is Euronest. Retrieved August 05, 2013, from http://www.euronest.europarl.europa.eu/euronest/

European External Action Service. (2013). Information on the EU-Ukraine Association Agreement. Retrieved August 05, 2013, from http://eeas.europa.eu/top_stories/2012/140912_ukraine_en.htm

European Union. (2008). Consolidated Version of the Treaty on the Functioning of the European Union. *Official Journal of the European Union, C115*, 47–199. Retrieved from http://eur-lex.europa.eu/LexUriServ/LexUriServ.do?uri=OJ:C:2008:115:0047:0199:en:PDF

European Union. (2010). Consolidated Version of the Treaty on European Union. *Official Journal of the European Union, C 83*, 13 – 45. Retrieved from http://eur-lex.europa.eu/LexUriServ/LexUriServ.do?uri=OJ:C:2010:083:0013:0046:en:PDF

European Union. (2012). EU cooperation for a successful Eastern Partnership. *Commission of the European Communities.* Retrieved August 05, 2013, from http://www.enpi-info.eu/files/publications/eastern_partnership_flyer_final_en.pdf

Freedom in the World. (n.d.). Freedom House. Data complied by the author based on the Freedom in the World Reports published between 2001 and 2013. Retrieved from http://www.freedomhouse.org/report-types/freedom-world

Freedom in the World 2013. (2013). Retrieved from http://www.freedomhouse.org/sites/default/files/FIW 2013 Booklet - for Web_1.pdf

Joint Declaration of the Prague Eastern Parntership Summit. (2009). 8435/09 (Presse 78). Council of the European Union. Retrieved from http://www.consilium.europa.eu/ueDocs/cms_Data/docs/pressdata/en/er/107589.pdf

Marchetti, A. (2008). Consolidation in Times of Crisis? The Setup of the

European Neighbourhood Policy and its Challenges. In L. Delcour & E. Tulmets (Eds.), *Pioneer Europe? Testing EU Foreign POlicy in the Neighbourhood* (pp. 21–34). Nomos Verlag, Baden-Baden.

Marin, Anaïs (2013): Trading off sovereignty. The outcome of Belarus' integration with Russia in the security and defence field. *OSW Commentary,* Centre for Eastern Studies. Warsaw. 2013.04.29.

Marshall, M. G., Gurr, T. R., & Jaggers, K. (2013). *POLITY^{TM} IV PRO-JECT Dataset Users' Manual POLITY IV PROJECT.* Retrieved from http://www.systemicpeace.org/inscr/p4manualv2012.pdf

Melikian, Roman (2013): The Eurasian Union, European Union and Armenian Complementarism. *Central Asia and the Caucasus. Journal of Social and Political Studies,* Vol. 14., Issue 2., from http://www.ca-c.org/online/2013/journal_eng/cac-02/05.shtml

Methodology, Freedom in the World. (2002). *Freedom in the World 2002, Freedom House.* Retrieved August 05, 2013, from http://www.free-domhouse.org/report/freedom-world-2002/methodology

Methodology, *Index of Economic Freedom.* (2013). In Index of Economic Freedom (pp. 477–489). The Heritage Foundation. Retrieved from https://thf_media.s3.amazonaws.com/index/pdf/2013/method-ology.pdf

Natural Gas Europe (2013): Russia Hints at Stopping Gas Deliveries to Moldova. *Natural Gas Europe,* 6 September 2013. Retrieved from http://www.naturalgaseurope.com/russia-dimitri-rogozin-moldova-gas-delivery Last accessed: 22 September 2013.

Panarmenian.net (2013): Fule says Customs Union Incompatible with AA/DCFTA. *Panarmenian.net,* 12 September 2013. http://www.panarmenian.net/eng/news/169897/

Petrov, R. (2011). Association agreement versus partnership an co-operation agreement. What is the difference? *EaP Community.* Retrieved August 05, 2013, from http://www.easternpartnership.org/community/debate/association-agreement-versus-partner-ship-co-operation-agreement-what-difference

Polish-Swedish Proposal on the Eastern Partnership. (n.d.). *Ministy of Foreign Affairs of the Republic of Poland.* Retrieved August 02, 2013, from http://www.enpi-info.eu/library/content/polish-swedish-proposal-eastern-partnership

Potocka, J. (2013). Poland warns EU-Ukraine bilateral agreement "clearly" at risk. *EurActiv.* Retrieved from http://www.euractiv.com/europes-east/sikorski-warns-ukraine-vinius-su-news-528869

Presidency Conclusions, 19/20 June 2008. (n.d.). *Council of the European Union, 11018/1/08 REV 1.* Retrieved August 02, 2013, from http://www.consilium.europa.eu/ueDocs/cms_Data/docs/pres sData/en/ec/101346.pdf

Presidency Conclusions, Extraordinary European Council, Brussels, 1 September 2008. (n.d.). *Council of the European Union, 12594/2/08*

REV 2. Retrieved August 02, 2013, from http://www.consilium. europa.eu/ueDocs/cms_Data/docs/pressData/en/ec/102545.pdf

Romsics, G., & Végh, Z. (2010). Támogatókkal, koalíció nélkül? A Keleti Partnerség támogatói és a kezdeményezés jövoje. *Külügyi Szemle,* (1), 107–134.

Shapovalova, N. (2009). The EU ' s Eastern Partnership?: still born? *FRIDE Policy Brief,* (May). Retrieved from http://www.fride.org/ download/pb11_ue_eastern_partnership_eng_may09.pdf

Stefan Batory Foundation. (2012a). Eastern Partnership Visa Liberalisation, Formal Stages Index. Retrieved July 27, 2013, from http:// monitoring.visa-free-europe.eu/formal-stage

Stefan Batory Foundation. (2012b). Eastern Partnership Visa Liberalisation Index. Retrieved July 29, 2013, from http://monitoring. visa-free-europe.eu/about

The Economist Intelligence Unit. (2013). *Democracy index 2012 Democracy at a standstill.* Retrieved from http://handlers/Whitepaper-Handler.ashx?fi=Democracy-Index-2012.pdf&mode=wp&campaignid=DemocracyIndex12

The European Neighbourhood Policy (ENP) and the Eastern Partnership (EAP). (2011). *European Parliament.* Retrieved August 02, 2013, from http://www.europarl.europa.eu/ftu/pdf/en/FTU_6.3.3.pdf

The Heritage Foundation. (2013). Economic Data and Statistics on World Economy and Economic Freedom. Retrieved July 15, 2013, from http://www.heritage.org/index/explore?view=by-region-country-year

Tulmets, E. (2006). Adapting the Experience of Enlargement to the Neighbourhood Policy: The ENP as a Substitute to Enlargement? In P. Kratochvíl (Ed.), *The European Union and its Neighbourhood: Policies, Problems and Priorities* (pp. 29–57). Insitute of International Affairs, Prague.

Ukraine Monitor. (2013). France Ready to Sign EU-Ukraine Association Agreement Say Reports From Paris. *PRNewswire.* Paris. Retrieved from http://www.prnewswire.com/news-releases/france-ready-to-sign-eu-ukraine-association-agreement-say-reports-from-paris-207684101.html

Various. (2010). Partnership and Cooperation Agreements (PCAs): Russia, Eastern Europe, the Southern Caucasus and Central Asia. *Summaries of EU legislation.* Retrieved August 05, 2013, from http://europa.eu/legislation_summaries/external_relations/relations_with_third_countries/eastern_europe_and_central_asia/r 17002_en.htm

Végh, Z. (2010). The Evolution of the Eastern Neighbourhood Policy of the European Union. In O. Ali, L. Artemenko, & J. Langer (Eds.), *The Eastern Partnership:New Perspectives for a New Europe* (pp. 15–33). Youth Eastern Partnershio, Cracow, Poland.

Végh, Z. (2011). *The Transformative Power of the European Union in its Eastern.* Eotvos Lorand Tudomanyegyetem, Budapest, Hungary.

Végh, Z. (2013). The Widening Implementation Gaps of the Eastern Partnership "Frontrunners." Conference presentation at the conference entitled "Challenging Eastern Limits – Intentions and Realities of the Eastern Partnership". 7 June 2013. Center for European Studies, Jagiellonian University, Cracow. Manuscript provided by the author.

Zagorski, Andrei (2012): Russia's neighbourhood policy. *EU Institute for Security Studies,* 14 February, 2012. http://www.iss.europa.eu/publications/detail/article/russias-neighbourhood-policy/

Notes on contributors

Dániel Bagameri holds an MA in International Relations from Eotvos Lorand University (Budapest) and an MA in European Studies from Central European University (Budapest). His research interests lie in the fields of European migration issues, cross-border regional cooperation within the EU, interest representation within the EU, as well as EU enlargement and neighborhood policy. His latest research investigates the European challenges in relation to the integration of third-country nationals, which will be compiled in a PhD thesis. He is currently affiliated with the International Organization for Migration (IOM) Budapest office.

Péter Balázs, PhD. is Jean Monnet professor at the International Relations and European Studies department of the Central European University. His research activities of are centered on the foreign policy of the European Union and problems of the modernization and integration of the Eastern part of the continent. He also researches the questions of European governance including the future of European institutions. Prof. Balazs heads the Center for EU Enlargement Studies at the CEU, combining his experience as a trained diplomat with academic research.

András Deák, PhD. is an Associate Fellow on Russia and Energy Security at the Hungarian Institute of International Affairs (HIIA). He worked as a senior researcher at the HIIA on Russian Foreign Policy during the 2000s. His extensive publication activity covers Central European relations with Russia, as well as post-Soviet energy policies with a special focus on gas and its European exports.

Anna Orosz is a PhD candidate at the Institute of International Studies at the Corvinus University of Budapest. In her dissertation she examines challenges related to the state-building process from the perspective of education policy. Geographically, she mainly focuses on the Western Balkan countries, and accordingly, she deals with these countries' European integration.

András Rácz, PhD. graduated at the Eötvös Loránd University in Budapest, defended his Ph.D. in Modern History 2008; currently is a senior fellow at the Hungarian Institute of International Affairs. His fields of expertise are: EU foreign and security policy towards Eastern Europe, Russian and post-Soviet politics, Hungarian foreign and security policy.

Péter Rada, PhD. is the president of the Corvinus Society for Foreign Affairs and Culture. He is Professor of International Relations at the Budapest College of Communication and Business and the Eötvös Loránd University. Dr Rada was a Fulbright visiting scholar at the SAIS Johns Hopkins University and at the SIPA, Columbia University. He has published several articles on security policy and state-building.

András Szalai is a PhD candidate at the Political Science Department of the Central European University, and a junior researcher of the university's Center for EU Enlargement Studies. His doctoral research centers on the role of foreign policy experts in policy formulation, while his professional interests include European foreign and security policy, transatlantic relations and foreign policy decision-making.

Fruzsina Tófalvi is a graduate of the Department of Political Science of the Central European University, author of several publications on Turkish democratization and foreign affairs since 2008. She currently works at the Hungarian Ministry of Defense as an analyst. The thoughts expressed in her chapter are her own and do not represent the view of the Ministry of Defense.

Katalin Varga is a PhD Candidate in Political Economy at the Doctoral School of Political Science, Public Policy and International Relations; Central European University, Budapest. Her research interests include financial systems and regulations, the Asian development model, and integration theories including new regionalism. Apart from analyzing the EU's measures to integrate its neighboring countries, she is currently researching the evolution of financial regulation in selected Southeast Asian countries.